Create Your Family History Book
with

Family Tree Maker®

Version 8

The Official Guide

Send Us Your Comments:

To comment on this book or any other PRIMA TECH title, visit our reader response page on the Web at **www.prima-tech.com/comments**.

How to Order:

For information on quantity discounts, contact the publisher: Prima Publishing, P.O. Box 1260BK, Rocklin, CA 95677-1260; (916) 787-7000. On your letterhead, include information concerning the intended use of the books and the number of books you want to purchase. For individual orders, turn to the back of this book for more information.

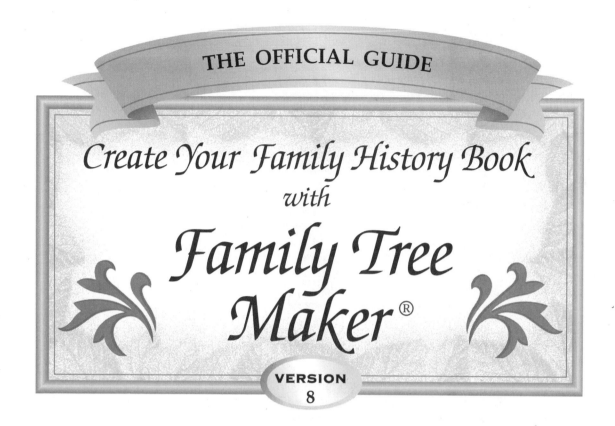

THE OFFICIAL GUIDE

Create Your Family History Book
with
Family Tree
Maker®

VERSION
8

Marthe Arends

PRIMA
TECH

A DIVISION OF PRIMA PUBLISHING

A Division of Prima Publishing

Prima Publishing and colophon are registered trademarks of Prima Communications, Inc. PRIMA TECH is a trademark of Prima Communications, Inc., Roseville, California 95661.

Family Tree Maker is a registered trademark and Broderbund is a trademark of Mattel Interactive, a division of Mattel, Inc., and its licensors. World Family Tree, FamilyFinder, Family Archive, GenealogyLibrary, and InterneTree are all trademarks and/or registered trademarks of Genealogy.com. All other trademarks are the property of their respective owners.

Important: Prima Publishing cannot provide software support. Please contact the appropriate software manufacturer's technical support line or Web site for assistance.

Prima Publishing and the author have attempted throughout this book to distinguish proprietary trademarks from descriptive terms by following the capitalization style used by the manufacturer.

Information contained in this book has been obtained by Prima Publishing from sources believed to be reliable. However, because of the possibility of human or mechanical error by our sources, Prima Publishing, or others, the Publisher does not guarantee the accuracy, adequacy, or completeness of any information and is not responsible for any errors or omissions or the results obtained from use of such information. Readers should be particularly aware of the fact that the Internet is an ever-changing entity. Some facts may have changed since this book went to press.

ISBN: 0-7615-3106-8
Library of Congress Catalog Card Number: 00-106644
Printed in the United States of America

0 01 02 03 04 II 10 9 8 7 6 5 4 3 2 1

Publisher:
Stacy L. Hiquet

Marketing Manager:
Judi Taylor

Associate Marketing Manager:
Jennifer Breece

Managing Editor:
Sandy Doell

Acquisitions Editor:
Emi Nakamura

Developmental Editor:
Kate Welsh

Project Editor:
Melba Hopper

Technical Reviewer:
Rhonda McClure

Copy Editor:
Betty Bolte

Proofreader:
Jeannie Smith

Interior Layout:
Marian Hartsough Associates

Cover Design:
Prima Design Team

Indexer:
Johnna VanHoose Dinse

To the Linger-Pals—
Vance Briceland, Kay Douglas, and Amber Tatnall

and the Musketeers—
Beverly Brandt, Lori Grube, and Libby Muelhaupt
Thanks, guys!

Acknowlegments

Who hasn't seen a movie awards presentation where the winner marches up to the microphone, clears his throat, and tossing back carefully coifed hair, thanks all the little people for helping make the award possible? That may be the style in Hollywood, but in the world of book publishing, there are no little people—every member of the team who works on a book has an important role, a fact that wise authors never take for granted. My appreciation and thanks go to the great group of people at Prima Tech who helped with this book, especially the acquisitions editor, Emi Nakamura, and the project editor, Melba Hopper. I would also like to thank the development editor, Kate Welsh; the copy editor, Betty Bolte; the proofreader, Jeannie Smith; the layout artist, Marian Hartsough; and the indexer, Johnna VanHoose Dinse. Special thanks go to Rhonda R. McClure, technical editor extraordinaire.

About the Author

Marthe Arends lives in the Pacific Northwest with her husband and three Rhodesian ridgebacks. She started on the road to genealogy when she was 18, guided by her grandmother who had always wanted to know what happened to the "three brothers who left the old country." In addition to spending long hours working on her family tree, Marthe has published and edited a computer genealogy newsletter, taught numerous online genealogy classes, written articles for a number of genealogical publications, and authored two books concerning genealogy and computers. Additionally, Marthe writes CD-ROM reviews for Broderbund and is the author of the popular "Internet Genealogy" lessons on Genealogy.com.

An interest in genealogy spawned a fascination with history, and now Marthe primarily spends her time researching and writing historical fiction. She is a member of several genealogy and writers' organizations and still manages to find time in a hectic schedule to do a little family research.

Contents
at a Glance

Contents at a Glance

Contents

Contents

Contents

Contents

Contents

PART II UNDERSTANDING BOOK ELEMENTS . . . 173

Chapter 6 *Exploring Custom and Miscellaneous Reports* 175

Contents

Contents

Contents

Contents

Contents

Contents

Contents

Introduction

Genealogy is said to be the third most popular hobby in the United States. If you approach any group of people and start talking about your illustrious (or not so illustrious) ancestors, the odds are good that someone in the crowd will feel compelled to join you in a discussion about his or her family history. For the most part, we are all fascinated with our family histories, not because we crave proof of a relationship with royalty or connection to a well-known historical figure, but because by learning about our ancestors, we have a clearer understanding of who we are and how we fit into the scheme of things. By connecting ourselves with the past, we become a part of history—albeit a very small part of history unless we are related to someone who had a profound influence on history. Because most of us cannot trace our ancestry back to such people, we must make do with those ancestors we possess by celebrating their lives and accomplishments.

It's my hope that this book will take you on a wonderful journey of exploration—exploration not only of your own family's history as you go about the task of researching, but also of the satisfaction that can be found by creating a book with the intention of sharing it with family and friends. Whether or not you realize it, writing a book is a very personal thing. Even if the book does not concern you directly—for example, if you write about ancestors who lived three hundred years ago—you still have a profound influence over what your readers will absorb. You act, in effect, as a filter, giving readers the information they need to understand the lives of the individuals you present.

It's a heady responsibility, writing, but not one that should intimidate you. Whether you are creating a book so that your children will know about their grandparents or a formal genealogy detailing all of the descendants of a particular pair of ancestors, Family Tree Maker will help you by taking over the onerous tasks, leaving you free to be imaginative and creative.

Whatever type of family history book you create, it will be uniquely *you*. Whenever I'm faced with the project of beginning a new book, I think of what Martha Graham said: "There is a vitality, a life force, a quickening that is translated through you into action, and there is only one of you in all time, this expression is unique, and if you block it, it will never exist through any other medium; and be lost." Those are wise words, and ones you should keep in mind as you begin the journey of creating a family history book. Don't let your unique expression be lost. Share yourself with this and future generations by creating a family history book from your heart.

What This Book Is About

For many people, the act of research alone is not enough. After all, they reason, why should the fruits of all that hard work sit in a filing cabinet benefiting no one? Enter the family history book—a book detailing the history, ancestors, or descendants of a specific individual, couple, or family. In most cases, family histories are written to share information with like-minded researchers, but for the purpose of this book, I use the term to indicate any sort of family-oriented book project. Thus, the book that is created to share a generation of grandchildren with a grandparent is as much a family history book as a formal, thoroughly researched, documented-within-an-inch-of-its-life genealogy.

This book will guide you through the intricacies of using Family Tree Maker to create a family history book — just what type of family history book you create is up to you! Writing a family history book is like any other creative process; you need to have imagination and creativity, yes, but you also need to do enough homework to make sure that the end product will be a success. That's where I hope to help you—by guiding you through the steps needed to envision, plan, organize, and carry out the tasks necessary to create the book of your dreams.

I walk you through the process of deciding what your focus will be, show you how to weigh all the issues connected with writing a family history book, give pointers on how to organize the book in the best manner; and most of all, I tell you how to push Family Tree Maker to its limits as you create your one-of-a-kind family history book.

Who Should Read This Book?

While this book is intended for genealogists who are already comfortable using Family Tree Maker, the novice user has not been ignored; steps are provided throughout the text so that if you don't know how to do a particular task, you will be able to follow along. Because most genealogists do not consider publishing a family history book until they have gathered enough information to make a book worthwhile, it is assumed that you have experience in conducting a family research project and that you have entered the results of your research into Family Tree Maker.

You don't have to be an expert researcher to use this book! One of the great benefits of Family Tree Maker is that it is suited for a wide range of user levels—the hobbyist can enjoy creating a family history book just as much as the dedicated researcher. This book explores a number of projects suitable to different levels of experience, both with the Family Tree Maker software and with genealogical research in general. Good genealogy practices are urged strongly, however—there is no excuse for conducting sloppy or incomplete research and then publishing the result. Whether you plan a detailed family history or a book to amuse your immediate family, this book will help you meet your goal with style and success.

How This Book Is Organized

I organized this book to be read from cover to cover, but if you are familiar with Family Tree Maker, you might want to dip into only specific chapters discussing subjects unfamiliar to you. Subject headers throughout the chapters will alert you to important discussions and ease you through the sometimes-complex process of creating a family history book. Here is a brief description of what you will find in the three sections.

Part I: "Preparing for a Family History Book Project" introduces you to the basics of planning and organizing your book, as well as explaining the standard trees and reports that you can create using Family Tree Maker. Chapter One, "Setting the Stage," starts you on your way. Chapter Two, "Organizing Your Family History Book," moves you into organizational mode. Chapter Three,

"Using Trees in Your Family History Book," takes a long hard look at the many and varied trees available. Chapter Four, "Using Miscellaneous Trees and Charts in Your Family History Book," offers details about the lesser known trees and charts. Chapter Five, "Using Narrative Reports in Your Family History Book," explores the sometimes-confusing differences between the Register Report and the NGS Quarterly Report.

Part II: "Understanding Book Elements" takes a closer look at those nonstandard Family Tree Maker items that you can use to add detail and interest to your book. Chapter Six, "Exploring Custom and Miscellaneous Reports," goes into more detail about how to create and use customized reports. Chapter Seven, "Using Graphics in Your Family History Book," dives into the wonderful addition that graphics can make to a book. Chapter Eight, "Adding Text to Your Family History Book," explores how you can add text to add flesh to your book. Chapter Nine, "Creating Your Family History Book," gets down to the basics of using the Book creation abilities of Family Tree Maker. Chapter Ten, "Printing and Publishing Your Family History Book," discusses various options you'll face when working with your final product.

Part III: "Pulling It All Together" takes you through the last stage of the journey. Chapter Eleven, "Family History Book Projects," gives you details on a variety of projects you can try your hand at, while Chapter Twelve, "Marketing and Promotion," gives you a heads-up on all the aspects of selling your book.

Conventions Used in This Book

Because you will probably read this book while you are at your computer, I've used several conventions to make the steps and information as clear as possible. If you keep these conventions in mind when you read this book, you should be able to easily follow the instructions in this book.

You select toolbar buttons or buttons found in dialog boxes by clicking the button with your mouse. In this book, *click* refers to the left mouse button, unless otherwise specified. *Double-clicking* refers to clicking the left mouse button twice in quick succession. You can also choose menus and menu commands by clicking them, even when the instructions are "From the File menu, choose Print."

Throughout the book, you are asked to select an option within a dialog box—you do so by clicking the specified item.

Pressing and holding one key while pressing another one is called performing a *key combination*. In this book, key combinations are indicated by a plus sign (+) between the keys you need to press. For example, for CTRL+S, you press and hold the Ctrl key while you press the P key.

Here are some other special elements that you will find in the book:

> **CAUTION** *Cautions generally tell you how to avoid problems.*

> **NOTE** *Notes provide additional helpful or interesting information.*

> **TIP** *Tips give you helpful ideas related to the subject being discussed, show you how to accomplish tasks easier, and sometimes provide shortcuts that only the experts know.*

PART I

Preparing for a Family History Book Project

CHAPTER ONE

Setting the Stage

Anybody can make history.
Only a great man can write it.

—Oscar Wilde, Aphorisms

n this age of computers and technology, genealogists who do not use a genealogical database program are putting themselves at a distinct disadvantage. Computer software programs such as Family Tree Maker make organizing and maintaining research much more efficient.

Family Tree Maker makes it easy for anyone—from novice to experienced researcher—to enter genealogical data into the program. Once you enter the data, you can do any number of things with the information: sort it, calculate relationships among distant relatives, create eye-catching trees and charts, work with custom reports, share data with your friends, build a library of source materials, and create a family history book.

Though writing a book about your family might seem like a complicated goal, it can be a rewarding endeavor. What other book will feature you, your family, and your ancestors? You can compare the process of writing such a book to undertaking a stage production—you must plan, organize, and create a product for an audience. Think of yourself as the director. You select the play (the focus of your book), hire the actors (choose which members of your family to include), and give them direction (decide which format to use). All these aspects of writing a family history book are discussed in this chapter.

More than likely, by now, you have a clear picture of your goals with regard to your family history book. You know who your audience is, you have an idea about the type of book you want to create, and you have selected a family line or individuals to include. In the next chapter, you move from the visualization stage to the pre-publication stage, with a look at organizing your book in a manner that is coherent and cohesive.

By the time you finish this chapter, you should have a better understanding of the following:

- ❄ What makes up a family history book
- ❄ Whether your data is ready to be placed into a family history book
- ❄ How to visualize your audience and select the right format and scope for that audience

    ❄ **NOTE** ❄ *Each chapter in this book contains information or details that you should consider before moving on to the next step in creating your family history book. Users who are experienced in genealogy and familiar with the use of Family Tree Maker might want to skim the sections that detail specific options and items. Users new to Family Tree Maker should take the time to read the sections on those items of interest before tackling a book project. As an additional help for new users, the sidebar "Family Tree Maker Basics," later in this chapter, provides steps for accomplishing a few basic tasks.*

The Family Tree Maker Toolbar

Because I anticipate that some of you might be new to Family Tree Maker, I've included Figure 1.1, which illustrates all the buttons on the Family Page that you might employ as you follow the examples and steps in this book. Please use Figure 1.1 as a guide when you are referred to a button on the Family Page in this chapter and subsequent chapters.

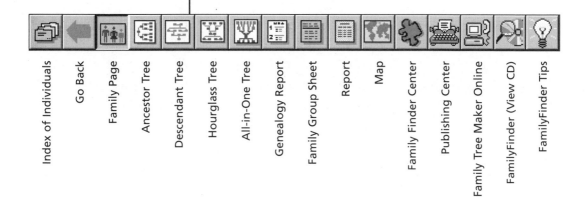

Figure 1.1

Here are the buttons you will need to access from the Family Tree Maker toolbar.

❧ NOTE ❧ *While writing this book, I used a beta copy of Family Tree Maker (that is, a working copy of the software while it is still in the testing stage). I found that occasionally an extra button—the Scrapbook button familiar to users of previous versions of Family Tree Maker— occasionally "adds" itself to the toolbar. Since I cannot duplicate the steps needed to re-create that effect, I assume it is an odd quirk of the program. Should the same thing happen to you, don't panic, just enjoy the addition of another button!*

What Is a Family History Book?

Imagine that you've collected your family data, fought your way through the poison ivy covering an ancestor's headstone, stared down the most daunting county clerk, and found that elusive source for a fact that has been a thorn in your researching side for many a year. You've scanned in your family photos; swapped GEDCOMs with other researchers; and verified, sourced, and documented until you can recite the first ten generations of your ancestry without peeking at your notes. Now what do you do with all that information?

❧ NOTE ❧ *GEDCOM stands for Genealogical Data Communication, which is the standard by which genealogical data is transferred from one genealogy program to another. A GEDCOM is nothing more than a text file specially created so that other GEDCOM-compliant genealogy-database programs can read the information contained in the GEDCOM.*

If you are like most people, you want to share the fruits of your labor with family members or other researchers. Although many family historians do not begin their research with the intention of publishing it, at some point, the idea of creating and publishing a family history book often becomes attractive. Unfortunately, some people are confused about the term *family history*. Is it a genealogy? Is it a historical accounting of a specific family?

The answer is simple. A family history can be whatever you want it to be! Whether you write the story of your great-grandparent's ancestors in the old country, detail the line of descent from King Edward III to yourself, or create a fiftieth wedding anniversary book for your parents that features your brothers and sisters, you're writing a family history.

Family Tree Maker enables you to create the sort of book you want to create, no matter how detailed or informal; everything you want to include in your book can be inserted quickly and easily—graphics, additional text, trees and reports, *front matter* (such as an introduction, foreword, title page, table of contents, and so on), as well as an index that can be regenerated as you add book elements. In Figure 1.2, you see an example of a title page produced with the Family Tree Maker Book feature.

> ❧ **NOTE** ❧ *You can find information on creating a title page in Chapter Nine, "Creating Your Family History Book."*

As a rule, a family history book focuses on a specific individual and details either that person's ancestors or descendants, but you are not limited to just those options. Using Family Tree Maker's Book feature, you can also create

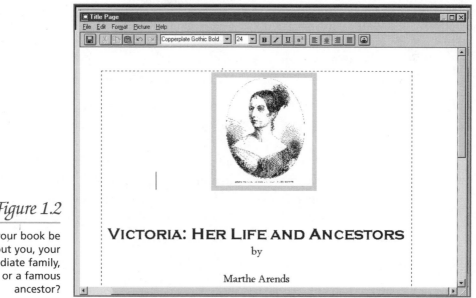

Figure 1.2

Will your book be about you, your immediate family, or a famous ancestor?

your autobiography or write a biography of a beloved grandparent or famous ancestor. If you are blessed with an ancestor's diary or journal, you can create a memoir complete with photos, ancestry, and descendants. You can find an example of a project devoted to one individual in Chapter Eleven, "Family History Book Projects."

Family History Book Types

You can choose from several formats to present your family history. Whether you choose to write an autobiography, biography, family history, or memoir, you should understand what constitutes each format. The following is a brief list of formats that you might want to investigate when making a decision about your book.

- **Autobiography.** The biography of a person narrated by that person. An autobiography can include information about the individual's ancestors and descendants, although generally the focus is on his or her life.

- **Biography.** An account of an individual's life, written by someone other than the individual. Biographies, like autobiographies, tend to focus on the individual's life more than on his or her ancestry or descendants.

- **Family history (aka genealogy).** An account of the descent or ancestry of a person or family. This can include the descendants of an individual (or couple) or the ancestors of a specific person. Family histories can also be comprised of the study of family pedigrees for groups of people not related by birth—for example, a group of people with something in common (settlement in the same location, travel together, birthplace, and so on).

Memoir. A narrative composed from personal experience, written by the person featured in the account. Memoirs are almost exclusively focused on a person's life, and not his or her ancestry. Memoirs usually feature either a particular time of great interest or episodes of great interest (for example, a memoir might focus on the time an individual spent decoding reports while working for military intelligence, or it might cover the many exciting points in a politician's life).

Using Family Tree Maker to Make Your Family History Book

In the old days, before computers and programs such as Family Tree Maker, writing a family history book meant organizing innumerable charts, forms, documents, and photographs so that the data therein could be typed in a fashion that was useful and meaningful to family historians. Mistakes and typos meant time-consuming corrections to the original manuscript. New information was usually added as an addendum in the back because correcting the original was too costly. Indexes were created by hand, a tedious task and prone to error. Sources, documents, or even whole families could be left out if authors lost track of where they were in their stack of items to include.

With Family Tree Maker, however, these problems are solved. Using the program, you can easily do the following:

- Create customized forms

- Correct and reorganize information

- Add graphics and digitized images

- Update information and generate trees, reports, and charts

🏃 Conduct spell-checks and error-checks

🏃 Generate an index

Creating a family history book with Family Tree Maker is simply a matter of a little planning, a few decisions, and a short amount of time at the computer.

Finding Your Focus

People have many reasons for creating a family history book. Your reasons for creating your book will directly influence the format and focus of the book. For example, researchers who create a professional family history containing several generations' worth of thoroughly documented data have different priorities than do researchers who want to present their families with a book filled with information, photos, and details about their siblings, parents, and grandparents.

Figure 1.3, which shows the creation of a family history book using the Book feature (discussed in Chapter Nine), displays the types of items you can include in a family history book. The focus of your book will determine the items you include in it.

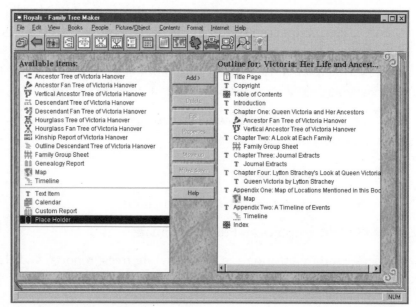

Figure 1.3

Select only those items that fit the focus of your book.

❧ **NOTE** ❧ *Although you will be using Family Tree Maker as the main source for your book, the program gives you the flexibility to supplement your book with material created in other programs, such as a word processor. For example, using a word processor, you can include transcriptions of journals, diaries, and documents; or you can write a narrative about specific individuals, locations, or eras. More about adding in text using a word processor or other program can be found in Chapter Eight, "Adding Text to Your Family History Book."*

Here are several questions to ask yourself as you begin working on your family history book:

- ❧ Who is the audience for your book?

- ❧ What type of book do you want to create—a formal family history, autobiography, memoirs, or something else? If you are unsure, check out the different book projects presented in Chapter Eleven.

- ❧ Which individuals do you want to include in the book—and whom do you want to exclude? Knowing which individuals will be included will help you give focus to your book. For example, if you want to create a book about your great-grandparents' lives after they immigrated to the United States, you probably will not want to include five generations of their ancestors.

In addition, here are some things you might want to think about:

- ❧ Have you conducted adequate research to support the focus of your book? In other words, do you have enough data entered to fulfill your goal for the book?

- ❧ Do you have all the family data entered into Family Tree Maker and sourced properly?

Family History Books for the Novice

Before creating your family history book, you might want to read one of the many books available about planning and writing a family history. Such books can give you an idea about what a typical family history book project consists of and can offer examples of how different family history books are arranged. They can also provide information about different narrative styles that you might want to use. Here are a couple that you might like to try:

❋ *Producing a Quality Family History* by Patricia Law Hatcher, published by Ancestry, Incorporated

❋ *Writing a 'Non-Boring' Family History* by Hazel Edwards, published by Hale & Iremonger

❋ How will you publish the book? A discussion of publishing your book is found in Chapter Ten, "Printing and Publishing Your Family History Book."

Scrutinizing Your Data

You're poised at the computer, fingers itching to fire up Family Tree Maker and get your family history book underway, while visions of the first Pulitzer Prize awarded to a family history book dance in your head. Eyes sparkling, a thousand ideas dashing about your brain, your breathing is erratic as you reach for the mouse to begin your journey . . . but wait! Are you sure you're ready to get under way?

❧ **NOTE** ❧ *You should be somewhat familiar with Family Tree Maker before diving into a family history book project. You should also have some data entered. If you do not have data entered into the program, do so before continuing so that you won't have to interrupt the creation of your book to enter your family information.*

If you are not familiar with the program, check out the sidebar "Family Tree Maker Basics," later in this chapter. In that sidebar, you will find a quick rundown of the steps for starting a Family File, entering basic information, adding a child, and entering sources for your events and facts. Throughout the book, I also provide steps for the specific tasks that you will perform as you create your book.

You can use the following bulleted list as a checklist before you begin working on your family history book in Family Tree Maker.

- Evaluate the information in your database. Is it complete? Have you verified every fact? Have you documented all events? Have you noted unverified information as such? Were you consistent in the manner in which you entered the information?

- Does your data consist solely of names and dates, or have you added as much supplemental information as is available? Names and dates are well and good, but boring unless accompanied by other information and details. Don't be afraid to enrich your family history by using anecdotes and local color.

- Do you have an audience? If you are creating a book on the descendants of Charlemagne with the intention of selling it to members of the Order of the Crown of Charlemagne society, have you verified that no such book already exists?

- Have you scanned in photographs and added them into an individual's or family's scrapbook? Have you scanned or digitized other items such as records, maps, cards, signatures, photographs of buildings, locations, headstones, and so on? Figure 1.4 shows how even a few graphics can liven up the dullest family.

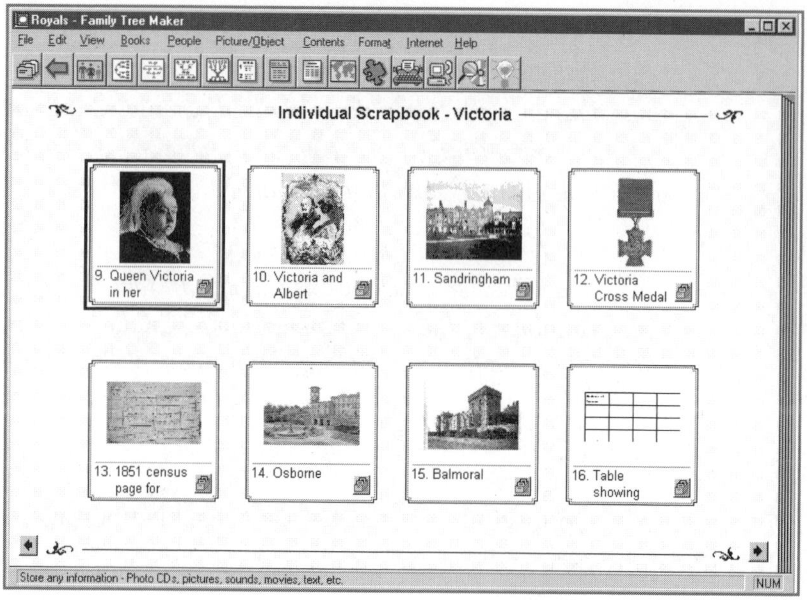

Figure 1.4

Photographs, scanned images, sound and video files, word-processor files, and OLE items can help to flesh out the individual or family.

NOTE OLE *(Object Linking and Embedding) technology allows information to be shared between applications within the Screens environment. OLE objects can be made up of almost any type of data—for example, graphics, tables, or text. You can add OLE objects to an individual's or marriage's Scrapbook, fleshing out the bare details with a wealth of information.*

- Have you used Family Tree Maker's error-checking feature to check for name errors or unlikely birth, death, and marriage dates? You'll find more information on error checking in Chapter Two, "Organizing Your Family History Book." Have you double-checked all information to make sure the data is correct?

  Remember to check for errors before beginning your family history book.

- Have you used Family Tree Maker's spell-check feature to proof your text and notes? More information about using the spell-check feature can be found in Chapter Eight.

✴ Have you visited a library and browsed through existing family history books? Checking other family history books can give you a good idea of what you like and dislike in a book and can provide ideas for items you might want to include in your own book. You also need to decide how you want the information formatted, what limits to set on the number of individuals you include, how to incorporate nonstandard items such as maps, document abstracts and extracts, scanned images, and so on.

✴ Have you examined your master source list and verified that your sources are cited properly? Are you using a consistent style when citing sources for all the information included in the database? Figure 1.5 shows how you can easily enter master source information. Whenever possible, sources should be entered for every piece of data in the database.

✴ Have you scanned your computer recently for viruses? Computer viruses can corrupt data, image files, or programs necessary for your computer to run correctly. Before undertaking a project that can't be duplicated easily, be sure to check your entire hard drive for viruses.

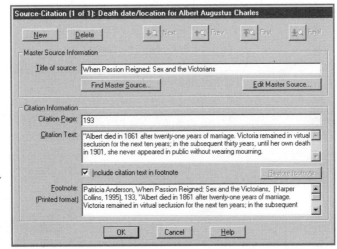

Figure 1.5

Be sure to include sources for all your information.

🦋 Have you created backups of your Family Tree Maker files? Before you begin your project, it's wise to make at least one backup of your precious family data! Although you might not think you'll need them, frequent backups have saved many researchers from having to start all over when their database files were corrupted or deleted. Figure 1.6 features the Family Tree Maker Backup Family File dialog box.

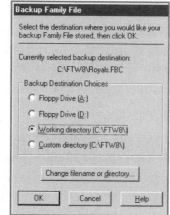

Figure 1.6

Backups are a necessity! Back up your database before making *any* changes.

Family Tree Maker Basics

The following information is intended for users who are new to Family Tree Maker. For more information about each task mentioned, consult the program's Getting Started manual, Family Tree Maker's Help file, or the book, *Family Tree Maker Version 8 Fast & Easy: The Official Guide,* by Rhonda R. McClure (published by Prima Tech).

To begin a new Family File, follow these steps:

1. Start Family Tree Maker.

2. From the File menu, choose New Family File.

3. In the New Family File dialog box, enter the filename you want to use in the File Name field and click Save.

   I generally use the family name so that I know which family is found in which file.

4. The Data Entry Wizard will now guide you through the first few steps of entering information about you, your parents, and grand-parents, as shown in Figure 1.7.

Start your Family Tree

Enter as many names as you know, starting with yours.
Include first, middle and last names if you know them, and use maiden
names for women.

	His father:	
Your father:		
	His mother:	
Your name:	Your gender: ○ Female ○ Male
	Her father:	
Your mother:		
	Her mother:	

Next >   Cancel   Help

Figure 1.7

Use the Startup
Wizard to enter
information in
the first few
steps.

Once you finish entering information in the Data Entry Wizard, you are sent to the Family Page (the main screen in Family Tree Maker), where you can enter or edit information for an individual's birth date and location, death date and location, burial date and location, marriage date and location, as well as add children, open an individual's Scrapbook, and more. Click the appropriate field to enter the information you want.

5. When you finish entering names and dates, add any children of the primary individual (and spouse, if applicable).

(continued)

NOTE *When you begin a new Family File, Family Tree Maker initiates a new Data Entry Wizard that guides you to enter basic information for yourself, your parents, and their parents (however, you do not need all that information to use the program). The Wizard asks you to enter names, birth information, death information, and whether you want to conduct a Family Finder Search. Once you fill out as much information as possible in the Wizard, you are sent to the primary individual's Family Page.*

To add a child, follow these steps:

1. On the Family Page, click the first row of the Children field.

2. Enter the child's first name (the surname is automatically filled in for you) and press either Enter or Tab to move to the next field.

3. Select the child's gender in the Sex field (if the child is not female, type an **M** over the F in the Sex field).

4. Click the Birth Dates field and enter the child's birth date.

5. Repeat the process for additional children.

To enter sources for an event or fact, follow these steps:

1. On the Family Page, click the field that you want to source (for example, an individual's death date).

2. From the View menu, select Source.

3. In the Source-Citation dialog box, enter the title in the Title of Source field (the title should be the name of the resource in which you found the information—for example, the name of a book or newspaper).

4. Click the Edit Master Source button and fill in as much information as possible in the Master Source dialog box. Click OK when you are finished.

   Family Tree Maker takes you back to the Source-Citation dialog box.

5. Click the Citation Page field and enter a page number.

6. Click the Citation Text field and enter the desired information about the item you are sourcing.

   You can include a quote from the source or a description of what you found.

7. If you want the information included in a footnote on trees and reports, click the Include Citation Text in Footnote check box.

8. The text for the footnote is automatically generated from the information you enter. If you want to change it, click the Footnote field and make your changes.

9. Click OK when finished.

To add More About Facts and Notes, follow these steps:

1. Click the More button that appears to the right of the name of the individual you want to work with.

   The More About screen opens, displaying the More About items: Facts, Address, Medical, Lineage, and Notes.

2. Click the item for which you want to enter information.

3. In the item's screen, enter your information. When you are finished, from the View menu, click Family Page to return to your starting point.

Giving Your Audience the Right Book

Making sure that your family history book is appropriate for your audience is an important part of the book's preparation. You should have a clear idea of why you are writing the book and who will be reading it. Will it be an informal collection of stories and pictures about your immediate family or a formal family history that will serve as a reference point for interested researchers? The book you write for your grandchildren showing their immediate family is going to be much different than the meticulously researched, 25-generation overview of your New England ancestors. Know your readers and gear the book to their needs.

Visualizing Your Audience

You must consider many factors when defining your audience, including what will please your readers, the book format, and which individuals to include and exclude.

When considering your audience, answer the following questions:

🏃 Will this book be for your immediate family? If so, you probably want to use an informal format and not worry about sources, detailed genealogy reports, evidences, and analyses of your findings. Instead, you might want to create one of the following:

- A book for your grandchildren telling about your life

- A book for your siblings detailing your parents' and grandparents' lives

- A biography of a parent or grandparent

- An autobiography

- A family scrapbook

🏃 Will this book be for a family gathering, such as a family reunion? If so, you'll probably want to use a more formal format and include your sources, use a variety of genealogical charts and forms to show the relationships in your extended family, and perhaps limit yourself to a few generations with all collateral lines shown.

* Will this book be used as a resource for persons interested in your family? If so, you'll probably want to use a formal format with sources, analyses of your findings and conflicting evidence, a variety of genealogical charts, a genealogy report in NGS Quarterly or Register format (both are discussed in detail in Chapter Five, "Using Narrative Reports in Your Family History Book"), a bibliography, an index, and other items geared toward serious researchers. Figure 1.8 shows an example of a family history in Register Report format, a more formal style that is not suited to all family history projects. See Chapters Three ("Using Trees in Your Family History Book"), Four ("Using Miscellaneous Trees and Charts in Your Family History Book"), and Five ("Using Narrative Reports in Your Family History Book") for details on the various trees, charts, reports, and other items you can include in your book.

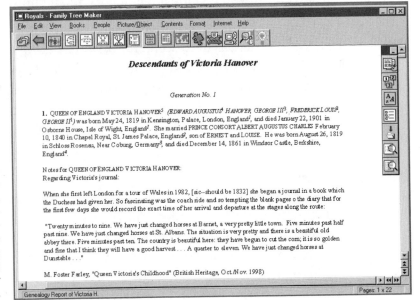

Figure 1.8

The book's audience will determine which items you include. For example, Register Reports are better suited for a detailed or formal family history than for a brief, informal book about your immediate family.

Choosing the Right Format

As demonstrated in the preceding section, your audience affects how you format your book. Once you decide on your audience, you need to make a decision about what form your book will take. Here are questions to consider when choosing the form (note that many questions apply to all forms).

* **Autobiography.** Will you include information about your parents, siblings, spouse, and children? Will you include photos and other items from your scrapbook as well as narrative?

* **Biography.** Will you include information about an individual's parents, siblings, spouse, and children? Will you include information about the individual's ancestry? If so, how many generations back will you go?

* **Informal family history.** Who is your target person? Will the book be ancestor-oriented or descendant-oriented? How many generations will you include? What charts and forms offer the most understanding to non-genealogists? Will you include photos and items as well as narrative? Will you include a mailing list of all family members?

* **Detailed family history.** Who is the target individual? Will the book be ancestor-oriented or descendant-oriented? How many generations will you include? Will you include *direct line* only (that is, direct descendants or ancestors without any cousins), or will you include everyone in the family? Will you limit information to just one family and exclude collateral lines? Which charts and forms present your information in an attractive and useful format?

* **Extensive family history.** Who is the target individual? Will the book be ancestor-oriented or descendant-oriented? How many generations will you include? Will you include direct line lineages, or include all of the family? Will you include analysis of your research and possible conflicting evidence? Will you provide a bibliography and summary of the sources you used? Will you include a Register- or NGS Quarterly–formatted report? Which charts and forms best present your information in a formal manner?

As you can see, you have many options for any family history book project, but don't worry at this point about committing yourself and not being able to change your mind later. Family Tree Maker enables you to easily reorder, add, and remove book items. In Chapter Nine, "Creating Your Family History Book," I go into more detail about each specific item, and in Chapter Eleven, "Family History Book Projects," I provide actual family history book projects.

Limiting the Scope of Your Family History Book

Imagine that you've spent years following leads and amassing information on your ancestors. You've tracked down sources; documented each and every fact; and photographed houses, headstones, barns, and relatives. You've transcribed wills and probate records, land records, and legal documents; you've scoured town vital record books for one more bit of evidence. You've scanned in photographs, photocopies, books, documents, and ephemera. You have information on thousands of individuals who make up your family tree, and now you are prepared to do them all justice by printing up a family history book.

Whoa—you want to do them *all* justice? Before you begin organizing your book and deciding which trees and charts to use, you should give some thought as to which individuals should be included. If your database is relatively small, you can get away with including everyone in the book. If you have 2,900 individuals listed, however, you're going to want to limit the number of individuals you include in the book. (If you are unsure whom to include, refer to the earlier section "Visualizing Your Audience" for help on understanding your audience.) Figure 1.9 shows the Family File Status dialog box, which tells you the database file size, the number of individuals in the database, and the number of records in the database. (To view this dialog box and find out how many people are in your Family Tree Maker database, open the Help menu and click Family File Status, or use the keyboard shortcut, Alt+F1.)

Why limit the number of individuals in your book? If you include too many people, your book might become unwieldy and cumbersome. Unless you have lots of experience organizing and writing a detailed family history book, too many individuals can cause the book to lose focus.

Figure 1.9

Do you really want
to include all 2,979
individuals?

Family File Status

Family File: Royals.FTW

Size: 6709 KB

Individuals: 2979

Text Records: 15650

Family Tree
Maker

OK

For example, maybe you want to create a book that will highlight all the fun ancestors in your family tree—Christopher the Revolutionary War veteran, Mary who sailed on the *Mayflower* with her father Isaac, Gottfried who escaped imprisonment in Prussia by the skin of his teeth, a noted historian by the name of Baskerville, and, oh yes, don't forget King Edward I. Even if you limit yourself to direct-line descent information, you'll probably end up with a book with no real focus; thus, the reader might start out following the Plantagenets in England, only to suddenly find herself elbow deep in a chapter about Gottfried's terrible experiences at the hands of a brutal Prussian general.

A wiser choice would be to create four separate books, each focusing on a target individual. Show ancestors or descendants as you like, but choose one person to be the target of your book, and use that focus to limit the number of individuals included to only those who are pertinent. Using Family Tree Maker, you can create several databases with just the family members you want, enabling you to include only people you want in your family history book.

❧ **NOTE** ❧ *When considering how to limit your book's scope, keep in mind that Family Tree Maker limits each book to contain only 500 items. That means you can have up to 500 different forms, trees, charts, text items, graphic items, and so on. It does not mean that your book can hold only 500 individuals—you could have 1,000 people listed in your book as long as you have 500 or fewer items. Because Family Tree Maker allows you to have 32 different books, however, you can be creative in working around the 500-item limit. For example, if you find yourself bumping up against the limit, you could create two books, each featuring a different ancestor.*

CHAPTER TWO

Organizing Your Family History Book

There is a history in all men's lives.
—William Shakespeare, *King Henry IV*

rganizing a family history book is not nearly as daunting as it sounds—arranging a book is similar to organizing a research plan. For example, you would not start out researching your family tree without some thought about which individuals you want to research, nor would you jump into the research without a minimal research plan in your head. Likewise, you must have a plan as to what type of book you want to create and which individuals you will include. You can use the same Family Tree Maker tool to organize your book that you use to organize your research.

By the end of this chapter, you will know how to do the following:

- ⚜ Organize your family history book project using Family Tree Maker's Research Journal.

- ⚜ Make sure that your database is ready for publication by conducting error checks.

- ⚜ Understand the basic copyright laws and how they apply to you.

- ⚜ Understand the importance of privacy issues.

Using the Research Journal

Family Tree Maker's Research Journal can be a great help when you are organizing and planning your family history book. Using the Research Journal, you can enter all the steps you need to plan and arrange your book—everything from visualizing the book to including step-by-step actions needed to complete your project. Both new and experienced users can find benefit in utilizing the organizational ability of the Research Journal; new users can use it to organize the process of research as well as to create a book, while experienced users can create detailed lists of steps they must accomplish to pull together a complex family history book.

One of the benefits of the Research Journal is its capability to create a To Do list to manage your tasks and to keep track of what you've accomplished, what you still need to accomplish, and what you plan to do next. Figure 2.1 shows an example of a plan you might create in the Research Journal to begin the process of creating a family history book.

To open the Research Journal screen, follow these steps:

1. From the Family Page toolbar, click the FamilyFinder Center button (refer to Chapter One to see this button on the toolbar).

   The FamilyFinder Center appears.

2. Click My Research Journal/To-Do List. Alternatively, from the View menu, you can click FamilyFinder and select Research Journal.

   The Research Journal screen opens, enabling you to enter new To Do items.

Follow these steps to add a new To Do item:

1. In the Research Journal, click the Click Here link at the top of the page.

   The New To Do Item dialog box opens (if you double-click an existing To Do item, the Edit To Do Item dialog box opens, allowing you to edit the item).

2. Enter your To Do text, set a priority, choose a category, and enter a date.

3. When you finish, click OK to return to the Research Journal screen.

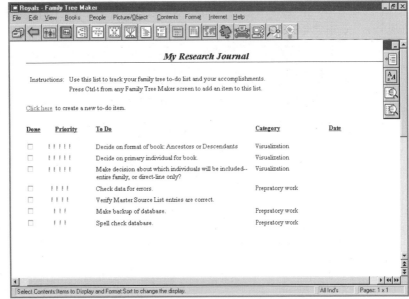

Figure 2.1

Use the Research Journal to plan, organize, and track the progress of your family history book.

The Research Journal has several useful features:

✻ Each task on the To Do List has a Done check box (refer to Figure 2.1) that you can check or uncheck to show items as complete or not complete. You can display items that are completed, not completed, or both.

To mark an item as completed, take this step:

1. In the Research Journal, click the check box located in the Done column.

   A check mark appears, letting you know that the task is marked as completed.

   If you change your mind, simply uncheck the box.

❋ You can assign a priority to each item; the Research Journal gives you one to five exclamation points to rate the priority of an item, so you will know at a glance which tasks you should focus on first. You might sort items in your list by priority.

To assign a priority to an item, follow these steps:

1. In the Research Journal, double-click the item to which you want to assign a priority.

   The Edit To Do Items dialog box opens, enabling you to edit the item.

2. Use the up and down arrows in the Priority box to assign a priority to that item.

3. Click OK to return to the Research Journal screen.

Here are the steps for sorting To Do items:

1. In the Research Journal screen, click the Format menu and select Sort Research Journal.

   The Research Journal screen appears.

2. Using the pull-down menu in the Sort Research Journal screen, select how you want your journal sorted—by category, date, or priority.

3. Click OK to return to the Research Journal screen.

❋ You can designate a category for each task. Then you can use the categories to sort the tasks in your To Do list by topic, day, or category. For example, I might want to arrange my tasks into visualization items (things to consider before beginning work on the book), organization items (tasks to be completed in the process of planning the book), and creation items (tasks to be completed to create the actual book). You can create as many categories as you like, customizing them to fit your needs.

To designate a category for an item, follow these steps:

1. In the Research Journal, double-click the item you want to assign a category.

   The Edit To Do Items dialog box opens, enabling you to edit the item.

2. In the Category field, enter a category.

   After you enter a category, it will be available for any other To Do items you enter via the pull-down arrow in the Category field of either the New To Do Item dialog box or the Edit To Do Item dialog box.

3. Click OK to return to the Research Journal screen.

❧ You can enter a date for each task, defining the date as you like—it can be the date you need the item completed, the date you began the item, or just the date you entered the item.

To enter a date for an item:

1. In the Research Journal, double-click the item for which you want to enter a date.

   The Edit To Do Items dialog box opens, enabling you to edit the item.

2. In the Date field, enter the date you want.

3. Click OK to return to the Research Journal screen.

The next two sections show you specific examples of how you can use the Research Journal to plan and organize a family history book—in this case, a formal family history book.

Planning a Formal Family History Book

Project: A formalized presentation of your research to date.

Description: A detailed family history showing the descendants of two New England ancestors.

Contents: The book will contain a number of descendant trees, charts, and reports; analyses of sources written elsewhere and imported into Family Tree Maker; scrapbooks for selected individuals; customized book items; and an index. Figure 2.2 shows some items included in the Research Journal for this project.

Here are the four basic steps to accomplish when creating this book:

1. Create the To Do list of items.

2. Set deadlines for items.

3. Assign priorities based on an item's importance.

4. Sort the items appropriately.

You may want to organize your book project differently—that's the beauty of the Research Journal. You can use it to fit your own needs, adapting the techniques that I'm about to show to suit your project.

Figure 2.2

Use the Research Journal to organize the tasks of creating a formal family history book.

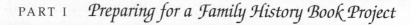

CREATING TO DO LISTS

Begin by listing tasks as To Do items. You'll want to include all the tasks you need to accomplish. To Do items can be as mundane as "outline book" or as exciting as "take manuscript to printer." Assigning each To Do item a category indicative of its place in the development of the book allows you to clearly differentiate separate stages.

In this example, five categories are shown (refer to Figure 2.1):

- ❧ Preliminaries (preliminary tasks needed to be accomplished in order to move ahead in the book's creation)

- ❧ Sources (tasks related to proper sourcing of data)

- ❧ Selection (choosing which items and individuals will be included in the book)

- ❧ Information (acquiring supplemental information needed to publish the book—in this case, verification of data and a list of interested researchers)

- ❧ Trees and charts (creation of specific Family Tree Maker trees, charts, and reports)

SETTING TO DO ITEM DEADLINES

You need to set deadlines to ensure that the tasks are completed in a timely manner. Note that a deadline is just one of the ways you can put the Date field to use. Instead of a deadline, you might want to enter the date only after you complete the task, or you might enter the date when you first include the To Do item. The choice is yours—for this example, I chose to use the Date field as a spot to enter my deadline, thus giving me a reminder of when I needed to have tasks completed.

ASSIGNING TO DO ITEM PRIORITIES

Assigning a priority to each task gives you the ability to see at a glance which items need to be accomplished first. Take a good look at your list of items and note whether some tasks need to be accomplished before others. If so, assign those prerequisite items a higher priority, and you'll be sure to complete them before you get to the next stage in your book's development.

When you sort your list by Priority, you will have a consecutive list of items organized by timeliness. In this example, the To Do list is sorted by priority so that I can be sure to attend to higher priority tasks before lower priority ones.

SORTING YOUR TO DO LIST

The last organizational stage of this project using the Research Journal is to decide how you want the list sorted. As you recall from the preceding discussion, you can sort by date, priority, or category. Because this example has tasks that you want completed before others, sort it by priority. Note that both completed and uncompleted tasks are included, offering the user an idea of what has been accomplished and what remains to be done.

> ❋**TIP**❋ *If you want to organize tasks in a specific order, number each one before you type the description. In Figure 2.2, the Research Journal is sorted by Priority; Family Tree Maker automatically alphabetizes the tasks within each level of priority. Thus, if you have four tasks assigned a level five priority, you can arrange them within that class by numbering each item so they will display in numerical order.*

MARKING ITEMS AS COMPLETED

Marking items as completed gives you a clear idea of which tasks are accomplished and which ones remain to be done. One way to keep from being overwhelmed by the sheer number of items on your list is to show only those items remaining to be completed. Marking off completed items allows you to focus on just those tasks that remain.

To show only items completed, only items not completed, or both, follow these steps:

1. On the Research Journal page, from the Contents menu, select Items to Include.

2. In the Items to Include dialog box that appears, select the choice you want to show in the list.

   You can also select to show only specific categories or all categories.

3. Make your choices and click OK to return to the Research Journal.

SETTING A CUT-OFF DATE

As you continue to research a family line, you'll still gather information, verify unsourced data, and find new leads to research resources. If your research project is a continuing one, it is important that you set a cut-off date, after which you will not include new information in your family history book.

Why is setting a cut-off date so important? If you do not set a date after which you will no longer include new information, you might repeatedly hold off the publication of your book while you investigate and evaluate each new tidbit of data. Although you want your book to be as complete as possible, you need to set a date for ceasing to include new facts in your database.

Once your book is planned, it's time to address one of the most important issues—making sure that your data is ready to be published in a family history book.

Preparing Your Database for Publication

One problem inherent in using a computer program that allows you to quickly and easily create a family history book is that users might be tempted to create and print copies of their family history before they should. Although no hard and fast rule governs how much data you need before you can print a family history, you should take a long look at your database and consider whether the information in it is complete.

Making Sure Your Database Is Complete

Using Family Tree Maker's Custom Report function, you can generate and print a report showing what sources are missing for those fields that you include in the report (for more information about the Custom Report, see Chapter Six,

"Exploring Custom and Miscellaneous Reports"). You can also create a report to show specific information and note obvious gaps in the data. Figure 2.3 shows an example of how you can use the Documented Events Report to show only those events that are *not* documented, while Figure 2.4 illustrates how you can set up a Custom Report to show what data you have—more importantly, the gaps show you what you still need to collect.

To create a Custom Report showing missing information, follow these steps:

1. In the Family Page, from the View menu, click Reports, Custom.

2. From the Format menu, select Report Format.

3. In the Report Format dialog box, scroll down to Documented Events, click it, and then click OK.

   The report appears listing all the events that have sources entered.

4. To show facts that do not have documentation, go to the Contents menu and select Options.

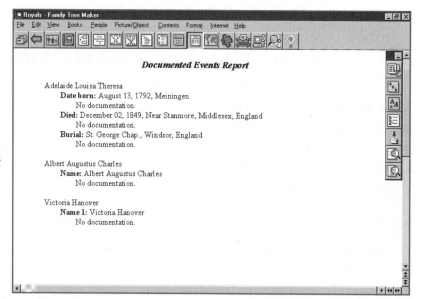

Figure 2.3

Here's an example of how you can use the Documented Events Report to show which facts are yet to be sourced.

5. Click List Events and Facts without Documentation.

6. Click OK.

The resulting report shows any facts or events you entered that are not sourced.

You can also make a customized report that shows the holes in your data. To do so, follow these steps:

1. In the Family Page, from the View menu, click Reports, Custom, or click the Reports button in the toolbar.

2. From the Format menu, select Report Format.

3. In the Report Format dialog box, select Custom and click OK.

4. From the Contents menu, select Items to Include (for more information about what items can be included in a report, see Chapter Three, "Using Trees in Your Family History Book").

Figure 2.4

You can create a Custom Report to show the information that you already have— and use the obvious gaps as a pointer to the information that you still need to gather.

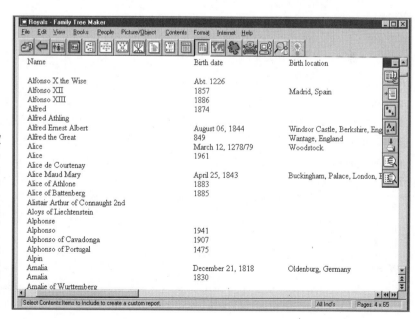

5. Select the items you want to appear on the report. (Note: more information about this report, and the options available for it, appear in Chapter Six, "Exploring Custom and Miscellaneous Reports.")

6. Click the right arrow to add the items to the report. When you are finished, click OK.

Don't be in a rush to publish your information! Take the time to make sure that the database is as complete as possible before you decide to print. If your report shows you are missing too much data, consider holding off printing your book until you have more data. Print the reports and charts you want to include in your book and examine them for empty fields, absent sources, and missing data. If at all possible, track down the sources and fill in the blank spots before you move on to the next step.

Checking Your Data for Accuracy

No matter how many attractive charts and trees, how many generations, or how many color pictures you insert in the document, the ultimate test of whether your book satisfies its readers lies in the accuracy of the information you present.

Even if you are creating a book intended only for your immediate family members, you are still obliged to ensure that everything in the book is as accurate as possible. Names, dates, events, sources, photograph descriptions, annotations, analyses, descriptive text, narratives, extracts, abstracts, and quotations from other publications must be checked for accuracy. Although much of the burden of accuracy lies directly on your shoulders, Family Tree Maker does make the task of error checking a bit easier by offering the user two functions: error checking and spell checking (spell checking an item is discussed in Chapter Eight, "Adding Text to Your Family History Book").

ERROR CHECKING

Say that you have only 25 individuals in your Family Tree Maker database; you still have a good amount of information entered, including dates and locations of events, names, source information, notes, and so on. It's easy for even the most meticulous researcher to make a mistake when entering data. An individual married to the wrong person, a child's date of birth before the parent's date of birth, or a person attached to the wrong branch of the family are some examples of mistakes that can be easily corrected. You can find such errors by utilizing the Data Errors Report, discussed later in this section.

Note that Family Tree Maker does some error checking automatically when you enter data, but the Find Error command enables you to check the database for errors that might not be readily apparent when you entered the information. Because the Data Errors Report function allows you to print a report of possible errors in your database, you have the opportunity to correct problems before you print your family history book.

Using the Find Error Feature

The Find Error feature checks your entire database for two specific types of errors: name errors and unlikely birth, death, and marriage dates. You can tell Family Tree Maker which type of error you want it to search for by using the Find Error command. Figure 2.5 shows the Find Error dialog box set so that a full search is executed for both types of errors.

Several types of name errors might crop up:

- Possible misplaced dash in a name
- Use of a title in the Name field
- Use of a name that contains an illegal character

Figure 2.5

Family Tree Maker will check the database for problem areas.

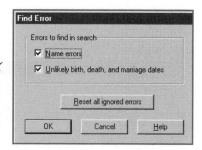

❀ Possible use of married name rather than maiden name

❀ Possible use of a name with too many or too few capital letters

❀ Possible use of a name that contains a nickname

Figure 2.6 shows typical name errors. As with other types of errors found using the Find Error command, Family Tree Maker tells you what it thinks is the problem with the data, and gives you the chance to correct the error or to ignore it if it is truly not an error.

A number of other data errors might also be detected:

❀ Born when parent individual was under 13.

❀ Individual's birth date is after mother's death date.

❀ Individual's birth date occurred too long after father's death date.

❀ Death date is before birth date.

❀ Individual's marriage to spouse occurred before age 13.

❀ Event date is empty.

❀ Death date is more than 120 years after birth date.

❀ Individual's birth date is more than 20 years after the marriage date of mother and father.

❀ Individual's birth date is before the marriage date of mother and father.

❀ Not in birth order in the children list.

❀ Mother is older than 50 at the time of child's birth.

Figure 2.6

A typical name error involves having too many or too few capital letters; in this example, Family Tree Maker didn't like the fact that this individual's name consisted of three capitalized words and one uncapitalized word.

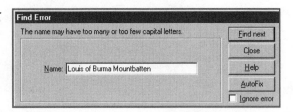

As all of these errors are self-explanatory, you should have no trouble determining whether the error is truly an error or whether it's one of the many situations in which the information is correct but "looks" wrong to Family Tree Maker.

Data Errors Report

The Data Errors printed report includes the preceding errors, as well as three others:

- **Is this *<name>* the same as *<name>?*** This error will show if you have two individuals who are named identically within the same family, with the same birth gender and birth dates. This error generally catches instances in which you have entered duplicate individuals.

  TIP *To merge duplicate individuals, from the People menu, click Merge Duplicate Individuals. Click Display Merge Report to display a list that lets you determine whether the individuals are the same, click Done when you're done with the report, and then click Merge Matching Information to merge the duplicate individuals in your database.*

- **No parents, no children, and no spouses.** This error pops up for individuals who are unrelated to anyone else in the database. If your person should be connected with someone in the database, you can use the Fix Relationship Errors function to add them to the appropriate person's family.

  TIP *To add an unrelated individual into a family by marriage, from the People menu, select Fix Relationship Mistakes. In the Fix Relationship Mistakes dialog box, select Attach Spouse. Click the name of the person you want attached as the spouse. Click OK.*

  To add an unrelated individual into a family as a child, from the People menu, select Fix Relationship Mistakes. In the Fix Relationship Mistakes dialog box, select Attach Child. Click the name of the person you want attached as the child. Click OK.

⚝ **<*Field name*> may have incorrect capitalization.** This error indicates that you typed an individual's name in all uppercase letters. You can correct this by using lowercase letters.

To create a Data Errors Report, follow these steps:

1. From the Family Page, click View, Reports, Data Errors.

2. If you want to change the Options (see Chapter Six, "Exploring Custom and Miscellaneous Reports," for more information on the report's options), from the Contents menu, select Options.

3. If you want to change the individuals included in the report, from the Contents menu, select Individuals to Include.

Figure 2.7 shows part of a Data Errors Report. Consult your Family Tree Maker manual for a full description of the errors and how to correct the problems.

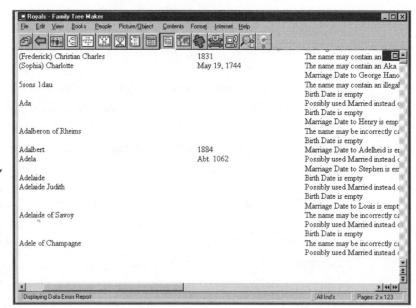

Figure 2.7

The Data Errors Report displays all the problems Family Tree Maker found in your database, including empty data fields.

❧ **NOTE** ❧ *Family Tree Maker's Find Error function includes an AutoFix feature that fixes errors that the program knows how to correct, or you can tell the program to ignore a problem. If you change your mind later, you can also reset the ignored errors so that they are once again recognized as errors.*

The Importance of Labeling and Describing Scrapbook Items

A picture is worth a thousand words, but many people have not taken the time to label all their family photos. This means that they are at a loss when they cannot put names to faces and fix the locations of pictures of houses, farms, buildings, and so on. It is important to properly label and describe each image you include in an individual's Scrapbook. Every bit of information you can gather about the picture—names of people in it, the location, reason for the picture, date—should be included. It all adds value to the picture and makes an item of much more interest to your readers. You should also include the information as a resource for interested researchers—sometimes the tiniest clue can lead other researchers to avenues of information that you had no idea were available! For example, mentioning that the house before which a group of children are posed is in a particular town might lead researchers to locate land records! Put whatever information you have about the picture's contents and circumstances into the Scrapbook item's description.

Figure 2.8 shows how easy it is to label and describe a Scrapbook item. You can find more information about the Scrapbook feature and about including graphics in your family history book in Chapter Seven, "Using Graphics in Your Family History Book."

Citing Your Sources

If you are creating an informal family history book or Scrapbook, you are probably not too concerned about making sure that your sources are comprehensive and correctly cited. But anyone who is planning to publish a book with the intent to inform other interested researchers or family members about the individuals included in the book needs to heed that age-old battle cry of genealogists: *Cite your sources.*

More About Picture/Object

Caption: Sandringham

Category: Locations

Date of origin: c.1870

Type: Picture

Description: Photo of Sandringham taken by the (then) Princess of Wales. Sandringham was a great favorite of the Queen, and she often stayed there in her later years, accompanied by family.

☐ Preferred Picture for Home Page

☐ Preferred Picture/Object #1 for trees

☐ Preferred Picture/Object #2 for trees

☐ Preferred Picture/Object #3 for trees

☐ Preferred Picture/Object for Labels/Cards

☐ Preferred Picture/Object for Fam Grp Sheets

Play Scrapbook
☑ Include in show

Printing
☑ Include in printed Scrapbook

Photo CD
CD #:
Picture #:
Resolution:

[OK]   [Cancel]   [Help]

Figure 2.8

Be sure to include as much information and descriptive details as you can for each of your Scrapbook items.

Sources are important because they show others where you found the information you are presenting—a sort of roadmap that indicates what specific document, book, or other resource you consulted to gain that data.

The Master Source feature of Family Tree Maker enables you to enter a great deal of detail about where you found the information for each event. For sources used for a number of events, you have to enter the information only once in the Master Source dialog box; then you call it up for each individual citation and note the page number and any citation text. Figures 2.9 and 2.10 show the two dialog boxes, that you will encounter when entering sources—the Source-Citation dialog box, where you will enter specific information about one event, and the Master Source dialog box, where you will enter a master source to be used in citations.

To enter a source for an item, follow these steps:

1. From the Family Page, click the field for which you want to enter a source.

2. From the View menu, select Source.

3. In the Source-Citation dialog box (see Figure 2.9), type your source's title, click the Edit Master Source button, and fill out the information in the Master Source dialog box (see Figure 2.10).

4. Click OK to return to the Source-Citation dialog box.

5. Enter the appropriate information in the Citation Page and Citation Text fields.

6. Click OK to return to the Family Page.

The Master Source dialog box allows you to enter a source that can be cited

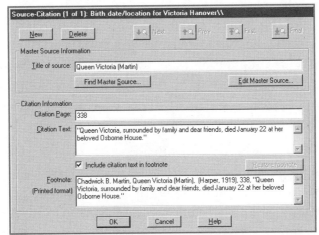

Figure 2.9

The Source-Citation dialog box allows you to enter all the pertinent information regarding a specific source of information. Be sure to be as complete as possible!

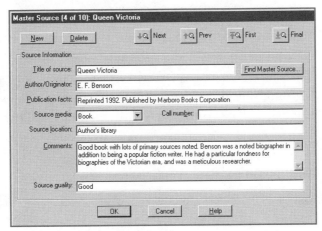

Figure 2.10

The Master Source dialog box allows you to create a source that you can later use in citations for more than one event via the Source-Citation dialog box.

again and again for various fields of data. Once you enter the source into the Master Source list, you can refer to that master source as many times as you like via the Source-Citation dialog box.

After you enter the basic information about a source (book title, author, and so on), you'll want to give the exact location within that resource for the information you are citing. Page numbers, source comments (quotes from the source, comments about its validity, and so on), or more information about the item you are sourcing can give your readers a better understanding about the resources you used to locate your information.

Safeguarding Your Data

In this age of global communication and rampant computer viruses, it's important that you protect the time and energy you pour into your research project by safeguarding your computer and the data it contains. Although no protection plan is guaranteed 100 percent safe, you can take two important steps to ensure that your precious genealogy data will not become the victim of an accidental or malicious act of computer mischief.

The first step is to invest in a frequently updated computer virus–detecting program. Several programs are available for many platforms of computers, most of which have weekly (or more frequent) updates available for download online. Programs such as McAfee's VirusScan and Norton Anti-Virus allow you to check your computer's memory, files that you download, or disks that you use for harmful viruses, worms, trojans, and their ilk.

The second step is to make frequent backups of your genealogical data and other valuable files. I use a two-disk system; after changes or additions are made, I back up the files to disk A. When I next make changes, I back up the files to disk B, giving myself an extra safeguard against the likelihood that my original backup disk will be confronted with one of the following:

* Be infected with a virus

* Become corrupted and made unreadable

* Be lost or destroyed

Viruses, Trojans, and Worms, Oh My!

A virus isn't just for living things anymore—computers can "catch" them as well, usually via files downloaded from the Internet, infected floppy disks, and sometimes files attached to e-mails. Every smart computer owner should be aware of the potential disaster posed by the following unholy trinity:

- **Virus.** A program or piece of code that runs without your knowledge. Viruses are man-made, and generally destructive in nature. Most can replicate themselves, spreading to other computers via e-mail or file transfers. The most destructive viruses will wipe out your hard drive, destroying everything on your computer.

- **Trojan.** A program that pretends it's one thing, while really it's another. Generally, trojans are destructive, but unlike viruses, they cannot replicate themselves.

- **Worm.** A special form of virus that can replicate itself and be very destructive, but that cannot attach itself to other programs (thus, for example, it cannot be sent inadvertently via e-mail).

The solutions to these evils? Frequent checks with current virus-detecting software and backing up all your important data to a safe (virus-free) location.

It's wise to follow a strict system of backups and virus checking when working on any project of import. Many people find it too bothersome to conduct periodic backups; others forget about them until it's too late. And many people think they are protected from viruses because they don't download files—but any computer can be infected! Don't lose your important data. Make a point of investing in current virus-detecting software and schedule frequent backups.

TIP *If you add both items to your To Do list, you'll be secure in the knowledge that you've done all you can to protect your precious data.*

Copyright Issues

You've found a painting of your great-great–grandfather hanging in a local history museum, and you want to include it in your book—because your family history book isn't really for profit and is just to disseminate information, it's okay if you use a picture of the painting without seeking permission, right?

Wrong! Despite the lure of photographs, maps, illustrations, portraits, analytical text, biographical notes, and similar works, you cannot include copyrighted items in your book without first gaining permission from their owners.

All authors need to be aware of the copyright laws in their countries and how those laws affect their books. In the United States, ignorance of the law does not excuse you from violations, and copyright laws are *very* vigorously enforced. Although some people feel the laws are too restricting, imagine how you would feel if someone took your family history book, put his or her name on it, and sold it.

Many people who violate copyright laws do so unknowingly and without malicious intent, but their actions are just as illegal and just as liable to punishment as are the actions of the person who intends to profit from copyright violations.

While such thoughts are daunting, you should not let them keep you from creating a family history book. As long as you think *before* you add a picture, illustration, or passage from a book to your own work and get permission to use the item—or make sure that it is in the pubic domain—you should be sitting pretty.

According to the U.S. Copyright Office, a copyright is as follows:

> . . . a form of protection provided by the laws of the United States (title 17, U.S. Code) to the authors of 'original works of authorship,' including literary, dramatic, musical, artistic, and certain other intellectual works. This protection is available to both published and unpublished works.

❧ **NOTE** ❧ *You can find more information about copyrights in the*
United States by contacting

> *U.S. Copyright Office*
> *Library of Congress*
> *101 Independence Ave. S.E.*
> *Washington, D.C. 20559-6000*
> *http://lcweb.loc.gov/copyright/circs/circ1.html*
> *E-mail: copyinfo@loc.gov*

What Is Copyrighted and What Isn't

Copyrighted works fall into eight categories:

- Literary works
- Musical works
- Dramatic works
- Pantomimes and choreographic works
- Pictorial, graphic, and sculptural works
- Motion pictures and other audiovisual works
- Sound recordings
- Architectural works

The U.S. Copyright Office notes that "computer programs and most 'compilations' may be registered as 'literary works;' maps and architectural plans may be registered as 'pictorial, graphic, and sculptural works.'"

Of this list, the items most likely to affect family historians are literary, pictorial, and graphical works.

Items not covered by copyright include these:

- Intangible works (for example, improvised speeches or performances that have not been written or recorded)

- Titles, names, short phrases, and slogans; familiar symbols or designs; mere variations of typographic ornamentation, lettering, or coloring; mere listings of ingredients or contents

- Ideas, procedures, methods, systems, processes, concepts, principles, discoveries, or devices, as distinguished from a description, explanation, or illustration

- Works consisting of information that is public domain or common property (such as the layout of a standard calendar or lists and tables taken from public documents)

Also of interest to family historians are works that are public domain or common property. Many of the United States government publications, documents, and maps are public domain (for example, the U.S. Copyright Office's circular detailing copyright facts is public domain) and thus can be used without fear of copyright violation.

According to the U.S. Copyright Office, a work created on or after January 1, 1978, is

> . . . automatically protected from the moment of its creation and is ordinarily given a term enduring for the author's life plus an additional 70 years after the author's death.

For a work created before January 1, 1978, but not published or registered by that date, the duration of copyright is

> . . . computed in the same way as for works created on or after January 1, 1978: the life-plus-70 or 95/120-year terms will apply to them as well."

The 95/120-year term, according to the U.S. Copyright Office, is explained as the time period that anonymous and pseudonymous works will remain in copyright—that is, 95 years from publication or 120 years from creation, whichever is shorter.

For a work created and published before January 1, 1978

> . . . copyright was secured either on the date a work was published with a copyright notice or on the date of registration if the work was registered in unpublished form. In either case, the copyright endured for a first term of 28 years from the date it was secured. . . . Public Law 102.307, enacted on June 26, 1992, amended the 1976 Copyright Act to provide for automatic renewal of the term of copyrights secured between January 1, 1964, and December 31, 1977.

Understanding the Fair Use Exception

Just to make things more confusing, there's an exception to copyright law: the doctrine of *fair use* that allows limited use of a small portion of a copyrighted work without permission. Examples of situations that generally fall under the fair use rule include the following:

- 🏃 Quoting or excerpting a work in a review or criticism or for purposes of illustration

- 🏃 Quoting a short passage in a scholarly or technical work for illustration of the author's comments

Unfortunately, no hard and fast rules exist as to how much of a work you can use under the fair use rule. The U.S. Copyright Office says

> It is permissible to use limited portions of a work including quotes, for purposes such as commentary, criticism, news reporting, and scholarly reports. There are no legal rules permitting the use of a specific number of words, a certain number of musical notes, or percentages of a work. Whether a particular use qualifies as fair use depends on all the circumstances.

Copyright Summarized

Confused? You're not alone! Here are a few tips to guide you through what might otherwise be murky waters:

- If the literary or artistic work you want to use was published or created more than 100 years ago, most likely it is in the public domain, but you should investigate the date the copyright expired *before* you use the work. For example, although several of Arthur Conan Doyle's stories are now in the public domain, his later works (published in the 1910s and 1920s) are still under copyright because of the "seventy years after the death of the author" restriction.

- If the U.S. Government created the work you want to use, chances are it is in the public domain, but again, before you include it in your own work, you should verify whether you can use it without permission.

- If the work is copyrighted, you can invoke the fair use rule and use a small portion of the work, assuming that your use of the work qualifies under the fair use factors:

  - The purpose and character of the use, including whether such use is of a commercial nature or is for nonprofit educational purposes

  - The nature of the copyrighted work

  - The amount and substantiality of the portion used in relation to the copyrighted work as a whole

  - The effect of the use upon the potential market for or value of the copyrighted work

- If the work is copyrighted and you have permission to use it, you will probably be required to acknowledge the copyright holder and note the permission given for its use.

All the copyright laws boil down to one basic precept: If you're not sure a work is freely available for use, do not use it without first gaining permission.

Taking Note of Privacy Issues

Just as it's important to be aware of copyright restrictions on any information you include in your database, so you should take note of two particular issues pertaining to privacy: the inclusion of information about living individuals and the inclusion of information that might be considered sensitive.

Invasion of a person's privacy is a serious issue. The rule of thumb is to exclude any information for living individuals other than their names and relationship with family members, because other information might not only embarrass the individual, but also be used for illegal or nefarious purposes.

Although censorship is usually repugnant to authors, you might want to censor details that could be considered sensitive. Gossip has no place in a family history book unless the rumor can be substantiated and verified, and even then, you may prefer to exclude the story if the information might damage or hurt a family member. Examples of information you might want to exclude from your book include an adoptive relationship concerning a living individual who might not be aware of the situation, illegitimacy, police records, participation in heinous crimes, and so on. If you want to exclude such information, make a copy of your Family Tree Maker file, delete the information you do not want included in your book, and save the new file as your working file.

To make a copy of your Family File, follow these steps:

1. Make sure that the Family File you want to copy is loaded.

2. From the File menu, select Copy/Export Family File.

3. Enter a new name for the copied file in the Filename field.

4. Pick the type of file you want saved from the Save as Type pull-down menu (you can save the file as various versions of Family Tree Maker files or as a GEDCOM).

5. Click Save.

Once you load up your new version, you are free to go in and delete whatever bit of information you do not want to be printed. To delete information, simply highlight it and press the Delete key.

Before you print trees, charts, and reports, review your database for information about living individuals. If you want to include living individuals in your family history book, use Family Tree Maker's Privatize feature to keep birth, marriage, death, and More About Facts for living individuals from displaying, printing, uploading, or exporting. Keep in mind, however, that with Privatize enabled, you cannot see or modify any information for living individuals. Turn off the privacy feature to view the information again. Figure 2.11 shows Family Tree Maker's Privatize Information dialog box.

Figure 2.11

If you plan on sharing your files or printing data regarding living individuals, use the Privatize Information command to protect personal information.

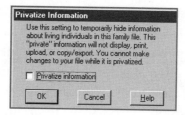

To use the Privatize Information command, follow these steps:

1. Open the Family File you want to privatize.

2. From the File menu, select Preferences, Privatize.

3. Read the information in the Privatize Information dialog box and click the Privatize Information check box if you want to continue.

   Family Tree Maker will then privatize your Family File, removing information about those individuals who are still living.

CHAPTER THREE

Using Trees in Your Family History Book

The subject of history
is the life of peoples and of humanity.
—Leo Tolstoy, *War and Peace*

amily Tree Maker creates a number of useful and interesting trees, reports, and charts that you might want to include in your family history book. Trees are divided into ancestor-ordered trees (that is, trees that show the *ancestors* of a specific individual) and descendant-ordered trees (that is, trees that show the *descendants* of a specific individual). The program has three main types of narrative reports: two descendant-ordered reports and one ancestor-ordered report. In addition to trees and reports, Family Tree Maker supports the use of several other items suitable for a family history book, including maps, a calendar, family group sheets, timelines, kinship reports, and a variety of customized reports.

This chapter explores the following trees:

- Standard Descendant Tree
- Fan Descendant Tree
- Outline Descendant Tree
- Standard Ancestor Tree
- Fan Ancestor Tree
- Vertical Ancestor Tree

The chapter is divided into two main sections. The first section details the descendant-ordered trees and ancestor-ordered trees. The second section reviews options, format, and contents for each tree. Other types of items that you might want to include in your book, such as narrative reports, custom reports, and miscellaneous charts, can be found in Chapters Four, "Using Miscellaneous Trees and Charts in Your Family History Book," Five, "Using Narrative Reports in Your Family History Book," and Six, "Exploring Custom and Miscellaneous Reports."

For each type of tree, report, or chart listed in this and the following three chapters, you will find the following:

- A full description of the tree or report
- The pros and cons of the item with a view to inclusion in a family history book
- A discussion of options available for each tree and report

By the time you finish this chapter, you will be conversant with a number of standard trees and reports that you can create using Family Tree Maker. You will also have done the following:

- Consulted the details given for each tree and report to locate which ones are best suited for your family history book project
- Printed sample copies of the trees and reports
- Experimented with the options and format for the trees and reports you choose to use

Experimenting with Trees, Reports, and Charts

Before choosing which trees, reports, and charts to use in your book, I advise you to print samples and experiment with the preferences and options for each until you find ones that suit your needs. Try changing the information included or limiting the individuals found on the chart. Will you like the tree better if you change the font? What if you change the density of boxes on the tree? How will it affect your tree if you change the information displayed?

Printing Trees, Reports, and Charts with Family Tree Maker

Much of the information that will be given to you in this and the following three chapters concerns which format and content options make up a tree, report, or chart. I urge everyone to experiment with the format and content options by changing the settings and printing sample copies *before* deciding on a final format. Since the instructions for printing a tree, report, or chart are basically the same, you should only have to take note of the instructions below to successfully print any item from Family Tree Maker.

To print a tree, report, chart, or other item (Scrapbook pages, More About Notes, and so on), follow these steps:

1. Open the Family File that you want to work with.

2. Click the name of the individual for whom you want to print an item.

3. Using the toolbar or menu, select that item (tree, report, chart, and so on).

4. Once the item's screen is open, from the File menu, select Print *[object name]*.

If you want to set up the printer differently for Family Tree Maker (select a different default printer or switch from portrait to landscape mode, for example), you can do so by going to the File menu and selecting Print Setup. You can find more information about the various print options in Chapter Ten, "Printing and Publishing Your Family History Book."

In general, you can change the following items on trees:

- 🏃 Font (the type, style, and size)
- 🏃 Boxes (line width and style)
- 🏃 Border (line width and style)

❀ Tree format (density and structure)

❀ The information to be included on the tree

❀ The individuals to be included on the tree

Note that this list is not comprehensive for every tree, report, and chart; for specific details on what options are available for each specific tree and report, consult the section for that tree in this chapter or in the relevant sections in Chapters Four, Five, and Six.

> ❋**TIP**❋ *Don't try to put too much information into one tree—trees can quickly become cluttered, making them difficult to read. Include only the information that is necessary in order for your readers to gain value from the tree.*

Exploring Descendant-Ordered Trees

Descendant-ordered trees show a person's children, grandchildren, and so on—in other words, the individual's *descendants*. The target individual is shown at the top of the tree, while the descendants are displayed along horizontal "branches," each subsequent generation lower than the one before it.

Such trees are popular in family history books, although they can quickly become quite bulky and take up a number of pages if you have several individuals in each generation. Three descendant-ordered trees are available in Family Tree Maker:

❀ Standard Descendant Tree

❀ Fan Descendant Tree

❀ Outline Descendant Tree

To create a Standard Descendant Tree:

1. On the Family Page, click the individual for whom you want to create the tree.

2. From the toolbar, click the Descendant Tree icon and then click Standard.

   Alternatively, from the View menu, select Descendant Tree, Standard.

To create a Fan Descendant Tree, follow these steps:

1. On the Family Page, click the individual for whom you want to create the tree.

2. From the toolbar, click the Descendant Tree icon and then click Fan.

   Alternatively, from the View menu, select Descendant Tree, Fan.

To create an Outline Descendant Tree, follow these steps:

1. On the Family Page, click the individual for whom you want to create the tree.

2. From the toolbar, click the Outline Descendant Tree icon.

   Alternatively, from the View menu, select Outline Descendant Tree.

The Standard Descendant Tree

The Standard Descendant Tree displays an individual's descendants in horizontal rows, one generation per row, and has three custom formats (later in this chapter, you will find the specifics on the tree format options):

- Automatic
- Horizontal
- 1-column

Although the three formats look different from one another, Family Tree Maker lumps them all under the general name of *Custom Standard Descendant Tree*. Because the options are the same for all three formats, I refer only to Custom Standard Descendant Tree.

The Standard Descendant Tree is also available in *Book layout* format, which automatically divides the Standard Descendant Tree into pages, with each page containing a cross-reference to the previous and subsequent pages so that readers can follow the tree.

For the sake of comparison, look at Figures 3.1 and 3.2. Figure 3.1 shows a Custom Standard Descendant Tree for Queen Victoria in automatic format. As you can see, Queen Victoria and Prince Albert are on the top tier in the tree, while one of their nine children—Princess Alice and her husband, Louis of Hesse— are directly below. Below Princess Alice's row are some of Queen Victoria's grandchildren, great-grandchildren, and so on (for a total of seven generations shown on the tree).

Figure 3.2, on the other hand, shows a close-up of the Book layout format Standard Descendant Tree for Queen Victoria. As you can see in the figure, individuals who will not fit on that page are cross-referenced to another page where they can be found.

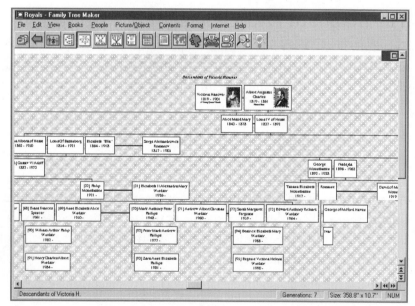

Figure 3.1

This Custom Standard Descendant Tree in automatic format for Queen Victoria stretches over several pages.

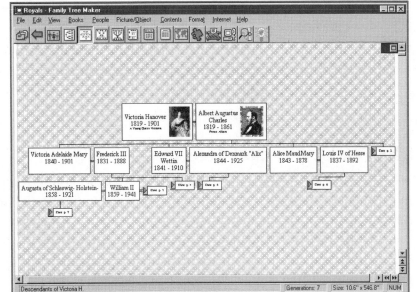

Figure 3.2

The Book layout version of the Standard Descendant Tree is formatted especially for use in a family history book, with references to previous and next pages for easy reading.

WEIGHING THE PROS AND CONS OF THE STANDARD DESCENDANT TREE

You have many factors to weigh when considering whether a tree or report is suitable for your family history book project. Here, I address a few of the more outstanding pros and cons related to the Standard Descendant Tree (in both Custom and Book layout):

- **Pros.** The Standard Descendant Tree enables you to see an individual's descendants at a glance. Non-genealogists can easily understand this tree, and it provides a graphical way to show the descendants of an individual or couple.

- **Cons.** If more than a few individuals per generation are included, the tree spills over several pages, making it difficult to follow who is related to whom (the Book layout format eases the problem by allowing cross-references to individuals on other pages). The more information you add to the tree, the more confusing it becomes, limiting the amount of data you can include on the tree. This tree is not the standard means of displaying descendant information in formalized genealogies; narrative reports are preferred for such projects.

The Fan Descendant Tree

A Fan Descendant Tree displays an individual's descendants around him or her in a circular or semi-circular pattern, one generation per level, with each subsequent generation shown a level away from the prior generation. (Think of an onion, with the outer skin being the generation farthest away from the primary individual.) You can choose from three shapes and three densities to create a Fan Descendant Tree.

The shapes and densities are mentioned later on in this chapter (see the entry for Fan Descendant Tree in the section "Selecting Your Format"), but for your convenience, I'll list them briefly here.

Here are the shapes you can choose from:

- Quarter Circle
- Semi-Circle
- Full Circle

Here are the densities available (in order from less to more dense):

- Generous
- Condensed
- Squished

Figure 3.3 shows one example of a Fan Descendant Tree; the example is created with the stipulation that it fit on one page. Because Queen Victoria, the primary individual on this chart, has so many descendants, Family Tree Maker eliminated those generations that would not fit on the page.

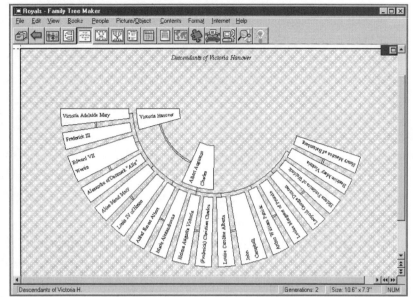

Figure 3.3

The Fan Descendant Tree for Queen Victoria, using the Fit-to-Page restriction.

WEIGHING THE PROS AND CONS OF THE FAN DESCENDANT TREE

When considering whether the Fan Descendant Tree is suitable for your family history book project, you'll want to weigh a few of its more outstanding pros and cons:

- **Pros.** This tree can display descendants in an attractive and easily followed format. Depending on the chart layout and density, you might be able to fit more individuals into a Fan Descendant Tree than in a Standard Descendant Tree.

- **Cons.** If you have more than a few individuals per generation, the tree will spill over to several pages, making it difficult to follow who is related to whom. Unlike the Standard Descendant Tree, no Book layout format exists for the Fan Descendant Tree. One way to avoid the multipage problem is to create Fan Descendant Trees for every few generations.

e Outline Descendant Tree

The Outline Descendant Tree is similar to the other descendant trees in that it displays an individual's descendants, but unlike the Standard Descendant Tree and the Fan Descendant Tree, this tree displays the descendants in a simple outline fashion. Each individual's information is one line, with each subsequent generation being indented farther than the prior generation. Spouses are indicated by a plus (+) sign. Figure 3.4 shows a portion of an Outline Descendant Tree for Queen Victoria.

WEIGHING THE PROS AND CONS OF THE OUTLINE DESCENDANT TREE

Is the Outline Descendant Tree suitable for your family history book project? You'll want to consider the following pros and cons before you decide:

- **Pros.** The information is presented in a non-graphical (that is, no boxes) format, making it easier to include a number of individuals.

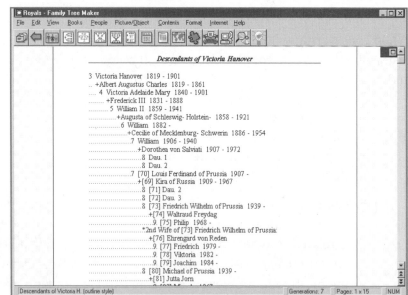

Figure 3.4

The Outline Descendant Tree presents information in a simple, text-only outline format.

Generation numbers help readers keep track of which individual belongs to which generation.

> ☀ **Cons.** Lengthy trees can spread over several pages, making it difficult to follow. If you turn off the Generation Number option, readers have a hard time following which generation is which.

Using Ancestor-Ordered Trees

Ancestor-ordered trees show a person's parents, grandparents, and so on—in other words, the individual's *ancestors*. The primary individual is shown in a central location on the tree, while the ancestors are displayed flowing out from the primary individual, each subsequent generation farther than the prior one. Unlike descendant-ordered trees, ancestor-ordered trees show only a direct-line relationship—no siblings, aunts, uncles, cousins, and so on of any individual are included.

Ancestor-ordered trees are popular in family history books, although as with descendant-ordered trees, they can quickly become quite bulky and take up a number of pages if you include several individuals in each generation. These three ancestor-ordered trees are available in Family Tree Maker:

> ☀ Standard Ancestor Tree
>
> ☀ Fan Ancestor Tree
>
> ☀ Vertical Ancestor Tree

The Standard Ancestor Tree

The Standard Ancestor Tree displays an individual's ancestry in a pattern that is commonly referred to by genealogists as a *pedigree chart*. The primary individual is located midway down the left side of the page, with paternal ancestors branching off above, and maternal ancestors branching off below, as shown in Figure 3.5.

The pedigree chart is one of the mainstays of genealogical charts because it presents the information about an individual's ancestors in an easily understood and concise manner. Three types of Standard Ancestor Trees are available in Family Tree Maker:

- **Custom.** Figure 3.5 shows an example of a Custom Standard Ancestor Tree (display options chosen were Detached Connections and Squished Layout).

- **Book layout.** Figure 3.6 shows an example of a Book layout Standard Ancestor Tree (the default display is Detached Connections).

- **Fit-to-Page.** Figure 3.7 shows a Fit-to-Page Standard Ancestor Tree (with the display option of Fishtail Connections).

All three versions of the Ancestor Tree are discussed in the following sections.

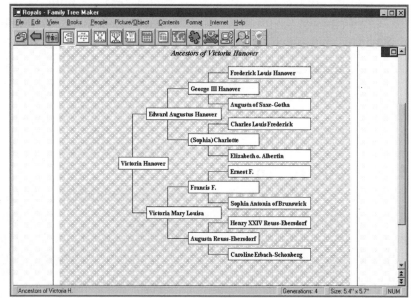

Figure 3.5

The Standard Ancestor Tree is more commonly called a *pedigree chart*.

Figure 3.6

In this example of a Book layout Standard Ancestor Tree, notice the difference between the Book layout and the Custom Standard Ancestor Tree— in the Book layout format, information is cross-referenced to individuals on other pages.

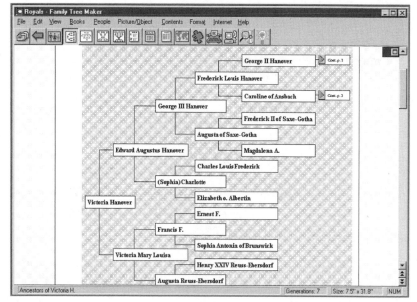

Figure 3.7

Here's an example of the third type of Standard Ancestor Tree: Fit-to-Page. Notice that fewer generations appear on this tree because Family Tree Maker has limited the amount of information to just what will fit on one page.

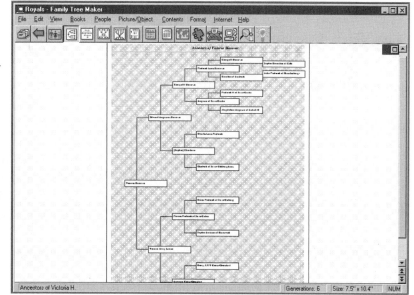

WEIGHING THE PROS AND CONS OF THE STANDARD ANCESTOR TREE

You need to weigh many factors when considering whether the Standard Ancestor tree is suitable for your family history book project. You'll want to take into account the following pros and cons:

- **Pros.** This tree is one of the standards of genealogical research; it presents information in an easy-to-read and easy-to-understand form. This tree's readability makes it useful for genealogists and non-genealogists alike. The Standard Ancestor Tree is available in Book layout format, which creates cross-references for individuals on prior and following pages.

- **Cons.** Individuals with a large number of ancestors might have charts that cascade for several pages (this problem can be overcome by using the Book layout format of the tree). Because this tree offers a graphical display of data, the amount of information that can be included on the tree is limited.

The Fan Ancestor Tree

The Fan Ancestor Tree displays an individual's ancestry in a circular, wedge, or semi-circular shape. The primary individual is in the center or bottom of the page, with ancestors branching off around him or her. The Fan Ancestor Tree comes in two styles:

- **Custom.** Custom trees allow you to select the shape and density of the tree (shapes allowed are Quarter Circle, Semi-Circle, and Full Circle; density choices are Generous, Condensed, and Squished). Figure 3.8 shows an example of a Custom Fan Ancestor Tree.

- **Fit-to-Page.** Family Tree Maker allows you to specify a restriction on the tree, formatting it so that only the information that can fit on one page will be included. All other information is removed from the chart, leaving you with a tree as shown in Figure 3.9.

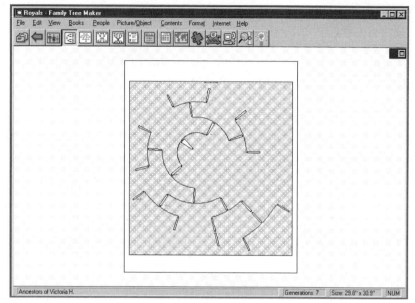

Figure 3.8

The Fan Ancestor Tree is another graphical way to display an individual's ancestors. Although you can't read the text at this zoomed-out view, you can see how this tree got its name from its fan shape.

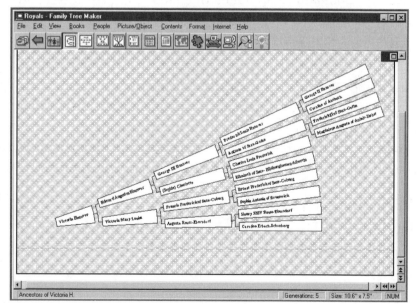

Figure 3.9

The Fit-to-Page Fan Ancestor Tree displays as much information as possible on one page only.

WEIGHING THE PROS AND CONS OF THE FAN ANCESTOR TREE

Should you use a Fan Ancestor Tree for your family history book project? Before you decide, you'll want to consider these pros and cons.

- **Pros.** The Fan Ancestor Tree is an attractively formatted graphical tree easily understood by non-genealogists. The tree presents information in a unique manner.

- **Cons.** The Fan Ancestor Tree is not a traditional tree used in more formal family history books; the Standard Ancestor Tree is more common. Due to the graphical nature of the tree, including too many items on the tree will make it unreadable.

The Vertical Ancestor Tree

The Vertical Ancestor Tree displays an individual's ancestry in a manner similar to the Standard Descendant Tree—that is, the primary individual is at the bottom of the page, while branches of his or her ancestors flow toward the top of the page. Figure 3.10 shows an example of a Vertical Ancestor Tree for Queen Victoria.

Just as the Standard Descendant Tree comes in two formats, the Vertical Ancestor Tree is available in Custom (shown in Figure 3.10) and Book layout. Family Tree Maker uses the Book layout version to arrange parts of the tree in printable sections with cross-references to prior and following pages. Figure 3.11 shows an example of a Book layout Vertical Ancestor Tree for Queen Victoria.

WEIGHING THE PROS AND CONS OF THE VERTICAL ANCESTOR TREE

When deciding whether the Vertical Ancestor Tree is right for your family history book, you'll want to consider the following pros and cons:

- **Pros.** The Vertical Ancestor Tree provides a unique way to display the ancestors of an individual in graphical format. Although not frequently used, such trees are easy to read and understand.

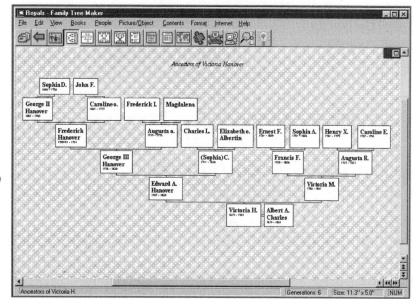

Figure 3.10

The Vertical Ancestor Tree displays an individual's ancestors in a sort of upside-down Standard Descendant Tree.

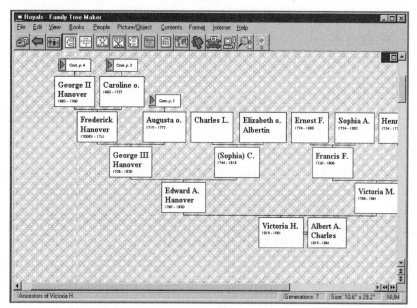

Figure 3.11

The Book layout Vertical Ancestor Tree is the best-suited version for inclusion in your family history book.

- **Cons.** Individuals with a large number of ancestors might have charts that cascade for several pages (this problem can be overcome by using the Book layout format of the tree). Due to the graphical nature of the chart, the amount of information that can be included without making the tree unreadable is limited. This is not a standard tree used in formal family history books.

Exploring Tree Suitability, Options, Format, and Contents

You have a number of choices to make regarding the options, format, and contents of the ancestor-ordered and descendant-ordered trees in Family Tree Maker. You must choose what to include, and exclude, on your trees—not an easy task with so much information you can include!

When viewing all the available choices, keep in mind your specific audience and your goal for the book. Formal family histories require different trees and information than informal family history book projects. By remembering your audience, you will have a better tool to judge whether a specific tree is suited to your project.

> **TIP** *Generally, the more informal your book, the more you will want to use trees rather than reports. Trees provide a graphical way to display information that is easily read and understood by non-genealogists. If you want to create a more formal family history book that is intended for an audience of interested genealogists, you'll want to use the more detailed reports rather than the less detailed trees.*

Testing the Tree for Suitability

This chapter and the following three chapters take a closer look at the suitability of each of the trees, charts, and reports available in Family Tree Maker for use in three different types of family history book projects.

The suitability of a tree, chart, or report is an important factor for you to consider when you are planning your book. If you want to create an informal book, you will not want to include hard-to-understand reports that will be incomprehensible to your audience. Likewise, if you are creating a formal family history book, you will not want to include those charts that are easy to understand and visually pleasing, but lack content.

For the purposes of example, consider these three levels of family history book projects (for more examples of projects, be sure to read Chapter Eleven, "Family History Book Projects," which shows several different types of family history book projects):

- An informal book intended to please immediate family members who are not genealogists

- An intermediate-level book that is thorough but not complete, and intended for an audience of genealogists

- A formal family history book that is complete, or near complete, with the highest standards of documentation and analysis, intended for serious genealogists

Keeping in mind that no hard and fast rule determines what you can and cannot include in your family history book, the suitability of the various descendant-ordered and ascendant-ordered trees described previously might be summarized as follows.

- **Standard Descendant Tree**

  - **Informal family history book.** This tree is useful and easily read by non-genealogists. Its graphical nature makes it a good choice for this project level.

  - **Intermediate family history book.** Although useful, this tree can be cumbersome if several individuals are included, thus you should be wary of including too much information on it. That said, the tree is a good choice for this level of project.

- **Formal family history book.** This tree is less useful than the more concise, and easier read, Outline Descendant Tree. For details about individuals or families, most genealogists prefer either the Register Report or NGS Quarterly report (discussed in Chapter Five).

Fan Descendant Tree

- **Informal family history book.** This tree is useful and easily read by non-genealogists. Graphically, this tree provides a pleasing layout of information.

- **Intermediate family history book.** Although useful, this tree can be cumbersome if several individuals are included. The tree is also somewhat wasteful of space.

- **Formal family history book.** This tree is not very useful when compared to the more concise, and easier read, Outline Descendant Tree.

Outline Descendant Tree

- **Informal family history book.** This tree contains a great deal of information, but might not be easily read by non-genealogists.

- **Intermediate family history book.** This is a useful and concise tree; a good choice for this project.

- **Formal family history book.** Easy to read and concise. This tree is a good choice for this project, although a more detailed version can be found in either the Register Report or NGS Quarterly report.

Standard Ancestor Tree

- **Informal family history book.** This is a good choice because this tree is easily read by non-genealogists.

- **Intermediate family history book.** This tree is a standard choice for inclusion in family history books. This tree is easy to read and understand.

- **Formal family history book.** Although suitable, this tree is not as common for a formal family history as for an intermediate-level family history.

⚸ Fan Ancestor Tree

- **Informal family history book.** This tree is a good choice because the tree is easily read by non-genealogists and is presented in an attractive format.

- **Intermediate family history book.** Traditional family history books would use a pedigree chart (Standard Ancestor Tree) instead of the fan version.

- **Formal family history book.** If you want to include a graphical version of an ancestor-ordered chart, the pedigree chart (Standard Ancestor Tree) is a more traditional choice.

⚸ Vertical Ancestor Tree

- **Informal family history book.** This tree is a good choice because this tree can be easily read by non-genealogists.

- **Intermediate family history book.** This tree is not a traditional choice; a pedigree chart (Standard Ancestor Tree) would be better suited for this sort of project.

- **Formal family history book.** If you want to include a graphical version of an ancestor-ordered chart, the pedigree chart (Standard Ancestor Tree) is a more traditional choice.

Considering Your Options

When you create a descendant-ordered or ancestor-ordered tree, various options enable you to customize how the tree is displayed. These options are found in the Contents menu and are listed below for your reference.

⚸ **Label Columns as Parents, Grandparents, and so on.** Select this option if you want each generation on your tree to have a label indicating what relationship they are to the primary individual. This option would be a good choice to use on an informal family history project, or for a book intended for a non-genealogist audience.

* **Include Duplicate Ancestors Each Time They Appear.** This option allows you to include those individuals who might appear more than once on your family tree (for example, if you have cousins who marry, much of their ancestry is duplicated). This can be useful if you want a complete family history, but is rather wasteful of space.

* **Include Siblings of Primary Individual.** If you want to include the brothers and sisters of the primary individual on your tree, this option allows you to do so. If the individual has several siblings, you might want to exclude them from the tree to keep it from being too cluttered.

* **Include Empty Branches.** This option allows you to include empty boxes indicating individuals for whom you have no information. No real pros or cons exist pertaining to including them—it's simply a matter of personal taste.

Note that not every option is available for every tree. For example, Figure 3.12 shows options that are available for the Standard Descendant Tree, which offers just two options.

The following lists show what options are available for each tree. To access options for any of the trees listed next, follow these steps:

1. From the selected tree screen, click Contents, Options.

2. Make your option choices (see the following lists for specific choices) and click OK.

Figure 3.12

The two available options for the Standard Descendant Tree are to label generations as Children, Grandchildren, and so on and to include duplicate descendants each time they appear.

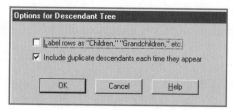

⚹ Standard Descendant Tree

- Label Columns as Parents, Grandparents, and so on.

- Include Duplicate Ancestors Each Time They Appear

⚹ **NOTE** ⚹ *Assuming you do not have too many individuals or too much information included on the tree, you might want to select both of these options because they serve to make the tree more understandable to people not familiar with genealogy.*

⚹ Fan Descendant Tree

- Include Duplicate Descendants Each Time They Appear

⚹ Outline Descendant Tree

⚹ **NOTE** ⚹ *Because the Outline Descendant Tree is a text-only tree (that is, it does not have any boxes and lines indicating relationships between individuals as the other trees do), the options available to it are different from the other graphical trees. Because this tree does not rely on a graphical layout to present information, all three choices are good ones to include for reasons of clarity and comprehension.*

- Print Spouses. Select this option to include the spouse on the tree.

- Include Duplicate Children of Intermarriages. This is similar to including duplicate individuals on graphical trees. If you want to include all children of every individual, regardless of whether they are found elsewhere on the tree, select this option.

- Mark Individuals with Multiple Spouses. This option alerts readers to the fact that an individual has more than one spouse.

⚹ Standard Ancestor Tree

- Label Columns as Parents, Grandparents, and so on.

- Include Duplicate Ancestors Each Time They Appear

- Include Siblings of Primary Individual

- Include Empty Branches

❧ **NOTE** ❧ *The Include Empty Branches option is not available for the Book layout Standard Ancestor Tree.*

Fan Ancestor Tree

- Include Duplicate Ancestors Each Time They Appear

Vertical Ancestor Tree

- Label Columns as Parents, Grandparents, and so on.

- Include Duplicate Ancestors Each Time They Appear

- Include Empty Branches

❧ **NOTE** ❧ *The Include Empty Branches option is not available for the Book layout Vertical Ancestor Tree.*

Deciding on Content

Depending on the tree, chart, or report you are configuring, you can include just a few or several items, all of which are found in the Contents menu. Family Tree Maker provides a long list of items you can include on your trees (and charts and reports). Although the list is a long one, take a moment to review it, because I refer to these items several times in this and the next three chapters.

Name	Age at Death
aka	Age at First Marriage
Birth Date/Location	Annulment
Marriage Date/Location	Baptism
Death Date/Location	Baptism (LDS)
Picture/Object	Bar Mitzvah
Adoption	Bat Mitzvah
Age at Birth of First Child	Blank Row
Age at Birth of Last Child	Blessing

Burial

Caste

Cause of Death

Census

Christening

City

Confirmation

Confirmation (LDS)

Country

Cremation

Custom Field

Death of One Spouse

Degree

Divorce

Divorce Filed

Education

Elected

Emigration

Endowment (LDS)

Engagement

Excommunicated

Fact 1

Fact 2

Fact 3

Fact 4

Fact 5

Fact 6

Fact 7

Fact 8

Fact 9

Fact 10

Fact 11

Fact 12

Fact 13

First Communion

Friends

Graduation

Height

Immigration

Individual Reference

Line in Box

Marriage Bann

Marriage Contract

Marriage Ending Date/Location

Marriage Fact

Marriage License

Marriage Picture/Object

Marriage Reference Number

Marriage Settlement

Medical Information

Military Service

Mission (LDS)

Namesake

Nationality

Naturalization

None-Ending

Number of Children	Retirement
Occupation	Sealed to Parents (LDS)
Ongoing-Ending	Sealed to Spouse (LDS)
Ordination	Separation
Other-Begin	Sex
Other-Ending	Single
Partners	Social Security Number
Phone	Spouse's Father
Private-Begin	Spouse's Mother
Private-Ending	State or Province
Probate	Street
Property	Temple
Reference Number	Unknown-Begin
Relationship Beginning Status	Unknown-Ending
Relationship Ending Status	Weight
Religion	Will
Residence	Zip or Postal Code

To access any of the items from the Items to Include list:

1. Open up the tree for which you want to modify the options.

2. From the Contents menu, click Items to Include.

3. In the Items to Include dialog box, select an item you want to include and click the right arrow to add it to the list of items that will be printed on your tree.

4. Repeat as necessary until you have all the items you want.

5. Click OK to return to the tree and see the changes you've made.

Most of the items in this list should be fairly self-explanatory. If you are confused as to what an item is, consult Family Tree Maker's Help file (look under the Help menu). You can also refer to Chapter Eleven for examples of when to include various items in a variety of family history book projects.

Although I'm sure it's obvious that no one would want to include all the items on the preceding, long list in a family tree, Family Tree Maker provides the list so you can best customize each tree, chart, and report to suit your needs. Take time to go over the list of items that can be included and select those that will best display your information.

Although it might be tempting to include lots of items on your tree, keep in mind space limitations and the number of pages you want to allow for each tree. Experiment with contents, printing out samples of trees until you strike a balance between information and readability. If your tree prints out with the text too dense, try deleting a few of the items you have included. If you have lots of white space and little information on the tree, add an item or two from the earlier list and check for readability.

Three other content choices are available:

> ☆ **Individuals to Include.** Selecting which individuals will be included on the tree is as important as deciding what information you will include. Unless you are creating an all-encompassing family history book, you'll probably want to limit your trees to those individuals upon whom you are specifically focusing. Family Tree Maker allows you to choose all the descendants of the primary individual (that is, collateral lines in addition to direct-line descendants) or only direct-line descendants (see Figure 3.13).

Figure 3.13

You might want to include all an individual's descendants, or only direct-line descendants.

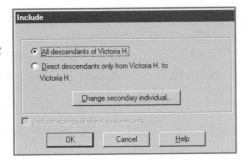

To access the Individuals to Include option, follow these steps:

1. Open the tree for which you want to modify the options.

2. From the Contents menu, click Individuals to Include.

3. In the Individuals to Include dialog box, select either all the descendants of your primary individual or the direct descendants from the primary individual to a secondary individual.

4. Click OK to return to the tree.

❋ **TIP** ❋ *Collateral descendants are those relatives who are not found in a direct line of descent between a primary individual and a secondary individual. For example, in a direct-line descent between your grandmother and yourself, her siblings and their issue are collateral lines.*

🏃 **Title & Footnote.** For each tree, you have the ability to change the title and footnote. Titles are best kept to simple, explanatory text, such as "Descendants of Queen Victoria" rather than something that might confuse readers (while a title of "A Dame and Her Progeny" might be amusing, it doesn't go very far explaining who the tree is for). Footnotes can be any sort of text you want; generally people put their name and date in a footnote to indicate who created the tree and when, but you can use other identifying text as a footnote if you would like.

Title and footnote options include using an automatic title, a custom title (which you select), and whether you want to include a title on every page. You can also specify whether you want the page numbers printed on each page (and what page number you want to start at), as well as whether you want to include the date and time of printing at the top of each page. Finally, you can have Family Tree Maker separate the text of the footnote by drawing a box around it.

To access the title and footnote options, follow these steps:

1. Open up the tree for which you want to modify the options.

2. From the Contents menu, click Title & Footnote.
3. In the Title & Footnote dialog box, make the choices (see list above) and click OK.

- **Number of Generations to Show.** Just as it's important to consider how many individuals you want included on your tree, so is it important to decide on the number of generations that will be included. Too many generations, and your tree can become unwieldy and bulky; too few generations, and little information is disseminated. As with other options, experiment with your trees by printing up several different trees using differing numbers of generations until you find the right balance between information and readability.

  To access the Number of Generations to Show option, follow these steps:

1. Open the tree for which you want to modify the options.
2. From the Contents menu, click Number of Generations to Show.
3. Use the up and down arrows to select the number of generations you want included on the tree.
4. Click OK to return to the tree.

You also have many content choices available for each tree.

- **Standard Descendant Tree.** You can select which items to include in each box (consult the long list earlier in this chapter for the items that can be included using the Items to Include feature), individuals to include, title and footnote, and the number of generations to show.
- **Fan Descendant Tree.** You can select which items to include in each box, individuals to include, title and footnote, and the number of generations to show.
- **Outline Descendant Tree.** You can select which items to include in each box, individuals to include, title and footnote, and the number of generations to show.

Standard Ancestor Tree. You can select which items to include in each box, title and footnote, and the number of generations to show.

 Fan Ancestor Tree. You can select which items to include in each box, title and footnote, and the number of generations to show.

 Vertical Ancestor Tree. You can select which items to include in each box, title and footnote, and the number of generations to show.

Selecting Your Format

Once you've decided what information you want to include on your tree, you'll want to decide how the tree is going to appear—that is, how it will be formatted. Changing the format of a tree can be as simple as changing the box style and font, or as complicated as changing the layout of the tree. You'll want to experiment with changing the formatting of each tree, report, and chart you use to find those features (layout, box and line style, font, and so on) that suit you and the tree you are creating. As with other tree options, strive for a format that is easy to understand and yet as comprehensive as possible without being unreadable.

Five basic format options are available:

 Tree Format. This allows you to specify how each individual tree will appear. For most trees, you have two options.

- **General Tree Format.** This format differs for each specific tree. Some trees, such as the Standard Ancestor Tree, allow you to select the type of tree you want—either Book layout or Custom. You can also choose to have the tree centered on the page, to make all the boxes the same size, or to have the boxes overlap page breaks. The last two choices are ones of purely personal preference. If you prefer a symmetrical tree, you'll probably want to have the boxes all the same size regardless of the information contained therein. Likewise, you can choose to have boxes not overlap page breaks if you find that distracting or confusing.

✻ **TIP** ✻ *Although it might seem like common sense to center your tree on a page, in some circumstances you do not want it so. For example, if you are printing and binding the book yourself, you might want to have the tree displayed off-center to allow for a binding margin along the left side.*

- **Layout Format.** Each tree comes with different layout options, which address how the tree itself is arranged—that is, how tightly the boxes are placed together and in some cases, the layout design of the tree (for example, the Standard Descendant Tree has three layouts: Automatic, Horizontal, or 1-Column).

✻ **Maximum Box Width.** Depending on the size of your tree (which is directly dependent on the number of individuals it includes), you might want to limit the box and picture/object widths on the tree. Shrinking the box widths gives you more room on the tree, but also gives you less space for the data included in the box. You'll want to carefully weigh the advantages and disadvantages of changing the box width. If you are unsure of the effect of changing the box or object width, try a test printout and see how readable the changes make the tree.

✻ **Box, Line, and Border Styles.** Family Tree Maker allows you to really customize the look of your tree by specifying the type of boxes, borders, and lines you want to use. Numerous format options for boxes are available; you can specify different formats for males, females, or those of undefined gender. For each of the three, you can specify the color for the box outline, fill, and shadow, as well as select one of six box styles. You can also choose to color each generation on the chart differently, making it easier to pick out which individuals belong to which generation. Another format option you have is to change the border style; six border styles are available, and you can specify border color and background color as well. The third format option you have is for lines; you can specify one of three line styles as well as line color. You can also choose to highlight the direct line relationship between the primary individual and another individual in a different color, and you can show non-natural parent-child relationships (for example, step-children) with a dotted line rather than a solid line.

❊ **Text Font, Style, and Size.** Family Tree Maker enables you to choose how you want text displayed on your trees. You can change the font, font size, font style (bold, italics, and so on), text color, and text alignment (center, left, or right) for all the items you have selected to include in your tree, including the title, footnotes, and generation labels. You can also choose to underline text if you want. Be aware that if you change the font size to a larger one, you run the risk of making the boxes on the tree larger, meaning that less information can be displayed per page. As with other format options, you should experiment with the text settings to find what works for you and your tree before deciding what to use.

❊ **Show Page Lines.** The last format choice you have is one that is strictly aesthetic: whether or not you want to have page lines shown on the screen. The lines will not appear on your tree itself, but they will give you an idea of how your tree will be printed, should it run to more than one page.

As with other options, not all format choices are available for every tree. The following lists what format choices are available for each tree (note that those trees that have Fit-to-Page, Book layout, and Custom formats available are detailed separately, because the format choices are different for each).

❊ **Standard Descendant Tree (Book layout)**

- Center Tree on Page

- Maximum Box Width

- Box, Border, and Line Styles

- Text Font, Style, and Size
- Show Page Lines

Standard Descendant Tree (Custom)

- Make Boxes All the Same Size
- Boxes Overlap Page Breaks
- Maximum Box Width
- Box, Border, and Line Styles
- Text Font, Style, and Size
- Show Page Lines

Fan Descendant Tree (Fit-to-Page)

- Flip Text

NOTE *This is a handy option if you have text on either side of the primary individual. Flip Text allows you to have the text on the right side of the page facing right, while the text on the left side of the page faces left, thus allowing you to read the text without turning the page upside down.*

Fan Descendant Tree (Custom)

- Make All Boxes the Same Width
- Rotate Tree to Center

NOTE *This format option allows the branches of the tree to form uniform angles away from the center of the tree. If you do not select this option, the branches will align with the bottom of the page.*

- Flip Text
- Quarter Circle Shape

- Semi-Circle Shape

- Full Circle Shape

- Generous Density

- Condensed Density

- Squished Density

❧ NOTE ❧ *Of the preceding items, the last six most affect how the tree will appear. The Quarter Circle, Semi-Circle, and Full Circle shape options are self-explanatory (see Figure 3.14 for a look at the format dialog box)—they refer to the shape the fan tree will emulate. Personal preference will lead you to choose whichever shape best suits your needs. The density choices refer to how tightly the boxes are placed onto a page; you should choose the Generous density for tree readability unless you have a great deal of information to include, in which case you might want to use a tighter density.*

- Maximum Box Width

- Box, Border, and Line Styles

- Text Font, Style, and Size

- Show Page Lines

Figure 3.14

The Fan Descendant Tree can be generated in three different shapes and densities.

⚘ Outline Descendant Tree

- **Indent with Which Character.** This option allows you to use something other than the traditional period (.) as an indent indicator. If you choose a different character, make sure it is something that is non-obtrusive.

- **Indent Each Generation by (in Inches).** If you have several generations to include on one tree, you might want to make the indentations less than the standard .30 inches so that all the generations can be included without indenting the information too far to the right. If you have only a few generations, you might want to increase the indent width so readers will be sure to notice which generation each individual belongs to.

- **Place Generation Number Before Each Descendant's Name.** This option can be helpful if your tree is lengthy or has a good number of generations. This options allows the reader to immediately identify the generation to which an individual belongs.

- **Starting Generation Number.** If you want to have the primary individual on your tree begin as a different generation number, this option allows you to change that. You might want to do so if you have the primary individual's ancestors on another chart, thus providing readers with a visual clue as to where the primary individual is in the line of descent.

- **Maximum Height (in Rows) for Each Individual.** This setting pertains to the number of rows you allot to each individual. If you have a number of items included for each individual (so that the information wraps to more than one line), you will want to make sure your maximum height number allows for the display of that information.

- **Number of Blank Lines Between Individuals.** If you like a tree with a less dense appearance, you can set this format option to leave spaces between each line in the tree, allowing white space to make your tree more readable.

- **Always One Page Wide.** This format option ensures that your information doesn't exceed the page width.

Standard Ancestor Tree (Fit-to-Page)

- Detached, Overlap, and Fishtail Connections

NOTE *These connections are unique to the Ancestor Tree and refer to the way the tree is laid out. A Detached connection indicates that the boxes are separated from one another by space, with lines drawn to indicate an individual's parents. An Overlap connection is the same as Detached, but without the white space around the boxes and the lines indicating parents (the exception is the primary individual, who does have the parents' lines shown). A Fishtail connection is one in which no lines or white space exist, and the boxes for parents do not appear alongside the child's box, but behind it instead. Which format connection you choose is up to you—there are really no benefits to one over the other.*

- Box, Line, and Border Styles

- Text Font, Style, and Size

Standard Ancestor Tree (Book layout)

- Detached, Overlap, and Fishtail Connections

- Center Tree on Page

- Maximum Width for Each Box

- Box, Line, and Border Styles

- Text Font, Style, and Size

Standard Ancestor Tree (Custom)

- Detached, Overlap, and Fishtail Connections
- Perfect, Collapsed, and Squished Layout

❧ **NOTE** ❧ *Like the connections format options, the layout option indicates how the tree will look—in this case, the density of the tree can be manipulated by selecting Perfect (lots of white space), Collapsed (the boxes are tighter together with less space surrounding them), and Squished (the boxes are as tight as possible with little space surround them). If you have a lot of individuals on your tree, you'll want to make the density of the tree tighter. If you have few individuals, use the Perfect layout.*

- Center Tree on Page
- Make All Boxes the Same Size
- Boxes Overlap Page Breaks

❧ **NOTE** ❧ *This option is available only with Detached connections.*

- Maximum Width for Each Box
- Box, Line, and Border Styles
- Text Font, Style, and Size

Fan Ancestor Tree (Fit-to-Page)

❧ **NOTE** ❧ *The Fit-to-Page type of Fan Ancestor Tree has restrictions due to its nature that will not allow you to specify the shape or density of the tree.*

- Flip Text
- Maximum Width for Each Box

- Box, Line, and Border Styles

- Text Font, Style, and Size

🦌 Fan Ancestor Tree (Custom)

- Quarter, Semi-Circular, and Circular Shapes

- Generous, Condensed, and Squished Densities

- Make All Boxes the Same Width

- Rotate Tree to Center

- Flip Text

- Maximum Width for Each Box

- Box, Line, and Border Styles

- Text Font, Style, and Size

Because the Fan Ancestor Tree is one that is not often seen, look at the different formats available before choosing one that fits your needs. Figures 3.15 and 3.16 show how customizable this particular tree is, and how the different format choices change the tree's appearance. Figure 3.15 shows an example of a Custom Fan Ancestor Tree in Quarter Circle shape, Squished density, with the Rotate to Center option selected.

If you have more ancestors, you might want to use the full circle shape to show the ancestors in a pleasing manner. Figure 3.16 shows an example of the Custom Ancestor Tree using the Circular shape and the Generous density.

> 🦌 **NOTE** 🦌 *If you choose a density other than generous, you won't get the Full Circle shape.*

Figure 3.17 shows an example of the Custom Fan Ancestor Tree using the Semi-Circular shape and Generous density. Notice that the shape is not quite a perfect semi-circle; as you add generations, you increase the ability for the tree to form the shape you want. Putting restrictions on the shape, such as the

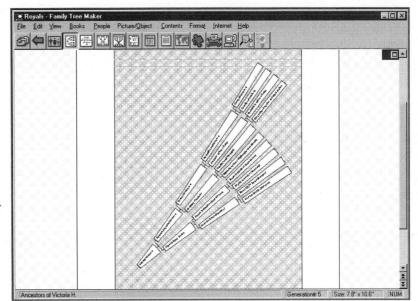

Figure 3.15

The Custom Ancestor Tree in quarter circle format, tree rotated to center.

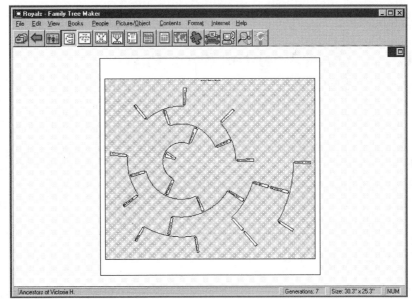

Figure 3.16

The Custom Ancestor Tree in circular shape with generous density.

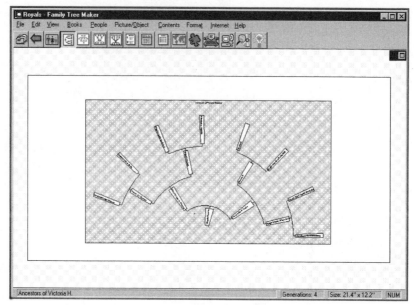

Figure 3.17

The Custom
Ancestor Tree in
semi-circular
shape with gen-
erous density.

Condensed and Squished densities, will affect how well the tree emulates the desired shape. For the best shape, use the Generous density.

USING TREES WITH THE BOOK FEATURE

One last set of options you can specify can be found once you add the tree to your family history book using the Book feature. This is the feature that you will use to create your family history book, and is described in detail in Chapter Eleven. When you select an item to be included in your book by means of the Book feature, you can modify some of the item's properties for your book. The significance of these properties will be discussed in full in Chapter Nine, "Creating Your Family History Book."

CHAPTER FOUR

Using Miscellaneous Trees and Charts in Your Family History Book

My history has been composed to be an everlasting possession, not the showpiece of an hour.

— Thucydides, *The Peloponnesian War*

amily Tree Maker presents a number of items that can be useful in a family history book, including two nontraditional trees (that is, trees not commonly seen in formal family history books) and charts. Not all the available items are suited to every genealogy project, though, so wise authors will evaluate the following trees and charts before deciding whether to include them in a family history book. As with other trees and reports, I recommend that you take the time to print samples and to play with the options and formatting of each before deciding whether a tree or chart is suitable for your project.

The available "miscellaneous" trees and charts are listed here. Of the items listed, only the Family Group Sheet is a standard item found in many family history books.

- All-in-One Tree
- Standard Hourglass Tree
- Hourglass Fan Tree
- Family Group Sheet
- Timeline
- Map
- Calendar

> ❧ **NOTE** ❧ *Although the last three items on the list are not, strictly speaking, a tree or a chart, I included them in this chapter for the sake of convenience.*

As with the two prior chapters, this one is divided into two main sections. The first section gives a description and samples of the miscellaneous trees and charts, and the second section reviews options, format, and contents for each item. You can find other types of items that you might want to include in your book, such as trees, narrative reports, custom reports, and miscellaneous charts, in Chapter Three, "Using Trees in Your Family History Book," Chapter Five, "Using Narrative Reports in Your Family History Book," and Chapter Six, "Exploring Custom and Miscellaneous Reports."

By the time you finish this chapter, you will be conversant with a number of the miscellaneous trees and charts you can create using Family Tree Maker. You will also have done the following:

- 🏃 Consulted the tree and chart descriptions to locate which ones are best suited for your family history book project

- 🏃 Printed sample copies of the trees and charts

- 🏃 Experimented with the options and format for the trees and charts you choose to use

Using an All-in-One Tree

The *All-in-One Tree* creates a graphical chart showing relationships in your database (an option allows you to specify whether you want to include everyone in the database or specify the number of ancestors and descendants). Although this might sound overwhelming—and if you have a large number of individuals in your database, it can easily be so—the All-in-One Tree allows you to examine the relationships between family members as displayed on one, often multipage, chart.

To create an All-in-One Tree, follow these steps:

1. Open the Family File with which you want to work.

2. On the Family Page, click the individual for whom you want to create an All-in-One Tree.

3. Go to the toolbar and click the All-in-One Tree button (or from the View menu, choose All-in-One Tree).

Figure 4.1 shows an example of a nine-generation All-in-One Tree for Queen Victoria; the tree includes four generations of her ancestors and four generations of her descendants. Notice that even with only nine generations, this tree is far too large to be printed on one page. Viewed as it is in Figure 4.1, it is also unreadable, but you can see the general shape of the tree.

Because the All-in-One Tree is a graphical tree, the same caveat applies for it as for other trees—namely, that the more information you include on the tree, the quicker the tree becomes confusing and unreadable. If you decide to use an

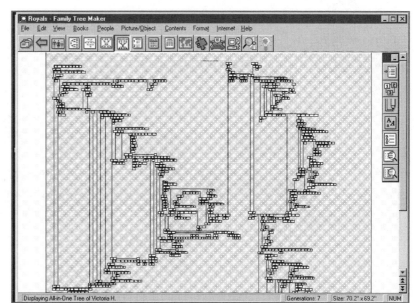

Figure 4.1

Queen Victoria's All-in-One Tree, shown using the Size to Window viewing command, is too large to be contained on one page.

All-in-One Tree, be wary of including too many items on the tree instead of creating several trees with different primary individuals.

Weighing the Pros and Cons of the All-in-One Tree

You have many factors to weigh when considering whether a tree or report is suitable for your family history book project. In this section, you consider a few of the more outstanding pros and cons related to the All-in-One Tree.

- **Pros.** This tree shows the connections between family members in a graphical format. You can select the number of generations to include, include everyone in the database, or just include the primary individual's ancestors and descendants.

- **Cons.** This tree can be cumbersome and confusing if you have numerous individuals in the database. Too much information included on the tree makes it difficult to understand. If more than a few individuals or generations are included, the tree will require several pages to print.

Using Standard Hourglass Trees and Fan Hourglass Trees

Hourglass Trees enable you to create a chart that shows, at a glance, both the ancestors and the descendants of a specific individual. This tree is unique in that it is a combination of the Standard Descendant Tree and the Vertical Ancestor Tree. Unlike the All-in-One Tree, which shows you how all the individuals in the database interact with one another (including stepfamily and unrelated trees), the Hourglass Tree shows only the direct-line ancestors and descendants of the primary individual.

Two basic types of Hourglass Trees are available in Family Tree Maker: *Standard* and *Fan*.

With the Family File that you want to work with open, follow these steps to create a Standard Hourglass Tree:

1. On the Family Page, click the individual for whom you want to create a tree.

2. Go to the toolbar and click the Hourglass button; in the menu that appears, select Standard. Or from the View menu, choose Hourglass Tree, Standard.

To create a Fan Hourglass Tree, just take these steps:

1. On the Family Page, click the individual for whom you want to create a tree.

2. Go to the toolbar and click the Hourglass button; in the menu that appears, select Fan. Alternatively, from the View menu, choose Hourglass Tree, Fan.

Using a Standard Hourglass Tree

The Standard Hourglass Tree displays an individual's family in a vertical, linear pattern; ancestors branch off above an individual, while descendants branch off below. The two types of Standard Hourglass Trees are as follows:

✵ **Book layout.** The Book layout version, shown in Figure 4.2, is recommended if you want to use the tree in a family history book. It includes cross-references to individuals found on prior and following pages.

Here's how you create a Standard Hourglass Tree in Book layout:

1. On the Family Page, click the individual for whom you want to create a tree.

2. Go to the toolbar and click the Hourglass button; in the menu that appears, select Standard.

3. From the Format menu, click Tree Format.

4. Under the General tab, click Book Layout.

Figure 4.2

A Standard
Hourglass Tree in
Book layout will
show you both
the descendants
and the ancestors
of an individual,
cross-referenced
to data on prior
and subsequent
pages.

5. Click OK.

🐾 **Custom.** If you want to create a tree that does not contain cross-references, the Custom version allows you to specify the layout of the tree for both ancestors and descendants. Figure 4.3 shows the Custom version of the Standard Hourglass Tree, with condensed ancestors and 1-column descendants (see the upcoming section on format options for more information).

To create a Standard Hourglass Tree in Custom layout, with the individual for whom you want to create a tree selected, follow these steps:

1. Click the Hourglass button and choose Standard from the menu that appears.

2. From the Format menu, click Tree Format.

3. Under the General tab, click Custom.

4. Click OK.

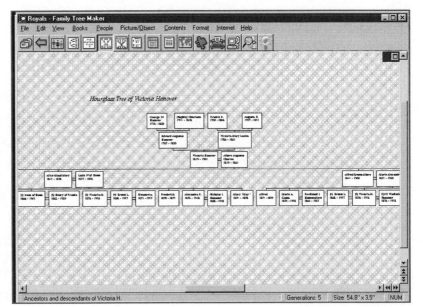

Figure 4.3

This zoomed-out view of the Custom version of the Standard Hourglass Tree shows how an individual's ancestors and descendants are displayed in a linear, horizontal format.

WEIGHING THE PROS AND CONS OF THE STANDARD HOURGLASS TREE

Is the Standard Hourglass Tree suitable for your family history book project? You'll want to consider the following pros and cons before you decide:

- **Pros.** This tree provides a graphically pleasing way to show an individual's ancestors and descendants on one tree. Customization options allow you to separately specify how the tree will display ancestors and descendants. Non-genealogists can easily understand this tree.

- **Cons.** This tree can be cumbersome if you have a large number of individuals or too much information is included. The Book layout version overcomes these problems by creating cross-referenced sections divided into pages. Too much information can make the tree unreadable.

Using a Fan Hourglass Tree

The Fan Hourglass Tree displays an individual's ancestors in a circular pattern—ancestors fan off above an individual, while descendants fan off below.

To create a Fan Hourglass Tree in Book layout, with the individual for whom you want to create a tree selected on the Family Page, follow these steps:

1. Click the Hourglass button; in the resulting menu, click Fan. Alternatively, from the View menu, click Hourglass Tree, Fan.

2. Click OK.

The Fan Hourglass Tree comes in two types of formats: Fit-to-Page and Custom.

* **Fit-to-Page.** This version of the Fan Hourglass Tree is created to appear on only one page; this standard, which is set by Family Tree Maker, means that the Fit-to-Page layout, shown in Figure 4.4, might limit the number of generations and items included in the tree.

   To create a Fan Hourglass Tree in Fit-to-Page layout, with the individual for whom you want to create a tree selected on the Family Page, follow these steps:

   1. Click the Hourglass button; in the resulting menu, click Fan.

   2. From the Format menu, click Tree Format.

   3. Under the General tab, click Fit-to-Page.

   4. Click OK.

* **Custom.** With the Custom version of the Fan Hourglass Tree, shown in Figure 4.5, more generations are included, but they are printed over several pages rather than on just one page, as in the Fit-to-Page version.

   With the individual of choice selected on the Family Page, follow these steps to create a Fan Hourglass Tree in Custom layout:

   1. Click the Hourglass button; in the resulting menu, click Fan.

Figure 4.4

The Fit-to-Page version of the Fan Hourglass Tree limits how many generations are displayed and, in order to better fit the tree on one page, might eliminate some of the items you want to include.

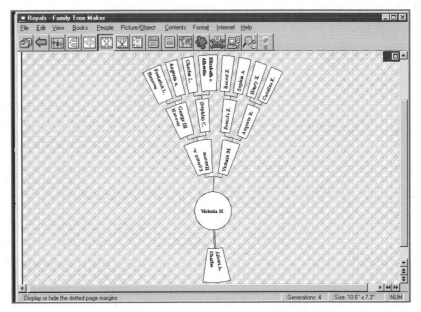

Figure 4.5

If you want to include several generations or more items on the tree, choose the Custom version of the Fan Hourglass Tree. Be warned, however, that a printed version will spill over onto several pages.

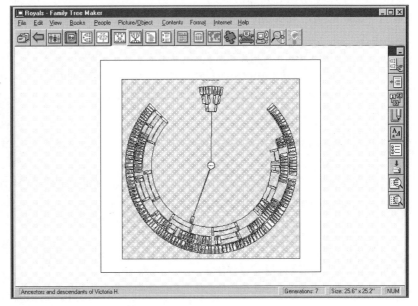

2.   From the Format menu, click Tree Format.

3.   Under the General tab, click Custom.

4.   Click OK.

> ❧ **NOTE** ❧ *If you want to include a Fan Hourglass Tree in your family history book, the Fit-to-Page version might be the better choice, although you will have to create several trees with different primary individuals to include the same amount of information as found on the Custom Fan Hourglass Tree.*

Figure 4.5 shows you the hazards of including too many generations on one tree—as you can see in this zoomed-out view, there are far too many people to be easily legible. Use few generations per tree for better readability.

WEIGHING THE PROS AND CONS OF THE FAN HOURGLASS TREE

When deciding whether to include a Fan Hourglass Tree in your family history book project, you'll want to weigh many factors. Consider these pros and cons:

- ❧ **Pros.** This tree provides a graphically pleasing way to show an individual's ancestors and descendants on one tree. This is a unique chart that is not commonly seen, but which is easily understood.

- ❧ **Cons.** This tree can be cumbersome and confusing if you have a large number of individuals included. One way to work around this is to use the Fit-to-Page version or to generate several trees for large ranges of generations. This tree is not standard to formal genealogies, and like other trees, may become unreadable with a lot of information included.

Family Group Sheet

The *Family Group Sheet* is one of the most easily recognized and frequently used forms by genealogists. It presents information by family unit (that is, two parents and their children) and allows researchers to quickly understand the nature of that family. Individuals who have more than one spouse are given a second (or however many are needed) Family Group Sheet to show that new family unit. Each of the children included on their parents' Family Group Sheet should also be given their own to show their family, if they have one.

With the individual for whom you want to create a Family Group Sheet selected on the Family Page, just follow these steps to create a Family Group Sheet:

1. Click the Family Group Sheet button on the toolbar. Alternatively, from the View menu, click Family Group Sheet.

2. The Family Group Sheet screen opens. If you want to change the options for the Family Group Sheet, see the section later in this chapter titled "Additional Family Group Sheet Options."

    ❧ **NOTE** ❧ *The basis of the Family Group Sheet is a family unit— couples do not have to be married in order to be included. Individuals who had relationships out of wedlock resulting in children should also be given their own Family Group Sheets.*

Figure 4.6 shows an example of a Family Group Sheet. Note that no siblings for either the husband or the wife are included on the sheet—only the husband, wife, their parents, and their children and spouses are included.

    ❧ **TIP** ❧ *Although you would not want to include one in your family history book, Family Tree Maker will print blank Family Group Sheets, which you can use to gather data as you research. These can be especially useful if you are at a family gathering or reunion—you can hand out blank Family Group Sheets and request that everyone fill in as much information as possible.*

Weighing the Pros and Cons of the Family Group Sheet

When deciding whether to include a Family Group Sheet in your family history book project, you'll want to consider the following pros and cons:

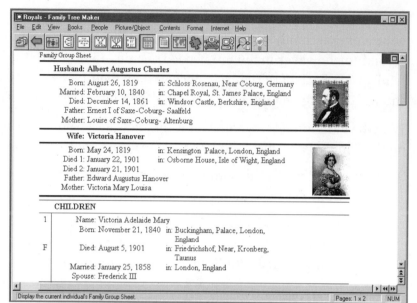

Figure 4.6

As you can see
from this partial
view, a Family
Group Sheet
presents details
about one
specific family
unit.

※ **Pros.** This chart is an excellent way to illustrate a family unit, allowing readers to quickly understand what children resulted from the union of two individuals. This chart is easily read and does not become confusing when lots of information is included in it.

※ **Cons.** Each family unit must be given its own Family Group Sheet. If you have a family with numerous children who have children themselves, those family units must be given their own Family Group Sheets, all of which can quickly add up. You might lose readers' attention if they cannot follow how families are related to one another.

Using a Timeline

A timeline is an interesting chart that shows you where an individual falls within a list of historical events. Each individual is represented by a horizontal Life Bar (a rectangular box with the person's name inside, or next to the box if the name is too long), as shown in Figure 4.7. Although timelines aren't usually included in formal genealogies, they are fun and interesting and would be well suited for use in a less formal family history, or other book project.

To create a Timeline, follow these steps:

1. On the Family Page, click the individual for whom you want to create a timeline.

2. From the View menu, click Timeline.

   The Timeline then appears. For details on changing the format of the Timeline, see the section later in this chapter titled "Selecting Your Format."

Family Tree Maker's Timeline can be customized to suit your needs; you can select which individuals you want to include, how you want them sorted, whether you want historical facts included (and where you want to find them), and more. Be sure to experiment with format options before settling on the form for the Timeline that suits you best.

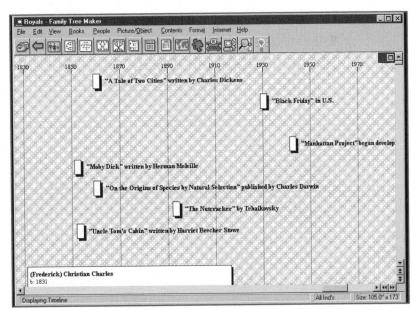

Figure 4.7

A timeline is a graphical and textual representation of where an individual's life fits in a list of historical events. Small white boxes mark historical events, whereas long rectangular boxes indicate individuals' lives.

Weighing the Pros and Cons of the Timeline

Should you use a timeline in your family history book project? Here are some points to consider as you make your decision.

- **Pros.** The Timeline is an excellent way to illustrate how an individual fits into the historical events of the time. A Timeline also shows you how individuals fall on a scale of years with relationship to one another, which can provide non-genealogists with a good sense of how family lines are made up.

- **Cons.** Too many individuals on one chart will make it print to several pages. Likewise, too much information included for each individual will overpower the chart and make it unreadable.

Using Maps

Maps go a long way toward giving readers a visual clue about the locations mentioned, which is why you might want to include several to accompany your family history. Family Tree Maker has a Map feature that automatically searches for all the locations connected with whatever events you specify and displays them on a map, as shown in Figure 4.8.

Follow these steps to create a Map:

1. Open the Family File that you want to work with.

2. Click the Map button on the toolbar. Alternatively, from the View menu, click Map.

   You are then taken to the Map screen. For more information about formatting the Map, see the section later in this chapter titled "Selecting Your Format."

Family Tree Maker comes with several maps that you can use: two for Europe (political and shaded relief), two for the world (political and shaded relief), one for North America (political), and one for the United States (shaded relief).

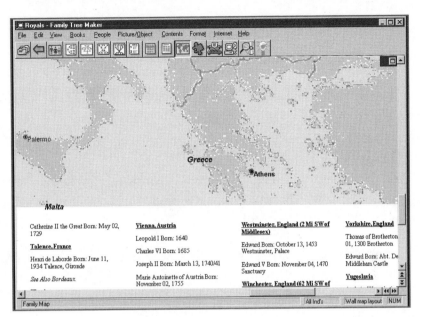

Figure 4.8

This political style map of Europe shows many of the locations of the births of individuals in a database. I chose to include only the individuals' names and birth dates/locations on this map, but I could have just as easily chosen other facts to be represented.

🌼 **TIP** 🌼 *You can include on the Map a location for an event that you have listed in the More About Facts or More About Marriage pages if you have selected either item on the Items to Be Included list. To enter a location, enter the fact name and date in the More About Facts screen, as well as any comments you have in the Comment/Location field and then follow the comments with a slash mark (/) and the location name. Family Tree Maker will search for locations following the slash mark and include them on a map.*

🌼 **NOTE** 🌼 *Family Tree Maker maps that are classified as political simply show the borders of countries in the traditional style of a map. Shaded relief maps show the contours of a country's terrain in relief format.*

Each of the six maps listed comes in two formats:

- **Book layout.** This format is for use in a family history book.
- **Wall Map layout.** This format is for printing out large, wall-sized maps.

Weighing the Pros and Cons of the Map Feature

You have many factors to weigh when considering whether using a map is suitable for your family history book project. You'll want to think about these pros and cons before you decide:

- **Pros.** A map is an excellent way to illustrate where individuals were when the events included on the map happened. Migration patterns can be tracked for several generations using maps.
- **Cons.** Too many individuals on one map will make it print to several pages, although the Book layout feature can repair this problem. Likewise, too much information included for each individual will overpower the map and make it unreadable. Wall Map layout requires a large number of pages to print.

Calendar

Like a map, a calendar is not a traditional item found in many family histories. However, it can be a fun and unique addition and should not be overlooked—particularly in informal family histories. Family Tree Maker allows you to create calendars with birthdays and anniversaries of living individuals, deceased individuals, or both.

To create a calendar, follow these steps:

1. Open the Family File that you want to work with.

2. From the View menu, click Calendar.

The Calendar screen appears. For more information about Calendar options, see the section later in this chapter titled "Additional Calendar Options."

You can select which individuals to include and which items you want displayed on the calendar, enabling you to customize the calendar to fit your project's needs. Figure 4.9 shows an example of a calendar that includes both living individuals and deceased individuals, but for privacy reasons, does not include the individuals' ages at the event.

⁂CAUTION⁂ *Do not include information about the birth year for living individuals unless you have their permission. Doing so without permission might constitute a violation of the individuals' privacy and is to be avoided, especially if your family history book will be available to people outside your immediate family circles.*

Figure 4.9

Calendars enable you to see who was born when and who celebrates an anniversary on what date. Although calendars are used most efficiently for living individuals, I find it fun to see who shares a birth date or anniversary with an ancestor.

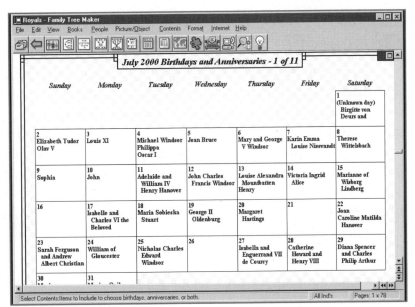

Weighing the Pros and Cons of the Calendar

Do you want to include a calendar in your family history book? Before you decide, you should consider these pros and cons:

* **Pros.** A Calendar is an excellent way to illustrate which individuals were born on which day. You might choose to print a calendar for living individuals only, providing a reminder of birthdays and anniversaries of family members; likewise, you could include dates for deceased individuals as a way to remember your ancestors and family members who are no longer with you.

* **Cons.** Very large databases might generate more than one page per calendar month, which can be confusing to the reader. Including deceased individuals, although interesting and informative, can also be confusing unless ages of the individuals are included, making it clear that someone who is celebrating their 130th birthday is deceased.

Exploring Tree and Chart Suitability, Options, Format, and Contents

You have many choices available regarding options, format, and content of the miscellaneous trees and charts in Family Tree Maker. Before choosing which trees and charts to use in your book, I advise you to print samples and experiment with the preferences and options for each until you find ones that suit your needs (for more information about printing trees, reports, and charts, see Chapter Three, "Using Trees in Your Family History Book"). Try changing the information included or limiting the individuals found on the chart. Will you like the report better if you change the font? What if you change the number of generations included in the report? How will it affect your tree if you change the manner in which notes and sources are included?

In general, the items you can change on trees and charts include the following:

* Font (the type, style, and size)

⚗ The individuals to be included on the tree

⚗ Whether to include More About notes and facts

⚗ Whether to include sources, and where they will be found within the tree or chart

Note that this list is not comprehensive for each tree or chart; for specific details on what options are available for each specific tree or chart, consult the section for that item in this chapter.

Testing the Tree or Chart for Suitability

The suitability of a tree or chart for your book is an important factor for you to consider when you are planning your book. If you have an informal book, you will not want to include hard-to-understand, detailed reports that will be incomprehensible to your audience. Likewise, if you are creating a formal family history book, you will not want to include those charts that are easy to understand and visually pleasing, but that lack content.

For the purposes of example, consider these three levels of family history book projects (for more examples of projects, be sure to read Chapter Eleven, "Family History Book Projects"):

⚗ An informal book intended to please non-genealogists' immediate family members

⚗ An intermediate-level book that is thorough but not complete—intended for an audience of genealogists

⚗ An advanced formal family history book that is complete, or near complete, with the highest standards of documentation and analysis—intended for serious genealogists

Keeping in mind that no hard-and-fast rule determines what you can and cannot include in your family history book, the suitability of the All-in-One Tree, Standard Hourglass Tree, Hourglass Fan Tree, Family Group Sheet, Timeline,

Map, and Calendar for the three types of projects might be summarized as follows:

 All-in-One Tree

- **Informal family history book.** This would be an interesting tree to use in an informal project; non-genealogists should easily understand the graphical nature of the tree as long as you have not included too many individuals in the tree.

- **Intermediate family history book.** This tree might not be the best choice for an intermediate-level family history book; a better choice of a graphical tree would be to create separate Standard Descendant and Standard Ancestor trees.

- **Formal family history book.** As with the intermediate-level book, the All-in-One tree could easily be replaced with descendant and ancestor trees, or better yet, a descendant-ordered narrative report and an Ahnentafel Report.

 Standard Hourglass Tree

- **Informal family history book.** This would be an interesting chart to use in an informal project; non-genealogists should easily understand the graphical nature of the chart.

- **Intermediate family history book.** This tree might not be the best choice for an intermediate-level family history book. If you want to include graphical trees showing an individual's ancestors and descendants, a better choice might be to create separate Standard Descendant and Ancestor trees, because you could fit more information on each tree.

- **Formal family history book.** As with the intermediate-level book, the Standard Hourglass Tree could easily be replaced with descendant and ancestor trees, or better yet, a descendant-ordered narrative report and an Ahnentafel Report.

❋ **Fan Hourglass Tree**

- **Informal family history book.** This would be an interesting chart to use in an informal project; non-genealogists should easily understand the graphical nature of the chart.

- **Intermediate family history book.** This tree might not be the best choice for an intermediate-level family history book. If you want to include graphical trees showing an individual's ancestors and descendants, a better choice might be to create separate Standard Descendant and Ancestor trees, because you could fit more information on each tree.

- **Formal family history book.** As with the intermediate-level book, the Fan Hourglass Tree could easily be replaced with descendant and ancestor trees, or better yet, a descendant-ordered narrative report and an Ahnentafel report.

❋ **Family Group Sheet**

- **Informal family history book.** A good choice, as it shows the relationship within a family unit. Easy to read and understand.

- **Intermediate family history book.** A traditional choice for many family history projects of this level.

- **Formal family history book.** Suitable, although not as widely used as narrative reports.

❋ **Timeline**

- **Informal family history book.** A good choice, as it shows the relationship of family members to one another against a backdrop of history. Easy to read and understand.

- **Intermediate family history book.** A different sort of chart to include if you are looking for something unique. Both genealogists and non-genealogists should be able to understand it.

- **Formal family history book.** Not a traditional choice for a formal family history, although it might be an interesting chart to include for individuals who were affected by historic events.

✵ Map

- **Informal family history book.** A good choice that is easily recognized by non-genealogists and that provides useful information at a glance.

- **Intermediate family history book.** As with an informal book, maps would be a good choice here because they provide geographical information in a graphical format.

- **Formal family history book.** Not a traditional choice for a formal family history, although it might be an interesting one to include if notes and facts are documented fully with locations.

✵ Calendar

- **Informal family history book.** A good choice that is easily recognized by non-genealogists, and one that provides useful information at a glance. Calendars offer a fun way to compare birth dates and anniversaries and are well suited to this sort of project.

- **Intermediate family history book.** As an appendix or other non-vital section in a book, a calendar could provide interest, but is not traditionally found in intermediate and formal family history books.

- **Formal family history book.** Not a traditional choice for a formal family history, although it might be an interesting one to include as an appendix or in a back section of the book.

Considering Your Options

When you create one of the miscellaneous trees or charts, you can select from multiple options that enable you to customize how that item is created and displayed. The options, accessed via the Contents menu, vary for each tree and chart. Below is a list of options for the trees and charts mentioned in this chapter (with the exception of the Family Group Sheet, Timeline, and Calendar, none of which have options available):

To access the options for any of the trees or charts mentioned in this chapter, follow these general steps:

1. Open the Family File that you want to work with.

2. Click the individual for whom you want to create the tree or chart.

3. Using the View menu, select the tree or chart you want.

4. Once you are in the item's view, from the Contents menu, select Options.

5. Make your Option selections (described in detail in this section) and click OK.

   - **Show Unconnected Stepfamily Trees.** This option is useful if you want to include stepfamily trees (for example, the family of a stepchild or stepparent), but it might be one that is confusing to readers. If you choose to enable this option, be sure your readers can tell that the step-family's tree is separate from the primary individual's tree. This option is available only for the All-in-One Tree.

   - **Show Unrelated Trees.** If you choose this option, you can also specify showing solitary, unlinked boxes. Like the stepfamily option, this option should be enabled only if you are sure that the separate trees can be differentiated as such. This option is available only for the All-in-One Tree.

   - **Display Siblings in Order Shown on Family Page.** This option allows you to have siblings presented on the tree in the order you entered them on the Family Page. This option is available only for the All-in-One Tree.

- **Use Thicker Line for Primary Individual's Box.** This is a good option to enable because it clearly shows which individual on the tree is the primary individual. This option is available only for the All-in-One Tree.

- **Label Columns as Parents, Grandparents, and so on.** This means each generation on your tree will have a label indicating its relationship to the primary individual. This option is a good choice to use on an informal family history project or for a book intended for a non-genealogist audience, as it makes the relationship clear even to those without genealogical knowledge. This option is available only for the Standard Hourglass Tree.

- **Include Duplicate Ancestors Each Time They Appear.** This option allows you to include those individuals who might appear more than once on your family tree (for example, if you have cousins who marry, much of their ancestry is duplicated). This can be useful when you want a complete family history, but you should be aware that including duplicate ancestors each time they appear might waste space. This option is available only for the Standard Hourglass Tree and the Fan Hourglass Tree.

- **Include Siblings of Primary Individual.** If you want to include the brothers and sisters of the primary individual on your tree, this option allows you to do so. If the individual has several siblings, you might want to exclude them from the tree to keep it from being too cluttered. This option is available only for the Hourglass Tree.

- **Include Empty Branches.** This option allows you to include empty boxes indicating individuals for which you have no information. There are no real pros or cons to choosing to include them—doing so is simply a matter of personal taste. This option is available only for the Hourglass Tree.

- **Allow Location Labels on Map to Overlap.** This can be useful if you require only a few labels on a map, but beware of using it if you have locations that are near each other or if you have many locations. Overlapped labels can quickly make the map unreadable. This option is available only for the Map.

Deciding on Content

As with other trees, one of the most powerful tools you have for deciding on the content of your tree or chart is the Items to Include option under the Contents menu. Depending on the tree you are configuring, you can choose to include any number of items from the list shown in Chapter Three. If you haven't viewed that list, take a moment to familiarize yourself with the types of information that can be included on trees and charts.

To access the options for any of the trees or charts mentioned in this chapter, follow these basic steps:

1. Open the Family File that you want to work with.

2. Click the individual for whom you want to create the tree or chart.

3. Using the View menu, select the tree or chart you want.

4. Once you are in the item's view, from the Contents menu, select the item you want (described in detail in this section) and click OK.

The caveat mentioned in Chapter Three bears repeating: Although you may be tempted to include a large amount of information on your trees and charts, keep readability in the forefront of your mind. If you have more information than can easily be presented on a tree or chart, consider printing more than one version. The first version can include a few of the items, while the second can include the remainder. For example, suppose that you want to include the following items:

- Name
- Birth Date/Location
- Marriage Date/Location
- Death Date/Location
- Picture/Object

- ✣ Burial
- ✣ Fact 1
- ✣ Fact 2
- ✣ Fact 3
- ✣ Marriage Fact
- ✣ Marriage Picture/Object
- ✣ Residence

That's a lot of information to include on any tree! If you are bound and determined to have this information on a Fan Hourglass Tree, you might choose to break up the information and print two copies of the tree—one containing the vital statistics information (birth, marriage, death, burial) and one including the facts and other information.

Likewise, you'll want to weigh carefully which individuals you plan to include on the tree and chart. Not all items give you the ability to specify which individuals you can include, so be sure to investigate whether the tree or chart of your choice has this capability.

The following is a list of standard items that can be included on trees and charts. Note that not all items are available for every tree and chart—following the list, you'll find another list showing which Contents items can be included for which tree and chart.

- ✣ **Items to Include.** This is the same list as shown in Chapter Three. You can select which items you'd like to appear on each tree and chart.

- ✣ **Individuals to Include.** This allows you to specify which individuals will be included.

- ✣ **Title & Footnote.** You can specify a title for each tree and chart, as well as create your own footnote. The footnote options for the Hourglass Trees are the same as for the standard trees; see Chapter Three for more information.

- **Number of Generations to Show.** This allows you to specify how many generations you want displayed on your tree or chart.

Following is a list of content choices available to you for each tree and chart (be sure to try out the various content choices to decide which ones are best suited to your needs):

- **All-in-One Tree.** For the All-in-One Tree, you can specify items that you want to include on the tree, whether to have titles and footnotes, and the number of generations to show.

- **Standard Hourglass Tree.** For the Standard Hourglass Tree, you can specify which items you want to include on the tree, which individuals you want to include, whether to have titles and footnotes, and the number of generations to show.

- **Fan Hourglass Tree.** For the Fan Hourglass Tree, you can specify which items you want to include on the tree, which individuals to include, whether to have a title and footnotes, and the number of generations to show.

  NOTE *The Number of Generations to Show option enables you to include only the direct line of descent between the primary individual and a secondary individual, as demonstrated in Figure 4.10. If you choose to use this feature, you will not be able to specify how many generations are to be included in your Fan Hourglass Tree—Family Tree Maker will automatically include the generations between the two selected individuals. For this reason, be sure that you set the number of ancestral generations you want to include on the tree before you select the direct-line descendant option.*

- **Family Group Sheet.** For the Family Group Sheet, you can specify which items to include and whether to use titles and footnotes. For information about accessing these options, see the upcoming section "Additional Family Group Sheet Options."

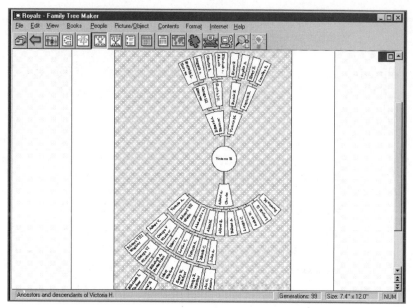

Figure 4.10

This Custom Fan Hourglass Tree was created using the direct-line descendant option, with siblings of each direct-line descendant included.

> ❧ **NOTE** ❧ *Family Group Sheets enable you to configure many more options than the two preceding ones. For more information about other types of options that are available with Family Group Sheets, see the section "Additional Family Group Sheet Options."*

❧ **Timeline.** For the Timeline, you can specify which items to include, which individuals to include, and whether to include titles and footnotes.

❧ **Map.** For the Map, you can specify which items to include, which individuals to include, and whether to use a title and footnotes.

❧ **Calendar.** For the Calendar, you can specify which items to include, which individuals to include, and whether to use a title and footnotes. However, the options found under Items to Include are different from those available for any other tree or chart, enabling you to select the year and month (or the entire year) to display.

> ❧ **NOTE** ❧ *Calendars enable you to configure more options than the preceding ones. For more information about what other types of options are available with Calendars, see the upcoming section "Additional Calendar Options."*

ADDITIONAL FAMILY GROUP SHEET OPTIONS

Unlike other trees, charts, and reports, where the contents' options are selected directly from the Contents menu, Family Tree Maker hides the contents' options for Family Group Sheets in the Items to Include dialog box. To see the options for Family Group Sheets, open the Contents menu and select Items to Include. In the Items to Include dialog box, select Standard Page on the right side (under the header Your Family Group Sheet Contains) and then click the Options button in the middle of the dialog box. You'll see the options available for Family Group Sheets, shown in Figure 4.11.

Figure 4.11

The options for a Family Group Sheet are hidden, but once you find them, you can greatly influence how the chart will appear.

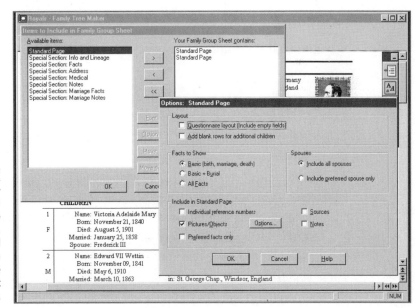

The options for the Standard Page fall into four categories: Layout, Facts to Show, Spouses, and Include in Standard Page. The options for these categories are as follows:

❊ **Layout**

- Questionnaire Layout (Include Empty Fields)
- Add Blank Rows for Additional Children

❊ **Facts to Show**

- Basic (Birth, Marriage, Death)
- Basic + Burial
- All Facts

❊ **Spouses**

- Include All Spouses
- Include Preferred Spouse Only

❊ **Include in Standard Page**

- Individual Reference Numbers
- Pictures/Objects
- Preferred Facts Only
- Sources
- Notes

❊ **TIP** ❊ *Like the Standard Ancestor Tree (pedigree chart), you can print copies of blank Family Group Sheets to use as worksheets while you research. Using the Questionnaire Layout option previously listed, you can also print Family Group Sheets that have empty fields included where you are missing information. Such a chart can be a great help when researching, but it is probably not the best layout choice for a family history book.*

Of the items shown in the preceding list, the ones you will probably most concern yourself with are those in the Include in Standard Page section:

- **Individual Reference Numbers.** Including individuals' reference numbers is handy if you want to use your family history book in conjunction with your database, but otherwise the numbers might be confused with those that the narrative reports (such as the NGS Quarterly Report) generate.

- **Pictures/Objects.** You can add objects that you have entered in an individual's (or marriage's) Scrapbook on the tree. Pictures add a fun way to increase your readers' awareness of which individuals are included, what they looked like, and so on. For a more detailed discussion on including pictures and objects in trees, reports, and charts, read Chapter Seven, "Using Graphics in Your Family History Book."

- **Preferred Facts Only.** When this option is selected, only those facts you designate as preferred appear on the chart (this is a good idea if you have alternate facts or conflicting evidence).

- **Sources and Notes.** You are given the option to include notes and sources on your Family Group Sheet, although you cannot specify where on the chart the notes and sources will appear. As with other reports and charts, it's always a good idea to include your sources, but you can opt to avoid notes, which can be bulky and disrupt the chart.

Other special options for Family Group Sheets accessed via the Items to Include menu include the following:

- **Info and Lineage.** This option allows you to include labels of empty fields and source information for the info and lineage sections.

- **Facts.** This option allows you to include source information for the facts and to display only those dates and locations that you specify as preferred.

⚹ **Marriage Facts.** This option allows you to include source information for the marriage facts and to display only those dates and locations that you specify as preferred.

One other option you have with Family Group Sheets that is not available on all the other trees and reports is the ability to include your name and address on the Family Group Sheet. This is useful when creating charts for research projects or exchanging with other interested researchers, but it is not necessary when used in a family history book unless you want to note which individual contributed which Family Group Sheet (see Chapter Eleven for information about such a project).

ADDITIONAL CALENDAR OPTIONS

In addition to the Calendar options, you can select how you want information about people displayed. You can opt to use any of the following:

⚹ Name Formats (Seven to Choose From)

⚹ Use Married Names for Female Family Members

⚹ Use aka If Available (Instead of the Name or Between the First and Last Names)

⚹ Last Name in Caps

⚹ Print Only If Alive (Allows You to Exclude Deceased Individuals)

In addition, you can choose which events to include: birthdays, anniversaries, or both. You might also want to include an individual's age on the calendar, although you should be wary of doing so for living individuals unless you have their permission.

Selecting Your Format

Once you decide what information you want to include on your tree or chart, it's time to turn an eye to how your tree or chart will be formatted. Family Tree Maker lets you make formatting changes for everything from the box style to the font or layout of the tree. Be sure to experiment with changing the formatting of each tree and chart you use to find which features (layout, box and line style, font, and so on) suit you best.

TREE FORMAT OPTIONS

Five basic tree format options are available (note that not all format options are available for all trees and charts; for more details about the options shown here, refer to Chapter Three):

* **Tree Format.** This is available only for trees and allows you to change the layout and general format of the tree. Generally, the format choices give you the chance to change the shape of the tree and the density in which information is presented.

* **Maximum Box Width.** Depending on the size of your tree or chart, you might want to limit the box and picture/object widths on the tree. Making the box widths smaller gives you more room on the tree, but it also gives you less space for the data included in the box. You'll want to carefully weigh the advantages and disadvantages of changing box width size.

* **Box, Line, and Border Styles.** You can customize the look of your tree or chart by specifying the type of boxes, borders, and lines you want to use. The number of format options available for boxes is numerous; you can specify different formats for males, females, or those of undefined gender. For each of the three, you can specify the color for the box outline, fill, and shadow, as well as select one of six box styles. You can also choose to color each generation on the chart differently, making it easier to pick out which individuals belong to which generation.

    You can change the border style. Six border styles are available, and you can specify border color and background color as well.

    You can specify one of three line styles and line color. You can also choose to highlight the direct-line relationship between the primary individual and another individual in a different color, and you can show non-natural parent-child relationships (for example, stepchildren) with a dotted line rather than a solid line.

⚹ **Text Font, Style, and Size.** You can choose how you want the text displayed on your trees and charts by specifying the font type, font size, and font style (bold, italics, and so on), text color, and text alignment (center, left, or right). You can also choose to underline text. Be aware that if you change the font size to a larger one, you run the risk of making the boxes on the tree larger, and thus less information can be displayed per page. As with other format options, experiment with the format settings to find what works for you and your tree before deciding on a final format.

⚹ **Show Page Lines.** The last format choice you have is one that is inconsequential because it won't affect the printed tree or chart: whether or not you want to have page lines shown on the screen. The lines will not appear on the tree itself, but they will give you an idea of how your tree will look when it's printed, should it run to more than one page.

To access the Format choices for any of the trees or charts mentioned in this chapter, follow these basic steps:

1. Open the Family File that you want to work with.

2. Click the individual for whom you want to create the tree or chart.

3. Using the View menu, select the tree or chart you want.

4. Once you are in the item's view, from the Format menu, select the item you want and click OK.

As with other options, not all format choices are available for every tree and chart. You should experiment with the format settings to find what works for you before deciding on a final format. The following is a list of the format choices that are available for each tree and chart mentioned in this chapter (you can also consult Chapter Three for more on these choices):

> ✗ **All-in-One Tree**
>
> > • **Maximum Width for Each Box & Picture/Object.** This format option is the same as for other trees.
> >
> > • **Box, Line, and Border Styles.** This format option is the same as for other trees.
> >
> > • **Text Font, Style, and Size.** This format option is the same as for other trees.
>
> ✗ **Standard Hourglass Tree**
>
> > • **Center Tree on Page.** This is a fairly straightforward option—if you want your tree centered on the page, select this item. If you prefer to have it offset to one side (for example, if you are manually inserting it into another document and want the left margin to be larger than other margins to allow for binding), you will not want this option selected.
> >
> > • **Make All Boxes Same Size (Not Available in Book Layout Version).** You should select this format feature if you want to ensure that all the boxes on the tree appear the same size regardless of the amount of information contained within. This is an aesthetic choice, although you should be wary of selecting it if you have a lot of information to present, because making the boxes all the same size wastes valuable space on the page.
> >
> > • **Boxes Overlap Page Breaks (Not Available in Book Layout Version).** If you print a tree that flows over more than one page, this feature enables you to let the boxes draw over page breaks. Because of the fractured nature resulting from such a format, I don't recommend it.

- **Perfect, Condensed, or Squished Ancestor Layout.** For more information about the three layout choices, refer to Chapter Three.

- **Automatic, Horizontal, or 1-Column, Descendant Layout.** This option is the same as for other trees.

- **Maximum Width for Each Box & Picture/Object.** This option is the same as for other trees.

- **Box, Line, and Border Styles.** This format option is the same as for other trees.

- **Text Font, Style, and Size.** This format option is the same as for other trees.

Fan Hourglass Tree

- **Hourglass, Semi-Circle, and Largest Number of Individual Shapes.** The last shape, shown by a pie chart symbol, will assign the bottom portion of the tree to the group—ancestors or descendants—that makes up the larger part of the tree. These shapes are similar to the ones shown in Chapter Three for the Fan Descendant Tree, and they indicate the shape that the fan tree will try to form within the limits of the database.

- **Make All Boxes Same Width.** As with the Make All Boxes the Same Size format feature, this one will make the tree print with all the boxes the same size, regardless of the amount of information you have for each person.

- **Flip Text.** This format feature is the same as the one discussed in Chapter Three; consult it for more information.

- **Generous, Condensed, or Squished Ancestor Layout.** This format feature is the same as for other trees.

- **Maximum Width for Each Box & Picture/Object.** This option is the same as for other trees.

- **Box, Line, and Border Styles.** This format option is the same as for other trees.

- **Text Font, Style, and Size.** This format option is the same as for other trees.

FAMILY GROUP SHEET FORMAT OPTIONS

Family Group Sheets offer only two format options:

> ❋ **Begin Each Person on a New Page.** Beginning each person on a new page is a good choice if you have lots of information for each individual, including pictures, objects, notes, and sources. If you do not have a lot of information or items for each individual, you probably will not want to select this format option because it causes the Family Group Sheet to consume several pages.

> ❋ **Text Font, Style, and Size.** These options are the same as for the trees and reports—that is, you can change the font, the style, and the size for all the text found on the Family Group Sheet.

TIMELINE FORMAT OPTIONS

You have numerous format options when it comes to timelines:

> ❋ **Years per Inch (20, 50, or 100).** This option should be used with care—if you try to pack too many people onto a timeline with a long range of years (for example, one using 100 years per inch), you run the risk of making the chart difficult to read.

> ❋ **Tick Mark Every *[your choice]* Decade(s).** This option sets the number of decades between tick marks displayed in the timeline; numbers range from 1 to 10.

> ❋ **Years Flow Left to Right, or Right to Left.** This option enables you to set the direction that the flow of years is displayed on the timeline—either left to right (for example, from 1700 to 1880) or right to left (from 1880 to 1700). You can choose which way you want them to be; either choice is fine, except that most people are used to seeing years flow from left to right.

※ **Display Historical Events.** If you choose to display historical events, you can display the events in the body of the timeline (refer to Figure 4.7, shown earlier in the chapter) or at the end of the Time-line. You can also specify which type of historical events you want included on your timeline via the Choose button on the formatting dialog box. Choices include events for Arts, Asia, Economics, Europe, Military, Politics, Religion, Technology, U.S., and World. Of course, you need not include historical events if you want simply to create a timeline to show how the individuals included in the chart fall chronologically in relationship to one another.

※ **Graphically Display Estimated Dates.** This option is useful if you do not have exact dates; Family Tree Maker estimates a birth or death date for you and draws the box for the individual accordingly.

MAP FORMAT OPTIONS

When working with maps, you have the following format options:

※ **Number of Columns.** The columns in the Number of Columns option, available for Book layout only, refer to the legend following the graphical portion of a map. Legends give readers a way to connect an individual with a location.

※ **Start on Page with Map.** The Start on Page with Map option, available for Book layout only, specifies that the legend start on the same page as the map.

※ **Column Width (in Inches).** This option is available for Wall Map layout only and affects the column width in the legend. If you have only a few columns, you can set wider widths than if you choose to have the legend spread over several columns.

※ **Include Legend.** The legend for the Family Tree Maker Map is composed of the facts for the location and the name and other information entered for individuals who were born in or near that location. For example, on a map I generated for Queen Victoria, the legend includes the following entry:

Goslar, Germany (24 mi. NW of Blankenburg)

On the next line is the entry for the individual born in this town:

Henry IV, Born November 11, 1050

❋ **Abbreviate State Names in Map.** If your United States map includes locations for a number of states, you might want to abbreviate the state name to avoid too much text on the map. As with trees and charts, the more text you include on an item, the greater the risk that the chart will become unreadable. Abbreviations can help eliminate text that isn't needed on the map.

❋ **Show Symbol Key.** If you want to display the symbols used to designate towns, cities, large cities, and counties, select this option. It is also useful when your map is not overrun with text from locations.

❋ **Make the Map Area Size Larger or Smaller (or Scale the Map to Fit Page).** This option gives you the ability to "blow up" the map size so that you can focus on a smaller geographic area. Enlarging the map area is useful if you have a high density of people located on a small area of map. As with any other feature, you should make sure that your map offers the reader as much information as can be read clearly and concisely.

❋ **Change Text Font, Size, and Style.** This option is identical to the ones related to trees, charts, and reports—that is, you can select the font type, font style, and font size for all the text on the map. Choose font types, styles, and sizes that are readable, but that don't take up too much space on the map. Experimenting with font size is a must.

❋ **Change Map to Another of the Available Maps.** Once you are through with the map currently in use, you can change to another map. This feature allows you to select from the maps that are

available to Family Tree Maker (see the section "Using Maps,"
earlier in this chapter, for information on the maps that are
available).

CALENDAR FORMAT OPTIONS

When working with calendars, you have various format options:

- **Three Box and Line Styles.** You can choose one of three line styles
  for the boxes and lines within the calendar: Thin, Medium, or
  Heavy. There is no particular reason to use one line style over
  another—it's purely an aesthetic judgment about what looks best.

- **Six Border Styles.** Six border choices are available for your
  calendar—the one you choose depends on which one you think
  best suits your calendar. As with other calendar format options,
  printing samples gives you a chance to see what format choices
  work best for you.

- **Line Color.** Family Tree Maker gives you the choice of 39 colors to
  use for line, fill, and border color (you must have a color printer to
  see the effect of the colors). Colors can add interest and variety to
  your calendar, but use them judiciously, lest you end up with a
  psychedelic calendar filled with all possible colors.

- **Fill Color.** As with the line color, you can select one of 39 colors as
  fill for each day's square. Make sure that your fill colors don't clash
  with the line and border colors!

- **Border Color.** If you want to change the color of the border, this
  option allows you to pick one of the same 39 colors available for line
  and fill.

Ancestors of George Howard Lafferty

Samuel Lafferty
1801 - 1873

Edwin E. Lafferty
1834 - 1907

Margaret McDowell
1803 - 1881

George E. Lafferty
1867 - 1936

Ernstus Fowler
1793 - 1875

Amelia Fowler
1814

Temperence Merrill
1796 - 1871

Nathan Wescott
1818 - 1900

Hiram Wescott

Sarah Ann McMichael
1820 - 1901

Wescott
1963

Samuel C. Amsden
1822 - 1899

Theresa Jerusa Amsden
1845 - 1934

Clarissa Hubbard
1820 - 1870

The History of George Howard Lafferty

George Howard Lafferty was born September 2, 1994 in Lenox township, Ashtabula County, Ohio, to Amber Amelia Wescott Lafferty and George Edwin Lafferty. A sister, Maud Irene, was born May 23, 1892.

A family of farmers, the Laffertys harvested the land where they lived. On May 9, 1919, they moved to Warren, Ohio, to a house on Forest Street NE. They lived next door to their daughter Maud, her husband Jay Rood Webster, and their three beautiful daughters, Reta, Shirley, and Marion.

As a youth, Lafferty went by "Howard" rather than "George" and signed his name as G. Howard Lafferty. After graduating from Lenox Township schools in 1911, he received a Teachers Certificate and became an educator and later a high school Principal. He then switched careers and ventured into banking just before World War I.

As a student at Ohio State University during the war, Howard Lafferty hoped to join the army but was classified 5G due to his glasses and other restrictions. In 1923 he received an L.L.B. degree and passed

Using Narrative Reports in Your Family History Book

A man may write at any time,
if he will set himself doggedly to it.

— Samuel Johnson, from James Boswell's,
Life of Johnson

Although trees and charts can be pretty and display information in a graphical manner that is easily grasped by non-genealogists, narrative reports are the meat and potatoes of serious family history books. Narrative reports are used in most formal family history books because they display the maximum amount of information in a no-nonsense, straightforward manner.

Family Tree Maker enables you to create three types of narrative reports:

- The Register Report
- The NGS Quarterly Report
- The Ahnentafel Report

This chapter covers all three in detail, with examples of numbering systems and format options. You will also find out how to include notes and sources to your satisfaction.

You may be asking yourself why there are three different types of narrative reports, rather than just one, and why you would want to choose one over the other. Of the three reports, two—the Register Report and the NGS Quarterly Report—are very similar in style and format, so deciding which to use is a matter of personal preference (for an in-depth discussion of both types, consult the appropriate sections in this chapter). The third report, the Ahnentafel Report, is different in content and style, and instead of being a descendent-ordered report, it features the ancestors of a primary individual. There are no specific guidelines as to when you would use one report over another—your project needs and personal preferences will guide you in determining which is best for you.

By the time you finish this chapter, you will be conversant with the standard reports that you can create using Family Tree Maker. You will also have done the following:

- Consulted the descriptions to locate which reports are best suited for your family history book project
- Printed sample copies of the reports
- Experimented with the options and formats for the reports you choose to use

Choices for changing your report formats are limited. You can usually change font attributes and other text-related formats. You can also decide which individuals to include or exclude and whether you want to include notes. Sources can be included or left out, and you can choose where to position them in the report. You can explore the remaining options for each report in the related sections in this chapter.

> ❧ **NOTE** ❧ *The More About Notes feature allows you to enter miscellaneous data related to a specific person. You can use this feature to include information you have gathered that is not suitable for inclusion in an event or source—for example, a quote from another source, a journal extract, part of a letter, and so on. More About Notes can be printed in some reports, including the ones described in this chapter.*
>
> *To access the More About Notes for an individual:*
>
> 1. *Click the person's name for whom you want to enter a note.*
> 2. *Click the More About button.*
> 3. *In the More About screen, click the Notes button.*
> 4. *The Notes screen will open, allowing you to enter your text. Your text is automatically saved when you move on to another screen.*

Using Narrative Reports

Although both the descendant-ordered and ancestor-ordered trees mentioned in Chapter Three, "Using Trees in Your Family History Book," provide a graphical way to easily understand who an individual's descendants and ancestors are, the trees are limited as to how much information can be included. For that reason, genealogists who want to explore an individual's family in greater detail use a narrative style report. Family Tree Maker includes its narrative reports under the general term "Genealogy Report." Figure 5.1 shows the three narrative report styles available.

To create a narrative report, follow these steps:

1. Open the Family File you want to work with.

2. Click the name of the individual for whom you want to create a report.

3. Click the Genealogy Reports button on the toolbar or from the View menu, click Genealogy Report.

4. In the Report screen, select the type of report you want to create from the Format menu by selecting Genealogy Report Format.

5. In the Genealogy Report Format dialog box, select the report format you want (Register, NGS Quarterly, or Ahnentafel; see Figure 5.1).

6. Click OK to return to the report.

> ❧ **NOTE** ❧ *Not all the reports provided by Family Tree Maker are narrative reports. Also offered are the Kinship Report, the Custom Report, and a variety of miscellaneous reports, all of which are discussed in Chapter Six, "Exploring Custom and Miscellaneous Reports."*

Genealogical standards created in the late nineteenth and early twentieth centuries have evolved into the descendant-ordered reports used today. (*Descendant-ordered* simply means that the report begins with a primary individual and lists his or her descendants in a descending fashion.) This style is

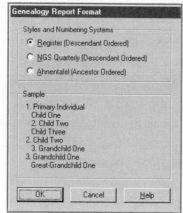

Figure 5.1

This dialog box shows the three narrative reports available in Family Tree Maker.

very similar to the descendant-ordered trees discussed earlier. Descendant-ordered narrative reports are the most frequently used reports in family history books, generally with one family unit (parents and their children) or generation featured per chapter.

Without some form of numbering system, it would not be easy to tell how an individual in a narrative report was related to the primary individual and individuals in the previous generations. For that reason, each of the narrative reports uses a numbering system to show those relationships—unfortunately, the numbering systems are unique to each report. Before you decide which narrative report you want to use in your family history book, you should print samples to see which style of report is understandable to you, and which will best present your information to your audience.

Numbering Systems

Numbering system is a term used to refer to the type of organizational format found in a narrative report. Several numbering systems have been developed over the years, but the standard and most frequently used ones are the three found in Family Tree Maker's narrative reports:

> ✲ **Register System.** Used in and referred to by Family Tree Maker as the Register Report.

⚘ **NGS Quarterly System.** Used in the NGS Quarterly Report.

⚘ **Ahnentafel System.** Used in the Ahnentafel Report.

> ⚘ **NOTE** ⚘ *Late in the nineteenth century, the editor of the prestigious* New England Historical and Genealogical Register *attempted to standardize the way genealogies were presented. The editor, Albert H. Hoyt, created a narrative report called the* Register Plan, *or* Register System. *The Register Report was later modified by the National Genealogy Society into what is now known as the* NGS Quarterly System *(named after the quarterly publication of the National Genealogy Society, this system was for a while also known as the* Modified Register System).

DEFINING THE REGISTER SYSTEM

In the Register System, which is used in Register Reports, the primary individual is assigned the number 1 and a superscript 1 (the superscript number indicates to which generation the individual belongs); each child is then numbered in order with lowercase Roman numerals (i, ii, iii, iv, v, and so on). If the child also had children, they would be given an Arabic number as well, in order of their birth. Figure 5.2 shows an example of a Register Report for Queen Victoria. (Note that Queen Victoria is shown by the superscript 5 as being in the seventh generation from the primary individual, Prince Ernest of Brunswick.)

DEFINING THE NGS QUARTERLY SYSTEM

Based on the Register System just described, the NGS Quarterly System was created so that each individual, whether or not he or she had children, was given a number. A plus sign (+) is used to indicate those individuals who did have children (for an example of the plus sign, see the section in this chapter titled "NGS Quarterly Report"). The NGS Quarterly format is an extremely popular narrative report style because all children are included in the numbering, not just those who had children themselves. Figure 5.3 shows the information contained in the preceding Register System report, but formatted in the NGS Quarterly System.

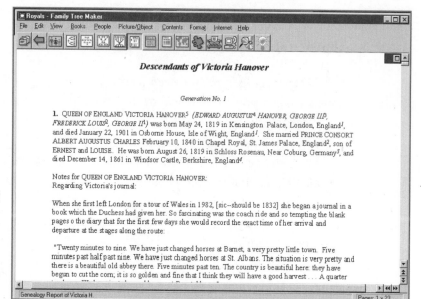

Figure 5.2

Here a Register Report for Queen Victoria shows the Register System of numbering.

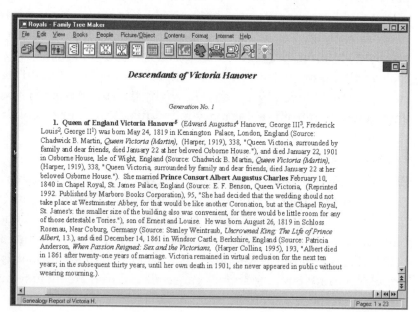

Figure 5.3

An NGS Quarterly—formatted narrative report for Queen Victoria.

DEFINING THE AHNENTAFEL SYSTEM

An Ahnentafel (German for "ancestor table") is an easy-to-understand ancestor-ordered narrative report showing a primary individual and his or her ancestors by generation. It is, in effect, a written version of the pedigree chart in which the primary individual is assigned the number 1. His or her ancestors are then numbered in the general pattern shown in the following table. Figure 5.4 shows an example of an Ahnentafel for Queen Victoria.

First Generation	**Second Generation**	**Third Generation**
Primary Individual #1	Father #2, Mother #3	Paternal Grandfather #4, Paternal Grandmother #5, Maternal Grandfather # 6, Maternal Grandmother #7, and so on

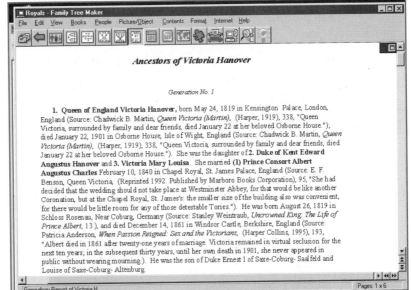

Figure 5.4

Excerpt of an Ahnentafel Report for Queen Victoria, showing the first, second, and part of the third generation.

Note that with the exception of the primary individual, men are always assigned even numbers, women odd numbers, and wives are always one number higher than their husbands. Thus, an individual's father is assigned a number twice his own, and the individual's mother is assigned a number twice his own plus one.

Register Reports

One of the most common narrative reports found in genealogies is the Register Report, a popular report that displays basic facts and biographical details about each individual in a descendant-ordered format, but does not include information about those individuals whose line did not continue. A slightly modified format of this style is still used by the New England Historical and Genealogical Society. Following is an example of how the Register report looks when printed.

> **NOTE** *Unlike the NGS Quarterly report, names are automatically put into capital letters. You might also notice that there are two sets of superscript numbers in the Register Report—the first set, directly following the primary individual and her male ancestors, is a generational indicator that tells the reader to what generation each individual belongs (based on a specified ancestor being the progenitor). The second set of superscript numbers—the ones in italics—is a source indicator, pointing out to the reader that each fact with a superscript number following it has a source. You should also notice, as mentioned previously, that Arabic numerals are assigned only to those children who have progeny of their own, but all children receive a Roman numeral to indicate their sibling order.*

Descendants of Victoria Hanover

Generation No. 1

1. QUEEN OF ENGLAND VICTORIA HANOVER[7] *(EDWARD AUGUSTUS[6] HANOVER, GEORGE III[5], FREDERICK LOUIS[4], GEORGE II[3], GEORGE I[2], ERNEST AUGUSTUS OF BRUNSWICK[1])* was born May 24, 1819 in Kensington Palace, London, England[1], and died January 22, 1901 in Osborne House, Isle of Wight, England[1]. She married PRINCE CONSORT ALBERT AUGUSTUS CHARLES February 10, 1840 in Chapel Royal, St. James Palace, England[2], son of ERNEST and LOUISE. He was born August 26, 1819 in Schloss Rosenau, Near Coburg, Germany[3], and died December 14, 1861 in Windsor Castle, Berkshire, England[5].

Children of VICTORIA and ALBERT CHARLES are:

2.   i.   PRINCESS ROYAL VICTORIA ADELAIDE MARY[8], b. November 21, 1840, Buckingham Palace, London, England; d. August 05, 1901, Friedrichshof, Near, Kronberg, Taunus.

3.   ii.   KING OF ENGLAND EDWARD VII WETTIN, b. November 09, 1841, Buckingham Palace, London, England; d. May 06, 1910, Buckingham Palace, London, England.

5.   iii.   PRINCESS ALICE MAUD MARY, b. April 25, 1843, Buckingham Palace, London, England; d. December 14, 1878, Darmstadt, Germany.

5.   iv.   PRINCE ALFRED ERNEST ALBERT, b. August 06, 1844, Windsor Castle, Berkshire, England; d. July 30, 1900, Schloss Rosenau, Near Coburg.

6.   v.   PRINCESS HELENA AUGUSTA VICTORIA, b. May 25, 1846, Buckingham Palace, London, England; d. June 09, 1923, Schomberg House, Pall Mall, London, England.

   vi.   PRINCESS LOUISE CAROLINE ALBERTA, b. March 18, 1848, Buckingham Palace, London, England; d. December 03, 1939, Kensington Palace, London, England; m. DUKE OF ARGYLL JOHN CAMPBELL, March 21, 1871, St. George Chap., Windsor, England; b. 1845; d. 1915.

7. vii. PRINCE ARTHUR WILLIAM PATRICK, b. May 01, 1850, Bucking-ham Palace, London, England; d. January 16, 1942, Bagshot Park, Surrey.

8. viii. PRINCE LEOPOLD GEORGE DUNCAN, b. April 07, 1853, Buck-ingham Palace, London, England; d. March 28, 1884, Cannes.

9. ix. PRINCESS BEATRICE MARY VICTORIA, b. April 14, 1857, Buck-ingham Palace, London, England; d. October 26, 1944, Bantridge Park, Balcombe, Sussex, England.

Endnotes

1. Chadwick B. Martin, *Queen Victoria (Martin)*, (Harper, 1919), 338, "Queen Victoria, surrounded by family and dear friends, died January 22 at her beloved Osborne House."

2. E. F. Benson, *Queen Victoria*, (Reprinted 1992. Published by Marboro Books Corporation), 95, "She had decided that the wedding should not take place at Westminster Abbey, for that would be like another Coronation, but at the Chapel Royal, St. James's: the smaller size of the building also was convenient, for there would be little room for any of those detestable Tories."

3. Stanley Weintraub, *Uncrowned King: The Life of Prince Albert*, 13.

5. Patricia Anderson, *When Passion Reigned: Sex and the Victorians*, (Harper Collins, 1995), 193, "Albert died in 1861 after twenty-one years of marriage. Victoria remained in virtual seclusion for the next ten years; in the subsequent thirty years, until her own death in 1901, she never appeared in public without wearing mourning."

To create a Register Report, follow these steps:

1. Click the name of the individual for whom you want to create the report.

2. Click either the Genealogy Report button on the toolbar or from the View menu, select Genealogy Report.

3. Once the Report screen opens, from the Format menu, select Genealogy Report Format.

4. Click Register and then click OK.

5. If you want to change the report's options, you can do so via the Contents menu. (Click Options, and make the changes you want. For more information about the options available for the Register Report, see the section "Considering Your Options," later in this chapter.)

WEIGHING THE PROS AND CONS OF THE REGISTER REPORT

You have many factors to weigh when considering whether a report is suitable for your family history book project. In this section, you'll look at a few of the more outstanding pros and cons related to the Register report.

- **Pros.** The Register Report is one of the standard narrative-style reports used by dedicated genealogists, and thus is recognizable and easy to read. Its concise manner is highly suited to allow the inclusion of lots of information, notes, sources, and so on. The report is a familiar one to most genealogists.

- **Cons.** A major drawback (in some people's minds) is that individuals who did not have children are not included in the numbering system. Thus, the report may be confusing or difficult to understand by non-genealogists or those not interested in a detailed family history. A better choice in that situation would be a Standard Descendant Tree.

NGS Quarterly Report

The NGS Quarterly Report is, like the Register Report, a popular narrative report that displays information, basic facts, and biographical details about each individual in a descendant-ordered format. It differs from the Register Report in that the NGS Quarterly numbering system assigns numbers to individuals whose line did not continue. The numbering system has been used by the National Genealogy Society in its scholarly journal, *The NGS Quarterly*, since its publication in 1912. Following is an example of how the NGS Quarterly Report looks when printed.

❦ NOTE ❦ *The NGS Quarterly report is as popular and widely used as the Register report, so your decision of which of the two descendant-ordered reports to use is one of personal preference. I prefer the NGS Quarterly report only because those individuals whose lines did not continue are given a number.*

Descendants of Victoria Hanover

Generation No. 1

1. Queen of England Victoria Hanover[7] (Edward Augustus[6] Hanover, George III[5], Frederick Louis[4], George II[3], George I[2], Ernest Augustus of Brunswick[1]) was born May 24, 1819 in Kensington Palace, London, England[1], and died January 22, 1901 in Osborne House, Isle of Wight, England[1]. She married **Prince Consort Albert Augustus Charles** February 10, 1840 in Chapel Royal, St. James Palace, England[2], son of Ernest and Louise. He was born August 26, 1819 in Schloss Rosenau, Near Coburg, Germany[3], and died December 14, 1861 in Windsor Castle, Berkshire, England[5].

Children of Victoria and Albert Charles are:

+ 2 i.   Princess Royal Victoria Adelaide Mary[8], born November 21, 1840 in Buckingham Palace, London, England; died August 05, 1901 in Friedrichshof, Near, Kronberg, Taunus.

+ 3 ii. King of England Edward VII Wettin, born November 09, 1841 in Buckingham Palace, London, England; died May 06, 1910 in Buckingham Palace, London, England.

+ 4 iii. Princess Alice Maud Mary, born April 25, 1843 in Buckingham Palace, London, England; died December 14, 1878 in Darmstadt, Germany.

+ 5 iv. Prince Alfred Ernest Albert, born August 06, 1844 in Windsor Castle, Berkshire, England; died July 30, 1900 in Schloss Rosenau, Near Coburg.

+ 6 v. Princess Helena Augusta Victoria, born May 25, 1846 in Buckingham Palace, London, England; died June 09, 1923 in Schomberg House, Pall Mall, London, England.

   7 vi. Princess Louise Caroline Alberta, born March 18, 1848 in Buckingham Palace, London, England; died December 03, 1939 in Kensington Palace, London, England. She married Duke of Argyll John Campbell March 21, 1871 in St. George Chap., Windsor, England; born 1845; died 1915.

+ 8 vii. Prince Arthur William Patrick, born May 01, 1850 in Buckingham Palace, London, England; died January 16, 1942 in Bagshot Park, Surrey.

+ 9 viii. Prince Leopold George Duncan, born April 07, 1853 in Buckingham Palace, London, England; died March 28, 1884 in Cannes.

+ 10 ix. Princess Beatrice Mary Victoria, born April 14, 1857 in Buckingham Palace, London, England; died October 26, 1944 in Bantridge Park, Balcombe, Sussex, England.

Endnotes

1. Chadwick B. Martin, *Queen Victoria (Martin)*, (Harper, 1919), 338, "Queen Victoria, surrounded by family and dear friends, died January 22 at her beloved Osborne House."

2. E. F. Benson, *Queen Victoria*, (Reprinted 1992. Published by Marboro Books Corporation), 95, "She had decided that the wedding should not take place at Westminster Abbey, for that would be like another Coronation, but at the Chapel Royal, St. James's: the smaller size of the building also was convenient, for there would be little room for any of those detestable Tories."

3. Stanley Weintraub, *Uncrowned King: The Life of Prince Albert*, 13.

5. Patricia Anderson, *When Passion Reigned: Sex and the Victorians*, (Harper Collins, 1995), 193, "Albert died in 1861 after twenty-one years of marriage. Victoria remained in virtual seclusion for the next ten years; in the subsequent thirty years, until her own death in 1901, she never appeared in public without wearing mourning."

If you compare the preceding example to the Register Report shown earlier in this chapter, you'll notice that instead of capitalizing names, the NGS Quarterly Report formats the names in bold. Also note the plus (+) signs next to individuals whose lines continued.

Follow these steps, to create an NGS Quarterly Report:

1. Click the name of the individual for whom you want to create the report.

2. Click either the Genealogy Report button on the toolbar or from the View menu, select Genealogy Report.

3. Once the Report screen opens, from the Format menu, select Genealogy Report Format.

4. Click NGS Quarterly and then click OK.

5. If you want to change the report's options, you can do so via the Contents menu. (Click Options and make the changes you want. For more information about the options available for the NGS Quarterly Report, see the section titled "Considering Your Options," later in this chapter.)

WEIGHING THE PROS AND CONS OF THE NGS QUARTERLY REPORT

By now, you have probably gotten the idea that I've stressed for the last few chapters—not every tree or report is suited for every project. For that reason, you'll want to evaluate the narrative reports to see which type will work best with your project. The following is a brief list of pros and cons for the NGS Quarterly Report:

- **Pros.** One of the most popular narrative-style reports used by dedicated genealogists. Easy to read and understand. The format of the report allows you to display a good deal of information without cluttering up the report.

⚡ **Cons.** Non-genealogists might have difficulty understanding the report. Generational numbers might confuse readers not familiar with this style of report.

Ahnentafel Report

The Ahnentafel Report is, unlike the Register and NGS Quarterly Reports, a narrative report that displays information in an ancestor-ordered format; that is, it shows the information about a target individual's ancestors, rather than their descendants. Although Ahnentafels are a familiar sight to many genealogists, they are not often found in family history books (they can, however, provide a nice, easily read list of an individual's ancestors by generation). The following is an example of an Ahnentafel Report (note that the information in the report has been abbreviated for inclusion).

> ⚜ **NOTE** ⚜ *Family Tree Maker's Ahnentafel Report differs from the standard Ahnentafel. In a traditional Ahnentafel, no information about a couple's children is included, as it is in the Family Tree Maker version shown here:*

Ancestors of Victoria Hanover

Generation No. 1

    1. Queen of England Victoria Hanover, born May 24, 1819 in Kensington Palace, London, England; died January 22, 1901 in Osborne House, Isle of Wight, England. She was the daughter of **2. Duke of Kent Edward Augustus Hanover** and **3. Victoria Mary Louisa**. She married **(1) Prince Consort Albert Augustus Charles** February 10, 1840 in Chapel Royal, St. James Palace, England. He was born August 26, 1819 in Schloss Rosenau, Near Coburg, Germany, and died December 14, 1861 in Windsor Castle, Berkshire, England. He was the son of Duke Ernest I of Saxe-Coburg- Saalfeld and Louise of Saxe-Coburg-Altenburg.

Generation No. 2

2. Duke of Kent Edward Augustus Hanover, born November 02, 1767 in Buckingham House, London, England; died January 23, 1820 in Sidmouth, Devon, England. He was the son of **5. King of England George III Hanover** and **5. (Sophia) Charlotte**. He married **3. Victoria Mary Louisa** July 11, 1818 in Kew Palace.

3. Victoria Mary Louisa, born August 17, 1786 in Coburg; died March 16, 1861 in Frogmore House, Windsor, England. She was the daughter of **6. Duke Francis Frederick of Saxe-Coburg** and **7. Countess Augusta Reuss-Ebersdorf**.

Child of Edward Hanover and Victoria is:

  1   i.   Queen of England Victoria Hanover, born May 24, 1819 in Kensington Palace, London, England; died January 22, 1901 in Osborne House, Isle of Wight, England; married Prince Consort Albert Augustus Charles February 10, 1840 in Chapel Royal, St. James Palace, England.

Generation No. 3

5. King of England George III Hanover, born June 04, 1738 in Norfolk-House, St. James Square, London, England; died January 29, 1820 in Windsor Castle, Windsor, Berkshire, England. He was the son of **8. Prince of Wales Frederick Louis Hanover** and **9. Augusta of Saxe-Gotha**. He married **5. (Sophia) Charlotte**.

5. (Sophia) Charlotte, born May 19, 1744 in Mirow; died November 17, 1818 in Kew Palace. She was the daughter of **10. Duke Charles Louis Frederick** and **11. Elizabeth of Saxe- Hildburghausen Albertin**.

Children of George Hanover and (Sophia) are:

       i.   King of England George IV Hanover, born August 12, 1762 in, London, England; died June 26, 1830 in Windsor Castle, Berkshire, England; married (1) Maria Anne Fitzherbert 1785; born 1756; died 1837; married (2) Caroline Amelia of Brunswick April 08, 1795 in Chapel Royal, St James Palace, England; born 1768; died 1821.

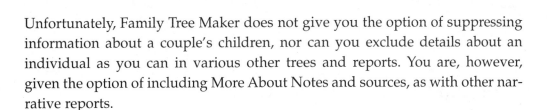

Unfortunately, Family Tree Maker does not give you the option of suppressing information about a couple's children, nor can you exclude details about an individual as you can in various other trees and reports. You are, however, given the option of including More About Notes and sources, as with other narrative reports.

To create an Ahnentafel Report, follow these steps:

1. Click the name of the individual for whom you want to create the report.

2. Click either the Genealogy Report button on the toolbar or from the View menu, select Genealogy Report.

3. Once the Report screen opens, from the Format menu, select Genealogy Report Format.

4. Click Ahnentafel and then click OK.

5. If you want to change the report's options, you can do so via the Contents menu. (Click Options and make the changes you want. For more information about the options available for the Ahnentafel Report, see the section titled "Considering Your Options," later in this chapter.)

WEIGHING THE PROS AND CONS OF THE AHNENTAFEL REPORT

Is an Ahnentafel Report right for your project? Before making a final decision, you'll want to consider the pros and cons:

 ☀ **Pros.** A popular report style that is familiar and understood by genealogists. This report provides an excellent way to detail an individual's ancestors. Because it is a narrative report, a good deal of information can be included in it without confusing the reader.

 ☀ **Cons.** This report might not be easily understood by individuals unfamiliar with an ancestor-oriented narrative report or by non-genealogists. Generational numbers may confuse readers not familiar with this style of report. Family Tree Maker's forced inclusion of children in the report may bother some purists.

Exploring Report Suitability, Options, Format, and Content

You have a number of choices to make regarding the options, format, and contents of the narrative reports in Family Tree Maker. You must choose what to include in your reports—not an easy task when there is so much information that you can include!

Testing the Report for Suitability

This section examines the suitability of each of the reports mentioned in this chapter with regard to use in three different types of family history book projects. Suitability of a report is an important factor for you to consider when you are planning your book. If you want to publish a book for your family's enjoyment, you will probably want to use different reports than you would if you were publishing a book for the use of family historians everywhere.

For the purposes of example, consider these three levels of family history book projects (for more examples of projects, be sure to read Chapter Eleven, "Family History Book Projects," which shows several different types of family history book projects):

- An informal book intended to please immediate family members who are not genealogists

- An intermediate-level book that is thorough but not complete and intended for an audience of genealogists

- An advanced formal family history book that is complete, or near complete, with the highest standards of documentation and analysis, intended for serious genealogists

Keeping in mind that no hard-and-fast rule determines what you can and cannot include in your family history book, the suitability of the Register Report, the NGS Quarterly Report, and the Ahnentafel Report for the three projects might be summarized as follows:

 Register Report

- **Informal family history book.** This report's numbering system might not be understood by non-genealogists, although the report does present biographical information in a readable format.

- **Intermediate family history book.** A useful addition and suitable for this level project.

- **Formal family history book.** A useful report when sources and notes are included and one common to formal genealogies. This numbering system is accepted by *The New England Historical and Genealogical Register.*

 NGS Quarterly Report

- **Informal family history book.** This report's numbering system might not be understood by non-genealogists, although the report does present biographical information in a readable format.

- **Intermediate family history book.** A useful addition and suitable for this level project.

- **Formal family history book.** A useful report when sources and notes are included and one common to formal genealogies. This numbering system is accepted by *The NGS Quarterly.*

 Ahnentafel Report

- **Informal family history book.** This report's numbering system might not be understood by non-genealogists, although the report does present biographical information in a readable format.

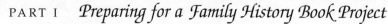
- **Intermediate family history book.** A useful addition and suitable for this level project.

- **Formal family history book.** A useful report when sources and notes are included and one common to formal genealogies. This numbering system is accepted by *The NGS Quarterly*.

Considering Your Options

When you create a narrative report, several options are available that will enable you to customize how the report is created. These options can be found in the Contents menu, and consist of the following:

⚹ **Include Individual Notes.** One way to give your reader details about an individual is to include within the narrative report notes that you have entered for that person. Notes can be anything you want to record—personal information, comments regarding conflicting evidence, information found in other sources, extracts of information from official records, abstracts from official records, and so on. Unless you have a good reason for keeping your narrative report abbreviated, you should always include your notes when you create a report.

⚹ **Include More About Facts.** This option allows you to include all the information you have recorded in the More About section of Family Tree Maker. Like notes, the More About Facts serve to round out the picture of the individual you are detailing and should be included unless you have a good reason not to. Without such additional information, your family history book will be nothing more than a collection of names, dates, and locations. Don't be afraid to put some flesh on your ancestral skeletons! You also have the option of displaying only those facts that you designate as preferred dates and locations—that is, those dates and locations that you know without a doubt to be valid and correct.

Following is an example of how More About Facts can enhance a report. The example is from the endnote sources for a Register Report and includes individual More About Notes for both Queen Victoria and Prince Albert, and a More About Fact for their marriage. (See the two upcoming sections "Including Source Information as Endnotes" and "Including Source Information as Inline Notes" for a discussion of how to include sources in your narrative report.)

More About QUEEN OF ENGLAND VICTORIA HANOVER:

Burial: Royal Mausoleum, Frogmore, Berkshire, England[5].

More About PRINCE CONSORT ALBERT AUGUSTUS CHARLES:

Burial: Royal Mausoleum, Frogmore, Windsor, England[6].

More About ALBERT CHARLES and VICTORIA:

Marriage: February 10, 1840, Chapel Royal, St. James Palace, England[7].

* **Include Marriage Notes.** This option allows you to include the notes you enter about a couple's marriage. As with individual notes, it is recommended that you include these because they help provide the reader with more information about a family.

* **Include More About Marriage Facts.** In addition to marriage notes, you can include those facts you entered for a couple under the More About section. Like the individual More About Facts, you can also choose to include only those dates and locations you specify as being preferred.

🏃 **Include Titles.** If you have entered titles in your database (Dr., Rev., Col., and so on), you can use this option to have them included in the narrative report. This is not a vital bit of information to be included, but it is a courtesy to include someone's title when possible. Unless the title is honorary or was not used by the individual, it is recommended that you include it when possible.

🏃 **Automatically Find the Oldest Ancestor.** When you create a Register Report or an NGS Quarterly Report, you can tell Family Tree Maker to automatically look through the ancestors for the primary individual and find the oldest ancestor. Family Tree Maker will then designate that person as being the first generation and will number the direct-line descent to the primary individual. An example of this can be seen in the excerpt from an NGS Quarterly Report directly following this bullet. In that sample, the superscript numbers following Queen Victoria's name (and her male ancestors immediately following her) indicate the generation number of each individual with regards to the oldest ancestor, Ernest Augustus of Brunswick.

Descendants of Victoria Hanover

Generation No. 1

1. Queen of England Victoria Hanover[7] (Edward Augustus[6] Hanover, George III[5], Frederick Louis[4], George II[3], George I[2], Ernest Augustus of Brunswick[1]) was born May 24, 1819 in Kensington Palace, London, England[1], and died January 22, 1901 in Osborne House, Isle of Wight, England[1].

✻ **Assume the Primary Individual Is the Immigrant Ancestor.** If you want to assign the superscript 1 to the primary individual (indicating that he or she is the oldest ancestor, or immigrant ancestor), this option allows you to do so.

The last three options available for the narrative reports are important ones, and because they can confuse people, I explore them in more detail here. These options all deal with how sources are presented within the narrative reports:

✻ Include Source Information as Endnotes

✻ Include Source Information as Inline Notes

✻ Do Not Include Source Information

Because sources and notes are very important to any family history book, you should weigh carefully how you want your sources and notes presented. Family Tree Maker enables you to include notes and sources within the body of the report (inline), at the end of the report (endnotes), or not at all (this last option is not recommended unless you have a particular reason for not documenting your information).

To access any of the options mentioned in this section, follow these steps:

1. Open the report you want to work with.

2. From the Contents menu, select Options.

3. In the Options for Genealogy Report dialog box, make your choices.

4. When you are satisfied with the changes, click OK to return to the report screen.

INCLUDING SOURCE INFORMATION AS ENDNOTES

In the following example, source information is included as *endnotes* for a Register Report:

Descendants of Victoria Hanover

Generation No. 1

1. QUEEN OF ENGLAND VICTORIA HANOVER[7] *(EDWARD AUGUSTUS[6] HANOVER, GEORGE III[5], FREDERICK LOUIS[4], GEORGE II[3], GEORGE I[2], ERNEST AUGUSTUS OF BRUNSWICK[1])* was born May 24, 1819 in Kensington Palace, London, England[1], and died January 22, 1901 in Osborne House, Isle of Wight, England[1]. She married PRINCE CONSORT ALBERT AUGUSTUS CHARLES February 10, 1840 in Chapel Royal, St. James Palace, England[2], son of ERNEST and LOUISE. He was born August 26, 1819 in Schloss Rosenau, Near Coburg, Germany[3], and died December 14, 1861 in Windsor Castle, Berkshire, England[5].

Endnotes

1. Chadwick B. Martin, *Queen Victoria (Martin)*, (Harper, 1919), 338, "Queen Victoria, surrounded by family and dear friends, died January 22 at her beloved Osborne House."

2. E. F. Benson, *Queen Victoria*, (Reprinted 1992. Published by Marboro Books Corporation), 95, "She had decided that the wedding should not take place at Westminster Abbey, for that would be like another Coronation, but at the Chapel Royal, St. James's: the smaller size of the building also was convenient, for there would be little room for any of those detestable Tories."

3. Stanley Weintraub, *Uncrowned King: The Life of Prince Albert*, 13.

4. Patricia Anderson, *When Passion Reigned: Sex and the Victorians*, (Harper Collins, 1995), 193, "Albert died in 1861 after twenty-one years of marriage. Victoria remained in virtual seclusion for the next ten years; in the subsequent thirty years, until her own death in 1901, she never appeared in public without wearing mourning."

As you can see in the preceding example, information that is sourced, such as that about Victoria and Albert's marriage, is noted in the sources found in the endnotes. The endnotes appear at the very end of the report, not after a section detailing information about a certain individual. Moving the source citations to the end allows the reader to focus on the information presented. Italicized superscript numbers tell the readers which facts have been sourced so that they can turn to the endnotes and consult the citations as desired. When sources' citations are placed in the endnotes, no source information appears in the body of the report.

Follow these steps to include your source information as endnotes:

1. Open the report you want to work with.

2. From the Contents menu, select Options.

3. In the Options for Genealogy Report dialog box, select Include Source Information as Endnotes.

4. Click OK to return to the report screen.

INCLUDING SOURCE INFORMATION AS INLINE NOTES

Source information can also be presented *inline*—that is, within the body of the report, directly following the basic facts for the individual(s) being discussed. The following is an example of inline source citations for an NGS Quarterly Report.

Descendants of Victoria Hanover

Generation No. 1

1. Queen of England Victoria Hanover[7] (Edward Augustus[6] Hanover, George III[5], Frederick Louis[4], George II[3], George I[2], Ernest Augustus of Brunswick[1]) was born May 24, 1819 in Kensington Palace, London, England (Source: Chadwick B. Martin, *Queen Victoria (Martin)*, (Harper, 1919), 338, "Queen Victoria, surrounded by family and dear friends, died January 22 at her beloved Osborne House."), and died January 22, 1901 in Osborne House, Isle of Wight, England (Source: Chadwick B. Martin, *Queen Victoria (Martin)*, (Harper, 1919), 338, "Queen Victoria, surrounded by family and dear friends, died January 22 at her beloved Osborne House."). She married **Prince Consort Albert Augustus Charles** February 10, 1840 in Chapel Royal, St. James Palace, England (Source: E. F. Benson, *Queen Victoria*, (Reprinted 1992. Published by Marboro Books Corporation), 95, "She had decided that the wedding should not take place at Westminster Abbey, for that would be like another Coronation, but at the Chapel Royal, St. James's: the smaller size of the building also was convenient, for there would be little room for any of those detestable Tories."), son of Ernest and Louise. He was born August 26, 1819 in Schloss Rosenau, Near Coburg, Germany (Source: Stanley Weintraub, *Uncrowned King: The Life of Prince Albert*, 13.), and died December 14, 1861 in Windsor Castle, Berkshire, England (Source: Patricia Anderson, *When Passion Reigned: Sex and the Victorians*, (Harper Collins, 1995), 193, "Albert died in 1861 after twenty-one years of marriage. Victoria remained in virtual seclusion for the next ten years; in the subsequent thirty years, until her own death in 1901, she never appeared in public without wearing mourning.").

In the preceding text, notice that there are no superscripts other than the generational numbers for each individual; instead, the source citations directly follow each sourced fact.

> ❧ **NOTE** ❧ *Where you want to place your source information is strictly a matter of personal preference. Some people feel that the inline sourcing of information is not preferred for family histories because it makes for a distracting read. Others find it handy to have the source information presented immediately after the facts, saving them the trouble of turning to the end of the report to hunt down source citations. My personal preference is to use sources in endnotes, but you may prefer otherwise. If you are unsure which source placement is the best, consider asking a couple of friends to view the report and offer their opinions about which makes for the easiest read.*

To include your source information as inline notes, follow these steps:

1. Open the report you want to work with.

2. From the Contents menu, select Options.

3. In the Options for Genealogy Report dialog box, select Include Source Information as Inline Notes.

4. Click OK to return to the report screen.

OPTING NOT TO INCLUDE SOURCE INFORMATION

The third option you have for including source information in narrative reports is to *not* include it at all. The following is an example of the preceding information, but with no source citations whatsoever.

Descendants of Victoria Hanover

Generation No. 1

1. QUEEN OF ENGLAND VICTORIA HANOVER[7] (EDWARD AUGUSTUS[6] HANOVER, GEORGE III[5], FREDERICK LOUIS[4], GEORGE II[3], GEORGE I[2], ERNEST AUGUSTUS OF BRUNSWICK[1]) was born May 24, 1819 in Kensington Palace, London, England, and died January 22, 1901 in Osborne House, Isle of Wight, England. She married PRINCE CONSORT ALBERT AUGUSTUS CHARLES February 10, 1840 in Chapel Royal, St. James Palace, England, son of ERNEST and LOUISE. He was born August 26, 1819 in Schloss Rosenau, Near Coburg, Germany, and died December 14, 1861 in Windsor Castle, Berkshire, England.

This is a bare-bones sort of family history, and it is not recommended for family history books that will be consulted by other interested researchers. Sources are vital to any genealogy, and excluding them lessens the validity of your research and analysis. If you choose not to include any sources whatsoever in your reports, be sure that you have a valid reason to do so. Readers are going to want to be sure you have verified your information, and source citations provide them with proof that you've done your work.

Follow these steps when you don't want to include source information in the report:

1. Open the report you want to work with.

2. From the Contents menu, select Options.

3. In the Options for Genealogy Report dialog box, select Do Not Include Source Information.

4. Click OK to return to the report screen.

Deciding on Content

Due to the nature of narrative reports, you are not allowed to select which items you want to include in the report as you can with trees and charts. For example, you cannot specify if you want to have birth, marriage, or death information included—Family Tree Maker automatically takes all the information you enter and includes it in the report. As mentioned previously, you can specify whether you want individual and marriage notes and More About Facts included, as well as source information, but all other information will automatically be placed within the report.

The two content choices available to you, however, are to specify the title and footnote and to decide how many generations will be included on the report. It should be noted that the footnote choices for the narrative report are not the same as the footnote choices for trees—that is, you are not given the opportunity to create your own footnote. Instead, footnotes for narrative reports consist of page numbers, date, and time of printing. You can also designate the report's starting page number. This can be useful if you are manually inserting a copy of the report into another book.

To access the contents choices for the reports described in this chapter, follow these steps:

1. Open the report you want to work with.

2. From the Contents menu, select either Title & Footnote, or Number of Generations to Show.

3. Make your choices for the selected option (for more information about both Title & Footnote and Number of Generations to Show, refer to Chapter Three).

4. When you are satisfied with your choices, click OK to return to the report.

Selecting Your Format

The Format menu is where you tell Family Tree Maker what type of narrative report you want—Register Report, NGS Quarterly Report, or Ahnentafel

Report. The only other format options you have for narrative reports are selecting text font, style, and size, and whether you want the on-screen version of the reports to show page lines.

To access the text font, style, and size format choices for the reports described in this chapter, follow these steps:

1. Open the report you want to work with.

2. From the Format menu, select Text Font, Style, and Size.

3. Make your text choices.

4. When you are satisfied with your choices, click OK to return to the report.

PART II

Understanding Book Elements

CHAPTER SIX

Exploring Custom and Miscellaneous Reports

The life of every man is a diary in which
he means to write one story, and writes another.

—Sir James Matthew Barrie

n addition to the standard narrative reports, Family Tree Maker has two other types of reports that have the potential to be incredibly useful in a book. The first is called a *Custom Report*. Unlike a narrative report, a Custom Report is designed and created solely by you—*you* pick the fields the Custom Report will include, *you* select the individuals who will be in the report, and *you* tell the report how it will be formatted. The second type is filed by Family Tree Maker under the generic term *reports* (which, incidentally, includes the Custom Report). Although these reports are not created solely for use in a family history book, you might find that they will suit your project.

A third type of report—the *Kinship Report*—is considered by Family Tree Maker to be a narrative report because of its numbering system, but I consider it more a member of the generic report family and for practical purposes discuss it here.

You will notice one major difference between the reports presented in this chapter (with the exception of the Kinship Report) and the reports, trees, and charts in other chapters: The reports discussed here are not generated around a primary individual. Instead, they present information about the entire database or selected individuals, without reference to any one individual.

To create a Custom Report, follow these steps:

1. Open a Family File.

2. Click the Report button. The Report screen opens, allowing you to make format and option choices.

3. From the Format menu, select Report Format.

4. In the Report Format dialog box, select Custom Report and click OK.

By the time you finish this chapter, you should have a good idea about what makes up a Custom Report and the other miscellaneous reports that are available for use in your family history book. As in the previous three chapters, I will describe the items in this chapter in detail and provide information about the format and content options for each.

Using Custom Reports

A Custom Report is a report that you set up by selecting the fields to be included, the individuals to be featured, and the information to be presented. Figure 6.1 shows a Custom Report with five fields: Name, Birth Date, Marriage Date, Death Date, and Spouse.

The usefulness of a Custom Report lies in its capability to display only the information you want displayed; unlike other trees and reports, which might have information included that you do not desire or need, a Custom Report is made up solely of those fields you choose.

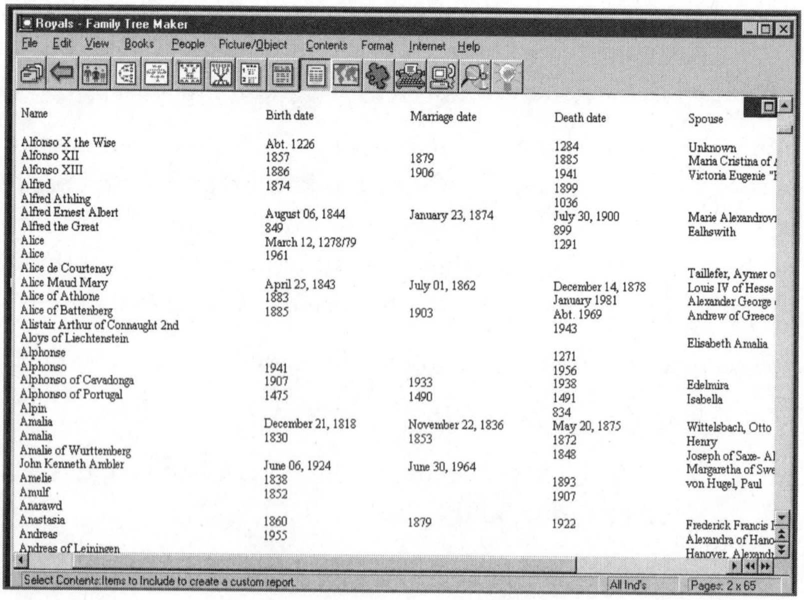

Figure 6.1

A Custom Report can feature as many or as few fields as you find useful.

Weighing the Pros and Cons of Custom Reports

Because you determine exactly how the Custom Report will appear, the report has few strikes against it. Nevertheless, you should consider the advantages and disadvantages before making a final decision on the contents and format of the Custom Report.

- **Pros.** Custom Reports provide you with a means to create a report that displays only the information you want. Because it is a text item, the report is easily followed by non-genealogists and allows you a useful way to present details and information. The capability to sort the report by any field makes it a particularly good way to present information in a meaningful manner.

- **Cons.** Be careful of providing too much information in the report—doing so makes the report less efficient in dissembling information. Non-genealogists might not easily understand detailed reports (reports that contain many fields of information).

Using Generic Reports

Family Tree Maker groups 11 miscellaneous reports under the title *reports*. These reports present specialized data, and although they are not standard items presented in a family history book, you might find them helpful. The reports are as follows:

- Alternate Facts
- Address
- Medical Information
- Birthdays of Living Individuals
- Marriage
- Parentage
- Bibliography
- Data Errors
- Documented Events

Although not all reports are useful for every project, you should take the time to familiarize yourself with each to determine whether the report suits your family history book project.

Using Alternate Facts Reports

As you've researched your family, you've probably come across one event or fact about an individual for which you have contradictory information—for example, two birth dates. If you are unsure which date is correct or have not established the validity of one fact over another, you will want to make use of Family Tree Maker's Alternate Facts function. Using the More About screen, you can enter information for a number of events and facts, including name, birth, death, and marriage information.

To create an Alternate Facts Report, with the Report screen open, follow these steps:

1. Choose Format, Report Format.

2. Select Alternate Facts Report and click OK.

The Alternate Facts Report searches the database and creates a report that displays all the alternate facts for each individual, as shown in Figure 6.2. Note that in the figure, two facts are displayed—the first is the preferred fact; the second is the alternate fact.

> ❋ **TIP** ❋ *In some of the figures, you might have noticed an instance where an individual's name is followed by two backslashes, such as Victoria Hanover\\. Family Tree Maker uses backslashes to indicate unusual or missing last names. For example, because of the tradition inherent with British nobility, Queen Victoria does not have a surname; instead, the name of her family's house (that is, the name given to the dynasty from which she is descended) is used, followed by two backslash characters to let Family Tree Maker know she is missing a last name. If I had not used the two backslashes, Family Tree Maker would have assumed that Queen Victoria's surname was Hanover.*
>
> *You can also place an unusual last name between backslashes to alert Family Tree Maker to the situation—thus, John \Golden Deer\ indicates a person whose last name is Golden Deer. If you had not included the two names within the backslashes, Family Tree Maker would have used Deer as the last name.*

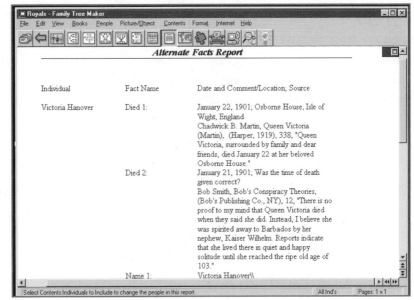

Figure 6.2

You can present details about conflicting information using the Alternate Facts Report.

WEIGHING THE PROS AND CONS OF THE ALTERNATE FACTS REPORT

As with other items in this chapter, this report is not a standard one included in traditional family histories. It's up to you to decide whether this report will enhance your book, though you might want to use it if you have many alternate facts recorded for individuals or marriages.

- **Pros.** This easy-to-read report displays the alternate information you entered for important events and facts. Experienced genealogists appreciate seeing all the information and evidence available because it allows them to determine the validity of the research.

- **Cons.** The idea of conflicting information and alternate facts might be beyond the scope of non-genealogists and therefore not important in their view. They might find the report confusing, because they will not know which fact is preferred.

Using Address Reports

The Address Report includes the addresses you entered for each individual. This report is not one I suggest using in a family history book; however, you might want to utilize the report to create mailing labels of interested persons or to create a list of addresses of family members for a family reunion.

> ❀ **NOTE** ❀ *Don't include this report in a book unless you first obtain permission from all the individuals in the report to print their addresses.*

To create an Address Report, with the Report screen open, follow these steps:

1. Choose Format, Report Format.

2. Select Address Report and click OK.

Using Medical Information Reports

The medical details you enter for an individual in the More About Facts section (height, weight, cause of death, and medical conditions) can be printed on a report. As with the Address Report, this is not a report that I recommend including in a family history book. If you have medical information you want included, it's better to place it in a note or custom text object instead.

If you do include this report, be aware of privacy issues and ask permission of living individuals involved (including individuals for whom information about a parent's hereditary medical condition could have meaning for living descendants).

To create a Medical Information Report, with the Report screen open, follow these steps:

1. Choose Format, Report Format.

2. Select Medical Information Report and click OK.

Using Birthdays of Living Individuals Reports

This report takes information from the database about those individuals who do not have a death date listed (thus, are presumed still alive) and creates a report with each individual's name, birthday, and age at next birthday. It should be noted that the report might not be valid if you have not entered a death date (or estimate of death date) for individuals.

To create a Birthdays of Living Individuals Report, with the Report screen open, follow these steps:

1. Choose Format, Report Format.

2. Select Birthdays of Living Individuals Report and click OK.

As you can see in Figure 6.3, this example report contains a few individuals who seem to have lived quite a long time—because those individuals do not have death dates entered, Family Tree Maker treats them as living.

WEIGHING THE PROS AND CONS OF THE BIRTHDAYS OF THE LIVING INDIVIDUALS REPORT

This report is not a standard one included in traditional family histories, so you need to decide whether it will enhance your book; however, I recommend using it if you are writing a family history book that is intended for an audience of

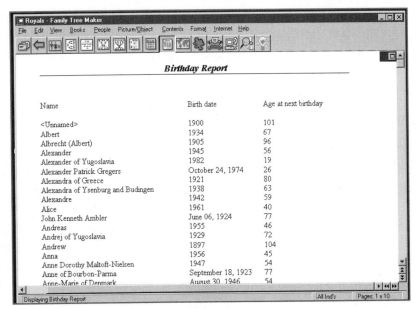

Figure 6.3

It is important to enter death dates or estimates of death dates whenever possible; reports such as this one use those dates to determine whether an individual is living or deceased.

immediate family members. This report isn't well suited to formalized family history books because it presents information that might infringe on privacy laws for living individuals.

> ✻ **Pros.** An easy-to-read report that displays the birth dates of all the individuals in your database who are presumed still living; information included can give readers an idea of individuals' birthdays and how old they were at their last birthday.

> ✻ **Cons.** Because of privacy issues, this report is not well suited to anything but publication for an immediate family, and this report is not one found in traditional family histories.

Using Marriage Reports

The Marriage Report enables you to create a document that shows information for each marriage in your database. Unlike other reports, you cannot specify which individuals or information to include; instead, Family Tree Maker automatically generates a report with the husband's name, wife's name, marriage date, and marriage ending status (if any). Figure 6.4 shows an example of a typical Marriage Report.

To create a Marriage Report, with the Report screen open, follow these steps:

1. Choose Format, Report Format.

2. Select Marriage Report and click OK.

WEIGHING THE PROS AND CONS OF THE MARRIAGE REPORT

Although this report is not traditionally used in family history books, you might want to include it as a concise overview of the marriages in your database.

> ✻ **Pros.** This informative report displays all individuals in your database who have been noted as married. The report is easily read and understood by experienced and novice audiences.

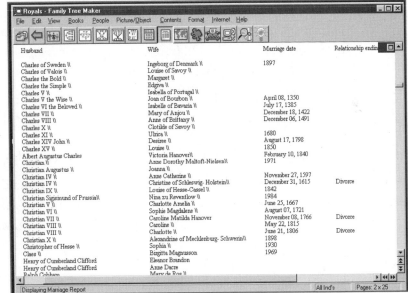

Figure 6.4

Marriage Reports offer a quick, useful way to see who married whom.

🦋 **Cons.** This is not a standard report found in family histories. The information presented in this report can be found in narrative reports, and it might be considered extraneous if you include one of these reports in your book.

Using Parentage Reports

The Parentage Report offers you a quick way to establish the identity of each individual's parents and the individual's relationship with his or her parents (natural, step, adopted, and so on). Unlike the Marriage Report listed previously, you can specify the individuals you want included in this report, giving it more versatility.

As with the other reports in this chapter, the Parentage Report is not a standard report and will not be found in traditional family histories, although this fact should not keep you from including it if you feel the report offers your readers a valuable way to view information.

❋ NOTE ❋ *Be aware that the Parentage Report will mention those individuals who are adopted into a family. If you want to include the report in a book, you should be sensitive to privacy issues and not include the report if it will infringe on an adopted person's privacy. Seek permission to publish the information from the person's parents (if the adopted person is a child) or from the adopted person if he or she is an adult.*

WEIGHING THE PROS AND CONS OF THE PARENTAGE REPORT

Whether you want to include this report in your book depends on how you want to present your information. Who an individual's parents are can be found on most of the reports, trees, and charts found in Family Tree Maker, but none of them present the information in as concise, uncluttered a manner as the Parentage Report does.

- ❋ **Pros.** This informative report displays information about individuals (all or selected) and their parents. The report is easily read and understood by experienced and inexperienced audiences.

- ❋ **Cons.** This is not a standard report in family histories. Because the basic information presented in this report can be found in other reports and trees (but not in this manner), the report might be considered extraneous.

Using Bibliography Reports

I admit freely to being a bibliophile. One of the first things I turn to in any non-fiction book is the *bibliography*—the list of print resources used by the author in the creation of the book. Including a Bibliography Report (the word *report* is redundant—I'll just refer to it as a bibliography) in your family history book is a very good idea, and one I strongly recommend.

To create a bibliography, with the Report screen open, follow these steps:

1. Choose Format, Report Format.

2. Select Bibliography and click OK.

By including a bibliography, you give your readers an exact list of the print resources you used, allowing them to locate and read those resources if they are interested. Family Tree Maker creates a bibliography for you automatically by taking all the books and other items found in your master source database and displaying them in a meaningful manner (see Figure 6.5 for an example of a bibliography).

Unless you have a specific reason for not sharing the list of your research resources with your readers (for example, if you are creating an informal family history book for which you did not consult printed resources), you should include a bibliography in your book.

Using Data Errors Reports

This is a report that should never find its way into a family history book—you only use it to note problems with your database so that you can fix the problems before you print your trees, reports, and charts.

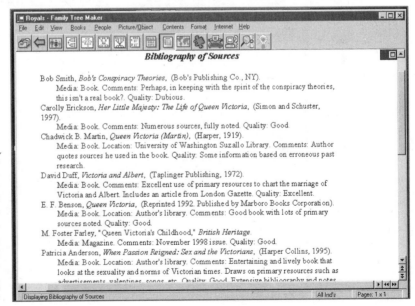

Figure 6.5

A bibliography adds a note of credibility to your family history book by giving readers a detailed list of your research resources.

To create a Data Errors Report, with the Report screen open, follow these steps:

1. Choose Format, Report Format.

2. Select Data Errors Report and click OK.

The Data Errors report will search your database and create a list of all problems it discovers (see Chapter Two, "Organizing Your Family History Book," for more on searching your database for errors and for an example of the kinds of errors the report might find). Although you can specify which individuals to include in the report, you have no influence over the report's output.

Using Documented Events Reports

This is another report that gives your reader insight into your research by displaying all the events for which you entered sources and notes. Although you will not normally find it in family history books, you could include it as an appendix or just print a copy for your own reference. Figure 6.6 shows an example of a Documented Events Report and the type of information found on it.

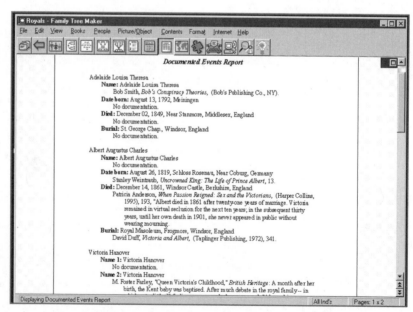

Figure 6.6

The Documented Events Report gives you an easy way to present all the events (or just events for specified individuals) that have source information entered.

To create a Documented Events Report, with the Report screen open, follow these steps:

1. Choose Format, Report Format.

2. Select Documented Events Report and click OK.

   ❧ **NOTE** ❧ *If you find that the information included in this report duplicates the source information found on other reports and charts, you might want to consider not using this report—more traditional family histories use source citations inline or as endnotes rather than in a separate report as just shown. For that reason, this report is best suited for use in a research reminder book (see Chapter Eleven, "Family History Book Projects," for an example of a portable research reminder book) or for an informal family history.*

WEIGHING THE PROS AND CONS OF THE DOCUMENTED EVENTS REPORT

Although this is not a traditional report included in most family history books, you might find that it offers a handy way to present sourced events.

❧ **Pros.** This informative report displays source information about events for individuals (all or selected). The report is easily read and understood by experienced and inexperienced audiences.

❧ **Cons.** This is not a standard report in family histories. If you include narrative reports with sources included (inline or endnotes), this information will be redundant.

Kinship Reports

You use a Kinship Report to show how one individual is related to others in the database. Family Tree Maker includes two styles of Kinship Reports: Canon & Civil and Relationship Only.

Using Canon & Civil Kinship Reports

Canon & Civil style Kinship reports show the degree of relationship between the primary individual's relatives (and their spouses). In genealogical terms, *degree of relationship* does not mean an exact relationship (for example, third cousin, twice removed), but the degree of distance between two individuals who are related by blood. (The *degree of distance* means the distance in the bloodline between the two individuals.)

To create a Canon & Civil Kinship Report, with the Report screen open, follow these steps:

1. Choose Format, Report Format.

2. Select Kinship—Canon & Civil Report and click OK.

The "Civil" part of the title refers to the degree of distance in the bloodline between the two individuals in steps. For example, if you wanted to calculate the degree of relationship in civil law between you and your cousin, count the steps between you and the common ancestor, in this case a grandparent, then count the steps between that grandparent and your cousin. Two steps up to your grandparent and two steps down to your cousin gives you a degree of four in civil law.

The "Canon" part refers to ecclesiastical laws, dating back to medieval times, that laid out rules as to who could marry whom, depending on how closely they were related by blood with regard to a common ancestor. For the preceding example, there are two steps up to your common ancestor, so your degree in Canon law is two.

In Figure 6.7, you can see that Aldophus Frederick V is Queen Victoria's first cousin, once removed (due to the inbreeding of European royalty, he is also related to her in numerous other ways, but you can ignore more distant relationships in this example). In Civil law, that would translate into there being five (indicated by the Roman numeral V) steps between the relationship of the two people; in Canon law, that translates into there being three (indicated by the Arabic numeral 3) degrees of descent from the two individuals' common ancestor.

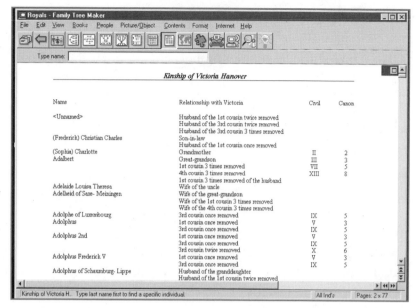

Figure 6.7

The Kinship Report: Civil & Canon version shows the legal degree of relationship.

✻ **TIP** ✻ *If you plan to include the Civil & Canon version of the Kinship Report in your family history book, consider also including a brief explanation of what the legal degree of relationship numbers mean. Readers unfamiliar with Civil & Canon law will appreciate your foresight!*

WEIGHING THE PROS AND CONS OF THE KINSHIP REPORT: CIVIL & CANON

Although this is not a traditional report included in most family history books, it would be an interesting addition and could be of much interest to your readers.

🦅 **Pros.** This informative report allows readers to view the legal degree of relationship between the primary individual and others in your database. Once the numbering system is explained, the report is easy to understand.

✤ **Cons.** This is not a standard report in family histories. Non-genealogists and those who do not have the advantage of an explanation of the numbering system might not understand the report easily.

Using Relationship Only Kinship Reports

If you want to include a Kinship Report, but don't want to overwhelm your readers with the somewhat intimidating Civil & Canon version, consider using the Relationship Only version. This report presents information about everyone in the database with respect to your primary individual. The relationship listed in the report is in standard format—that is, grandfather, second cousin first removed, and so on. Figure 6.8 shows an example of a Relationship Only Kinship Report. Notice that the report is not just limited to those individuals related by blood, but also includes spouses of relatives.

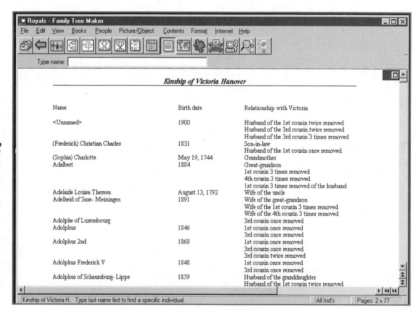

Figure 6.8

The Relationship Only version of the Kinship Report is a bit more reader-friendly for readers who are not savvy regarding Civil & Canon law.

To create a Relationship Only Kinship Report, with the Report screen open, follow these steps:

1. Choose Format, Report Format.

2. Select Relationship Only Kinship Report and click OK.

WEIGHING THE PROS AND CONS OF THE RELATIONSHIP ONLY KINSHIP REPORT

Although this is not a traditional report included in most family history books, it also might be an interesting addition for your readers, especially if they are not familiar with the legal degree of relationships.

- **Pros.** Genealogists and non-genealogists can easily understand this report. It concisely presents the relationships between the primary individual and everyone else in the database.

- **Cons.** This is not a standard report in family histories. If you have a large number of individuals in your database, the report can be quite lengthy.

Exploring Report Suitability, Options, Format, and Contents

You have a number of choices to make regarding the options, format, and contents of the custom and miscellaneous reports in Family Tree Maker. You must choose what to include in your reports—not an easy task when you have so much information that you can include!

Testing the Reports for Suitability

Not all the reports discussed in this chapter are suitable for a family history book. You must judge whether a particular report will give your readers the information you want them to have. It might help to consider these three levels of family history book projects (for more examples of projects, be sure to read Chapter Eleven, which shows several different types of family history book projects):

- An informal book intended to please non-genealogist immediate family members

- An intermediate-level book that is thorough but not complete, and intended for an audience of genealogists

- An advanced, formal family history book that is complete, or near complete, with the highest standards of documentation and analysis, and intended for serious genealogists

Keeping in mind that no hard-and-fast rule determines what you can and cannot include in your family history book, the suitability of the various reports discussed in this chapter for the three types of projects might be summarized as follows:

- **Custom Reports**

  - **Informal family history book.** Custom Reports are very suitable for this type of project because you can pick what information to present. Because the report is text-only, non-genealogists can understand it easily.

  - **Intermediate family history book.** Depending on the information chosen to be included in the report, a Custom Report is quite useful and suitable for this type of project.

  - **Formal family history book.** As with the intermediate project, a Custom Report can have great use in this type of project, assuming that the information presented is not duplicated elsewhere and is presented in a meaningful fashion.

- **Alternate Facts Reports**

  - **Informal family history book.** These reports are not very useful for this type of project because most informal family histories lack detailed facts and events.

- **Intermediate family history book.** Useful and appropriate, this report offers readers a chance to understand conflicting facts.

- **Formal family history book.** As with the intermediate project, this report is useful to readers in noting where alternate facts exist for events and details.

Address Reports

- **Informal family history book.** Depending on the type of project, a list of addresses might be well suited to this book. Remember the caveat regarding privacy before you decide to publish anyone's name and address.

- **Intermediate family history book.** This report is not suitable for this type of project unless the book is geared toward members of a family society or group who might want a list of member names and addresses.

- **Formal family history book.** This report is not suitable for this type of project unless you have a very good reason for it.

Medical Information Reports

- **Informal family history book.** A Medical Information Report is not well suited to this sort of book unless you are creating a medical family history.

- **Intermediate family history book.** If you have many individuals in your database who have a medical history, this report is suitable (although by no means traditional) for this type of book.

- **Formal family history book.** The same consideration applies as for the intermediate level book—if you have a substantial amount of medical information to present, the report is suitable for this type of project.

Birthdays of Living Individuals Reports

- **Informal family history book.** This report is an excellent choice for this type of project, assuming that the recipients are the people included in the report and that you remember to keep privacy issues in mind.

- **Intermediate family history book.** This report is not suitable for this type of project, especially because of privacy issues.

- **Formal family history book.** As with the intermediate-level project, privacy issues keep this report from being a good choice for this type of book.

Marriage Reports

- **Informal family history book.** This report is a suitable choice for this type of project because non-genealogists can easily understand it.

- **Intermediate family history book.** Not a standard item, but it might make an interesting appendix.

- **Formal family history book.** As with the intermediate-level project, this report is not a standard item included in formal family history books, but it might be of interest to readers.

Parentage Reports

- **Informal family history book.** The report is a suitable choice for this type of project because non-genealogists can easily understand it.

- **Intermediate family history book.** This report is not a standard item, but it might make an interesting addition.

- **Formal family history book.** As with the intermediate-level project, this report is not a standard item included in formal family history books, but it might be of interest to readers.

※ Bibliography

- **Informal family history book.** A bibliography is probably not applicable at this level because events and facts are unlikely to be sourced. If facts are sourced, I'd recommend including a bibliography.

- **Intermediate family history book.** I highly recommend including a bibliography in this type of project.

- **Formal family history book.** This is a must-have item for this type of project.

※ Data Errors Reports

- This report should not be included in any book.

※ Documented Events Reports

- **Informal family history book.** This report is probably not applicable at this level because events and facts are unlikely to be sourced.

- **Intermediate family history book.** If narrative reports are included with sources inline or as endnotes, this report will be redundant. Otherwise, the report is suitable for this level of project.

- **Formal family history book.** As with the intermediate project, this report will be redundant if narrative reports are included, but will make a suitable appendix.

※ Kinship Report: Civil & Canon

- **Informal family history book.** This report is probably not a good idea at this level because non-genealogists will not easily understand the system used to explain relationships.

- **Intermediate family history book.** A good choice for this type of project because the report shows how complex families are related.

- **Formal family history book.** As with the intermediate project, this report is well suited for this type of project. Most experienced genealogists understand what the Civil & Canon numbers mean.

 Kinship Report: Relationship Only

- **Informal family history book.** A better choice than the Civil & Canon Report, this is well suited to an informal book because it shows relationships in terms most people can understand.

- **Intermediate family history book.** This report could be used at this level of project, but for a more professional and detailed report, the Civil & Canon Report is a better choice.

 Formal family history book. Unless you have a particular reason not to include it, the Civil & Canon Report is more suited to this type of project because it presents the information in a formalized format that is understood and used by genealogists.

Considering Your Options

Because of the nature of the miscellaneous reports presented in this chapter, most do not have options available. The following is a list for those reports that do have options:

 Standard or Annotated Bibliography. This option enables you to create either a straight list of publications with citation information (publisher, publication date, and so on) or a list that includes your comments about the source, the quality of the resource, as well as standard publication information. I prefer an annotated list because it gives me insight into what the resource is and how valuable the researcher found it. This option is available for the bibliography only.

To access this option, with the Report screen open, follow these steps:

1. Choose Format, Report Format.

2. Select Bibliography and click OK.

3. Click Contents, Options.

4. Select Standard or Annotated Bibliography and click OK.

✹ **Include Footnotes without Referenced Sources.** This option enables you to include unsourced footnotes that you entered into the database. Because I am a stickler on sourcing everything, I don't recommend this option unless you have a good reason for using it (for example, if your footnote was a comment that is not suitable for sourcing—such as a dispute with the source that you have not yet proven, and thus don't want made public yet). This option is available for the bibliography only.

To access this option, with the Report screen open, follow these steps:

1. Choose Format, Report Format.

2. Select Bibliography and click OK.

3. Click Contents, Options.

4. Click the Include Footnotes without Referenced Sources box, and click OK.

✹ **Include Name Capitalization Errors.** This is a useful option to locate names that you might have mistyped. This option is only available for the Data Errors Report. Remember that I don't recommend including it in a family history book.

To access this option, with the Report screen open, follow these steps:

1. Choose Format, Report Format.

2. Select Data Errors Report and click OK.

3. Click Contents, Options.

4. Click the Include Name Capitalization Errors box and click OK.

✹ **Include Empty Birth and Marriage Date Field Errors.** As with the preceding option, this function is useful for locating problems with the database. Because this option is available only for the Data Errors Report, you won't include it in a family history book.

To access this option, with the Report screen open, follow these steps:

1. Choose Format, Report Format.

2. Select Data Errors Report and click OK.

3. Click Contents, Options.

4. Click the Include Empty Birth and Marriage Date Field Errors box and click OK.

 List Individuals and Marriages with Documentation, without Documentation or List All Individuals and Marriages Regardless of Documentation. These three options give you the ability to specify whom you want to include in your report. My rule of thumb is always to include documentation, unless you have a very good reason not to. This option is available only for the Documented Events Report.

To access this option, with the Report screen open, follow these steps:

1. Choose Format, Report Format.

2. Select Documented Events Report and click OK.

3. Click Contents, Options.

4. Click the option of your choice and click OK.

List All Events and Facts with Documentation and without Documentation or List All Events and Facts Regardless of Documentation. Like the preceding option, this one gives you the ability to specify what you want to include in your report—in this case, you can choose how you want the events and facts presented. I recommend that you include documentation whenever possible. This option is available only for the Documented Events Report.

To access this option, with the Report screen open, follow these steps:

1. Choose Format, Report Format.

2. Select Documented Events Report and click OK.

3. Click Contents, Options.

4. Click the option of your choice and click OK.

❋ **Show Footnote Format of Documentation.** This option enables you to have the documentation included in standard footnote format. If you desire brevity, this option is the best choice. This option is available only for the Documented Events Report.

To access this option, with the Report screen open, follow these steps:

1. Choose Format, Report Format.

2. Select Documented Events Report and click OK.

3. Click Contents, Options.

4. Click the option of your choice (whom to include, what to include, and how it should be printed) and click OK.

❋ **Show Complete Format of Documentation.** This option allows you to present the documentation in complete, detailed format, with full resource citation, comments, and quality of resource. This option is available only for the Documented Events Report.

To access this option, with the Report screen open, follow these steps:

1. Choose Format, Report Format.

2. Select Documented Events Report and click OK.

3. Click Contents, Options.

4. Click the option of your choice and click OK.

Deciding on Content

Family Tree Maker provides four standard content items that you can manipulate on the miscellaneous reports presented in this chapter. Not all items are available for each report—for example, some reports have a format prohibiting you from selecting which individuals can be included. With that thought in mind, I'll remind you of the standard recommendation of experimenting with reports to see what contents work best. The following is a list of content items that might be available, depending in the report. Next is a list of the items that are available for each report.

※ **Items to Include.** This is the same list as shown in Chapter Three, "Using Trees in Your Family History Book." You can select the items that you want to appear on each tree and chart.

To access this option, with the Report screen open, follow these steps:

1. Click Contents.

2. Select Items to Include and click OK.

※ **Individuals to Include.** This function allows you to specify which individuals will be included.

To access this option, with the Report screen open, follow these steps:

1. Choose Format, Report Format.

2. Select the Report you want to use and click OK.

3. Click Contents.

4. Select Individuals to Include and click OK.

※ **Title & Footnote.** You can specify a title for your report, as well as create your own footnote. See Chapter Three for information on footnotes.

To access this option, with the Report screen open, follow these steps:

1. Choose Format, Report Format.

2. Select the Report you want to use and click OK.

3. Click Contents.

4. Select Title & Footnote and click OK.

※ **Number of Generations to Show.** This function allows you to specify how many generations you want to display on your tree or chart.

To access this option, with the Report screen open, follow these steps:

1. Choose Format, Report Format.

2. Select the Report you want to use and click OK.

3. Click Contents.

4. Select Number of Generations to Show and click OK.

The following is a list of Contents choices available to you for each report. As with other reports and trees, you need to weigh each of the choices to determine which ones will be best for your book. Don't be afraid to experiment with the reports. Try varying the contents to see which ones display the maximum amount of information in the most readable format.

❋ Custom Report

- Items to Include

- Individuals to Include

- Title & Footnote

❋ Alternate Facts Report

- Individuals to Include

- Title & Footnote

❋ Address Report

- Individuals to Include

- Title & Footnote

❋ Medical Information Report

- Individuals to Include

- Title & Footnote

❋ Birthdays of Living Individuals Report

- Individuals to Include

- Title & Footnote

❋ Marriage Report

- Title & Footnote

❊ **Parentage Report**

- Individuals to Include
- Title & Footnote

❊ **Bibliography**

- Individuals to Include
- Title & Footnote

❊ **Data Errors Report**

- Individuals to Include
- Title & Footnote

❊ **Documented Events Report**

- Individuals to Include
- Title & Footnote

❊ **Kinship Report: Civil & Canon**

- Number of Generations to Show
- Title & Footnote

❊ **Kinship Report: Relationship Only**

- Number of Generations to Show
- Title & Footnote

Selecting Your Format

Because of the nature of the miscellaneous reports, few format choices are open to you. In most cases, you are limited to choices concerning the font and border style of the report. The following is a list of the format options available for the miscellaneous reports (not all options are available for all reports):

❊ **Maximum Width for Each Column.** This option enables you to have Family Tree Maker automatically set the column widths (dependant on the amount of information you include), or you can set the widths yourself. Be warned that Family Tree Maker will sometimes create widths that spread your report width-wise over multiple pages. In those situations, it's best to set the column widths manually or delete the number of items included in the report.

To access this option, with the Report screen open, follow these steps:

1. Choose Format, Report Format.

2. Select the Report you want to use and click OK.

3. Click Format, Maximum Width for Each Column.

4. Make the changes you want to the width and click OK.

✳ **Sort report.** This option allows you to tell Family Tree Maker by what field you want the report sorted. You can sort by any of the fields included in the report, in ascending or descending order. In addition, you can specify a secondary sort field (in ascending or descending order) to further arrange the report in a manner that is meaningful to you. You can also choose to have the individuals in the report not sorted by any field, which arranges them in ancestor or descendant order.

To access this option, with the Report screen open, follow these steps:

1. Choose Format, Report Format.

2. Select the Report you want to use and click OK.

3. Choose Format, Sort Report.

4. Select the order in which you want to sort the report and click OK.

✳ **Border Styles.** You can customize the look of your report by specifying the type of border at the top and bottom of the report. You can also specify border color, background color, and border thickness.

To access this option, with the Report screen open, follow these steps:

1. Choose Format, Report Format.

2. Select the Report you want to use and click OK.

3. Choose Format, Border Styles.

4. Make the choices you want to the border style and color and click OK.

✴ **Text Font, Style, and Size.** You can choose how you want the text displayed in your report by specifying the font, font size, font style (bold, italics, and so on), text color, and text alignment (center, left, or right). You can also choose to underline some text if you desire. Be aware that if you change the font size to a larger one, you run the risk of making the boxes on the tree larger, and thus less information can be displayed per page.

To access this option, with the Report screen open, follow these steps:

1. Choose Format, Report Format.

2. Select the Report you want to use and click OK.

3. Choose Format, Text Font, Style, and Size.

4. Make the changes you want to the font, style, and size and click OK.

✴ **Show Page Lines.** The last format choice you have is one that is strictly esoteric and won't affect the printed report—whether or not you want to have page lines shown on the screen. The lines will not appear in the report, but they will give you an idea about how your report will look when it is printed, should it run to more than one page.

To access this option, with the Report screen open, follow these steps:

1. Choose Format, Report Format.

2. Select the Report you want to use and click OK.

3. Click Format, Show Page Lines.

4. When you finish, click OK.

The following is a list of the format choices that are available for each report mentioned in this chapter. When considering format, be sure to keep in mind

both your reader (you want the book items to be easily read) and consistency (for a professional appearance, format all the trees, charts, and reports in a consistent manner).

✺ Custom Report

- Maximum Column Width
- Sort Report
- Border Style
- Text Font, Style, and Size

✺ Alternate Facts Report

- Sort Report
- Border Style
- Text Font, Style, and Size

✺ Address Report

- Maximum Column Width
- Sort Report
- Border Style
- Text Font, Style, and Size

✺ Medical Information Report

- Maximum Column Width
- Sort Report
- Border Style
- Text Font, Style, and Size

✺ Birthdays of Living Individuals Report

- Maximum Column Width
- Sort Report
- Border Style
- Text Font, Style, and Size

※ **Marriage Report**

- Maximum Column Width
- Sort Report
- Border Style
- Text Font, Style, and Size

※ **Parentage Report**

- Maximum Column Width
- Sort Report
- Border Style
- Text Font, Style, and Size

※ **Bibliography**

- Text Font, Style, and Size

※ **Data Errors Report**

- Sort Report
- Border Style
- Text Font, Style, and Size

※ **Documented Events Report**

- Text Font, Style, and Size

※ **Kinship Report: Civil & Canon**

- Border Style
- Text Font, Style, and Size

※ **Kinship Report: Relationship Only**

- Border Style
- Text Font, Style, and Size

CHAPTER SEVEN

Using Graphics in Your
Family History Book

A picture shows me at a glance
what it takes dozens of pages of a book to expound.

—Ivan Sergeyevich Turgenev, *Fathers and Sons*

ne of the joys of the computer age is the ability to digitize items for use in documents. Digital cameras, scanners, and video grabber devices make it extremely easy to include images of photographs, still shots of locations—just about anything you can take a picture of, you can include in your family history book.

As Turgenev implies in the preceding quotation, giving your reader a picture can save you a lot of work. Imagine that you have to describe each of your eight great-grandparents. It will take you a while to get through a detailed description of just the basics (height, weight, hair color, eye color, skin tone). Imagine how much more work it would be to go over things such as posture, body type, facial expression, hair styles, and so on. And yet all those things can be seen with one glance at a picture!

This chapter examines including graphical images in your family history book. You'll explore why you might want to add images and what types of objects you can include, and you take a look at Family Tree Maker's Scrapbook feature.

By the time you finish this chapter, you should be conversant with the following:

- 🏃 Why adding pictures can aid and enhance a book

- 🏃 What types of objects you can add to a Scrapbook

- 🏃 How to print Scrapbook pages

- 🏃 How to include pictures in various trees and charts

A Picture Is Worth a Thousand Words

Three basic reasons why you might want to include graphical items in your family history book are listed here:

- ⚑ To illustrate a point by providing visual information
- ⚑ To include items that might not be available to the average reader
- ⚑ To create a digital archive for rare and delicate items

Adding graphics to a book adds interest for your reader. Including graphics in your trees and charts can be a wonderful way to inform your reader, without wasting space on tedious descriptions and explanations.

Now take a closer look at how graphics can be used to enhance plain text into something with more meaning and clarity.

The following is a brief paragraph of text from Lytton Strachey's *Queen Victoria*, describing Queen Victoria's appearance when she was 18 years old:

> The great assembly of lords and notables, bishops, generals, and Ministers of State . . . saw a countenance, not beautiful, but prepossessing—fair hair, blue prominent eyes, a small curved nose, an open mouth revealing the upper teeth, a tiny chin, a clear complexion. . . .

That description is well and good. From it, you know Queen Victoria had fair hair, blue eyes, and unremarkable features. But compare that bare-bones text to the portrait of Victoria at age 18 (and imagine it shown in its original color, not a black and white representation) shown in Figure 7.1, and you'll see how effective graphic images can be.

With the addition of graphics, your readers can *see* all those things that you do not have the space to mention and can draw their own conclusions from the information you present. You can see from the picture that Victoria, indeed, had prominent eyes and a tiny chin—that she looked every bit a Hanover. Although you might mention this in print, including the picture helps your reader pull together the information you present.

Figure 7.1

A picture really can be worth a thousand words.

In addition to illustrating points in your text, you can include graphics as a way of presenting hard-to-locate or rare items. For example, you might want to include an image of a rare document, such as an indenture or a land grant that is not available to the public. Using a digital camera to take a picture of the document, you can include a digitized version in your family history book, making available an item that most people otherwise will not have the opportunity to view.

Likewise, with fragile or delicate items, you might want to include a digital version of the item as a way of preserving it as a sort of archive. For example, say that you have a very fragile *ambrotype,* a picture that was printed on glass during the middle of the nineteenth century. Because of the fragile nature of the picture, the ambrotype is not something you can share with family and friends. Yet, if you take a digital picture of it, you can include a copy in your book, not only making the item available to those who do not have access to it, but also giving yourself a bit of insurance against a catastrophe. Should something happen to the original, you have a digital copy of the item!

Creating Graphical Objects

Today a variety of ways are available for obtaining digital versions of items you want to include as graphics—flatbed and hand-held scanners and digital cameras—and keep in mind that companies that digitize photos as part of their processing are the best-known resources.

A *scanner*, either flatbed or hand-held, acts as a sort of photocopy machine, creating a digital image of an item placed within its viewing screen. The images are then saved directly to your computer's hard drive, where you can manipulate them at will in a graphics-editing program. With the addition of OCR (Optical Character Recognition) software, you can take a scanned image of text and convert it to readable text—that is, text that you can import into a word processor.

A digital camera acts as a normal camera, except that it saves images to RAM rather than to film. Images can be transferred directly to your computer for enhancement. If you prefer to use a traditional camera, various photo-development companies will, for a small fee, process your film and put your pictures on disk or CD-ROM, making it easy for you to import the graphics file into a word-processing program or a database such as Family Tree Maker.

Family Tree Maker uses graphics within the Scrapbook function (more about that in the section "Using the Scrapbook Feature in Family Tree Maker," later in this chapter). The Scrapbook acts as a storage area where you can enter and describe pictures and other objects for individuals or marriages. Family Tree Maker enables you to import any type of OLE (Object Linking and Embedding) object into the Scrapbook. Typical OLE objects might be video clips from a video capture device, sound clips, graphics, text from a word processor, or data from a spreadsheet or database.

In addition to OLE objects, you can import any of the following types of graphics:

- Screens bitmap (BMP)
- ZSoft (PCX)
- FlashPix (FPX)
- Photoshop 3.0 (PSD)
- JPEG (JPG)
- Tagged Information Format (TIF)
- PhotoCD (PCD)
- Screens Metafile (WMF)

A Closer Look at OLE Objects

According to Webopedia's (http://www.webopedia.com) definition:

> OLE is a compound document standard developed by Microsoft Corporation. It enables you to create objects with one application and then link or embed them in a second application. Embedded objects retain their original format and links to the application that created them.

Typical OLE objects are graphics, database tables, spreadsheets, and so on. Family Tree Maker allows you to import OLE objects into an individual or marriage Scrapbook. To do so, follow these steps:

1. Open the Scrapbook for the person or marriage you want to work with.

2. Once the Scrapbook screen opens, click in the Scrapbook screen where you want your object to appear and from the Picture/Object menu, select Insert Object.

3. The Insert Object dialog box, shown in Figure 7.2, opens, allowing you to select the object you want. If you are creating a new object, make sure that the Create New radio button is selected; then select the type of object you want to place into the Scrapbook from the Object Type box and click OK. The application used to create the object opens and allows you to create the object. When you finish, you can save the file and return to Family Tree Maker, where the object will be added to the Scrapbook.

4. If you want to include an existing object, click Create from File. In the File field, point to the file you want to include and click OK. The item you selected will be added into the Scrapbook.

It should be noted that not all OLE objects can be seen, let alone printed and included in a family history book. Some OLE objects, such as sound and video clips, might be excellent choices to include in a Scrapbook, but will not translate to the printed medium. In those instances, you will not want to include the OLE objects when you are printing a Scrapbook or selecting items to be printed in a New Text item, tree, or chart.

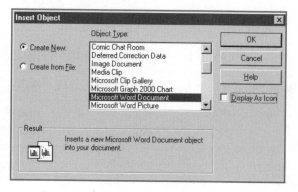

Figure 7.2

OLE objects can be created by any number of applications in formats that you may or may not be able to include in your family history book.

Most scanners and digital cameras can save graphics in one of the preceding formats, giving you the flexibility to choose whatever graphics format suits your needs. A discussion of the various pros and cons of each graphics type is beyond the scope of this book, but the most popular graphics formats used these days are JPG, PCX, and TIF.

Scanning Directly into a Scrapbook

If you have a scanner installed on your computer, you might want to bypass the additional step of scanning into your scanning software, saving the file, and then loading it into Family Tree Maker. Instead, you can scan the image directly into an individual's or marriage's Scrapbook.

If you plan on viewing the Scrapbook images only on-screen, lower the scanning DPI to about 150 DPI (dots per inch). This resolution will produce a nice image, as well as keep the file size manageable.

If you plan on printing your Scrapbook or images from the Scrapbook in reports or trees, the resolution you scan at should be a little higher. For example, if you are printing with an ink-jet printer at 300 DPI, you'll probably want to scan images at 200–300 DPI (keeping in mind that the higher the scanning resolution, the larger the resulting graphic file size).

I don't recommend scanning images at over 300 DPI unless you have a huge amount of storage space. For my 600 DPI laser printer, I scan images at resolutions between 200–300, depending on the size of the object (I scan smaller objects or ones that will be significantly cropped at 300 DPI and larger images at 200 DPI).

If you have a lot of images for an individual, don't feel that you need to include them all unless you have adequate storage space for the resulting graphic files. Keep in mind how many images you have scanned overall when adding images for individual's and marriage's Scrapbooks.

To keep scanned image file sizes down, you can scan at lower resolutions and use a graphic format that compresses the image (for example, TIF or JPEG). For more information on graphic file formats as related to scanned images, check out "Scanned Image File Size Issues," which appeared in the February 1999 issue of *PC Magazine UK*. This excellent article is also available online at http://www.zdnet.co.uk/pcmag/labs/1999/02/scanner/3.html.

If you want more information on how to scan, check out the tutorial, "Fundamentals of Digital Scanning," which you can find online at http://www.people.virginia.edu/~arch-con/Help/scanning/basics.html.

Investigating Types of Objects That Can Be Included in a Family History Book

When one thinks of graphics for a family history book, photographs generally come to mind first. Photos are an integral part of any family history book, but because the art of photography is relatively modern (the first photographic process, the *daguerreotype*, wasn't introduced until 1839), many individuals in your family tree were probably never photographed. Fortunately, other items are available that you can choose to include in your family history book to help flesh out the individuals, locations, and society in which your ancestors lived. Don't overlook unusual or eclectic items when building a Scrapbook for each

individual—just as you cherish those family stories and anecdotes, so should you cherish the tangible proofs of their lives.

❋ **TIP** ❋ *Before you include an item in your book, make sure that it is legal for you to do so. Obtain permission from its owner to use the item before you include scanned photos, verify that the image of a painting you want to use is in the public domain, and so on.*

The following is a list of some of the items that can be scanned or otherwise digitized (by means of a digital camera, video camera and video screen grab hardware, or traditional film digitized during processing):

- 🏃 Documents
- 🏃 Paper ephemera
- 🏃 Locations
- 🏃 Artwork and letters
- 🏃 Textiles
- 🏃 Memorabilia

❋ **NOTE** ❋ *This list is not comprehensive—anything that can be digitally reproduced can be included in a book, so do not limit yourself to including only those items traditionally seen in family history books.*

Documents

Many documents can be found that you might want to include in your family history book. *Documents* are generally public domain items (because they contain facts, which can't be copyrighted) and, as such, should be legal for you to include without seeking permission. Some of the documents your readers might like to see are vital records, such as certificates (for example, birth, marriage, and death certificates), naturalization records, religious documents (baptismal certificates, funeral cards, church membership lists), census records, and newspaper and magazine articles pertaining to the individual.

Suppose that you want to write a family history book about your great-great–grandparents, Nicholas and Elizabeth Benner, who emigrated from Germany to the United States. For this book, you might want to include scanned images of the German parish records showing Nicholas and Elizabeth's birth and marriage, the passenger list showing how and when they traveled to the

United States, their naturalization petitions and certificates, copies of their children's birth certificates, land records showing what tracts of land or houses they purchased, images from the census microfilms, and finally their funeral cards. Including such documents can go a long way to enhance the information that you present in your book.

> ❧ **NOTE** ❧ *Remember copyright laws! If you want to include a copy of a magazine article, newspaper clipping, maps, and so on in your Scrapbook, make sure that you can do so without violating the author's copyright. For more information about copyright laws, refer to Chapter Two.*

Paper Ephemera

In addition to documents, you can include other types of paper items to illustrate a point or enhance your book—for example, maps. Both ancient and modern maps can go a long way in helping your reader understand where a site—be it a field, building, town, or country—is located. City maps, fire insurance maps, town maps, and their ilk are all extremely useful and should be included whenever possible. Other types of paper items that can be included are newspaper and magazine articles about the individual (news stories, obituaries, marriage and birth notices) or about the location or society in which the individual lived.

Suppose that you want to write a family history book about your English Baskerville ancestors, a noble family of some repute. For this book, you could include maps of the county and town where the Baskervilles lived, newspaper articles about the history of the town and the family's relationship to it, local histories about Baskerville Hall, as well as postcards showing the house and the surrounding area.

Locations

Like maps, images of locations can greatly increase your readers' understanding of the environment in which your ancestors lived. Images of houses, buildings, battlefields, and other locations of importance can be included in conjunction with text. In addition, you can include pictures of headstones, monuments, and other markers; historic photographs of towns and cities; and so on.

Say that you want to write a family history book revolving around several key families who founded a town. In this book, you could include images showing the progress of the town as it grew, houses in which the founders lived, businesses and buildings that influenced the town's growth, rubbings or images from the founders' headstones, and pictures of important town events, all illustrating the interaction of the families with the local history of the town.

Artwork and Letters

Because the earliest photographic images date back less than two hundred years, family historians must rely on other sources for images of people. Portraits, statues and busts, miniatures, sketches, and paintings all enable your reader to see how people and objects appeared. In addition to formal portraits and paintings featuring individuals, you can include drawings and artistic endeavors by the individuals. Other forms of artistic media you might want to include are letters, poems, journals, or diaries kept or written by the individuals featured in the book. Such a personal and intimate look can only give your reader more insight into the person you are discussing.

Assume, for example, that you want to write a family history book for a grandparent. In this book you could include drawings and paintings by great-grandchildren, silhouettes created for you and your siblings, letters written to the grandparent, poems celebrating her life, footprints and handprints of great-grandchildren, and so on.

Textiles

Many families have some sort of textile keepsake in their family—it could be a quilt, sample, needlework cushion, dress, christening gown, and so on. Images of such items can go far to make real an otherwise lifeless individual. Like artwork or prose, anything created by or specifically for an individual adds immensely to the value of your text, so don't overlook including images of items that might not have been used in a family history book before.

Suppose that you want to write a family history book featuring an ancestor who traveled west on a wagon train. For this book, you could include digital images of the marriage quilt made once the family arrived on their homestead, the sampler created by one of the family's daughters, a handkerchief edged with handmade lace, and pictures of the gown made for the children's christenings.

Memorabilia

Almost every family has a collection of miscellaneous items that might have little monetary value, but great sentimental value. Including in your book military medals and honors, awards, trophies, keepsakes like curls from a child's first haircut, lockets, and so forth can put your reader in touch with the individuals about whom you are writing. Personal effects do not have to be spectacular to be interesting. Although the picture of a handsome antique engagement ring traditionally given to the brides of firstborn sons can be a spectacular item to work into a biography, a simple heart-shaped stone given to a sweetheart can bring poignancy and meaning to the tale of how two ancestors met and courted.

Suppose that you want to write a biography about a great-great–grandfather. In the book, you could include digital images of the military medals earned during his service, the cap that went with his Civil War uniform, the bullet removed from his body when he was shot during a battle, copies of his discharge and pension papers, and even—for the thorough and exacting researcher—images of advertisements for the type of prosthesis he wore after losing his leg. All these items have little meaning unless you connect them to an individual, but then they can serve to build a full and detailed picture of who the person was.

Using the Scrapbook Feature in Family Tree Maker

As I mentioned earlier in this chapter, Family Tree Maker adds graphics to reports, trees, and charts via the Scrapbook feature. The Scrapbook is aptly named; it acts as an electronic Scrapbook into which you can import photos, scanned images, OLE objects, or just about anything you can copy onto your computer's Clipboard.

Each individual in your Family File can have his or her own Scrapbook, or you can insert items to a Scrapbook created for a couple (wedding pictures, family photos, and so on are great objects to place in the marriage Scrapbook).

On the Family Page, you can tell at a glance whether an individual or marriage Scrapbook contains items; the Scrapbook button appears closed when no items are in the Scrapbook and open when there are items. Figure 7.3 shows an example of open and closed buttons.

Follow these steps to open a new or existing Scrapbook:

1. Go to the Family Page for the individual whose Scrapbook you want to open. Alternatively, you can go to the Family Page that contains the marriage of those whose Scrapbook you want to open.

2. Click the Scrapbook button (refer to Figure 7.3) for the individual or marriage.

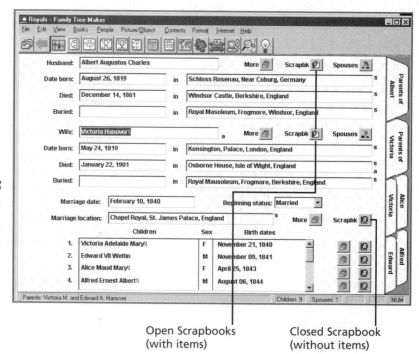

Figure 7.3

Queen Victoria and Prince Albert have items in their Scrapbooks, but nothing is in the Scrapbook for their marriage.

Open Scrapbooks
(with items)

Closed Scrapbook
(without items)

When you finish with the Scrapbook, you can close it by returning to the Family Page or by clicking one of the buttons on the toolbar.

As you can see from Figure 7.4, which shows an example of the Scrapbook screen, each object added into the Scrapbook appears as a thumbnail (small) version of the original object.

Scrapbooks can be used in three ways with regard to a family history book project:

🌸 They can be printed separately for an all-graphics version of a family history book (with only object descriptions and information as text).

🌸 They can be used in conjunction with a family history book to add life to sections regarding specific individuals or marriages.

🌸 The images contained within the Scrapbook can be used in selected reports and trees without printing the entire Scrapbook.

However you use the Scrapbook feature, you will find that it adds real value to your book.

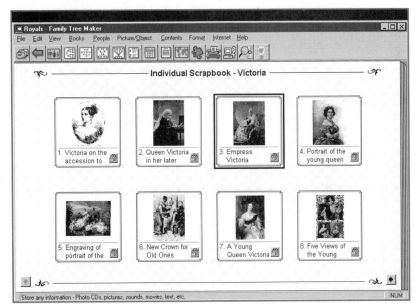

Figure 7.4

Each individual and marriage has a Scrapbook attached, which you can use to illustrate that person's or couple's life.

Inserting Objects into a Scrapbook

Before you can include items from the Scrapbook in your trees, charts, and text items, you have to add them to an individual or marriage Scrapbook. Unlike the old days when you had to sit down with a pot of paste, scissors, and construction paper, Family Tree Maker makes it easy for you to insert an item into the Scrapbook and manipulate it until it fits your needs. Follow these steps to insert an object into the Scrapbook:

1. Go to the Family Page for the individual whose Scrapbook you want to open (or the Family Page that contains the marriage of the people whose Scrapbook you want to open).

2. Click the Scrapbook button for the individual or marriage.

3. From the Picture/Object menu, select the type of object you want to include and click one of the following:

   • Insert PhotoCD Picture

   • Insert Picture from File

   • Insert Picture from Scanner/Camera

   • Insert Object (this is for OLE objects)

   ❋ **TIP** ❋ *You can also paste objects directly from your computer's Clipboard by opening the Edit menu and choosing Paste or Paste Special (Paste Special applies only to OLE objects).*

4. From the Look In drop-down list, pick the drive and directory where the graphics file you want is located and type the filename of the item you want to include.

5. If the Preview Picture box to the left of the dialog box is clicked, you will see a thumbnail representation of the item you are inserting.

6. Click the Open button. If the object is a picture, it appears in the Edit Picture dialog box. If the object is not a picture, the object appears as an icon (a sound icon for sound files, video icon for video clips, and so on). Click OK to return to the Scrapbook.

7. If you are adding a picture, you can edit the picture by rotating it, cropping it, or flipping it horizontally or vertically.

> ❋ **NOTE** ❋ *You can manipulate a picture by any of the means just mentioned: rotating, cropping, or flipping. For example, to crop a picture, simply click and drag your mouse over the picture to create a crop box and click the Crop button (see Figure 7.5). Family Tree Maker will then crop the picture down to the area you specified. If you change your mind, you can click the Cancel button to return to the original picture.*

8. When you finish editing, click OK, and your picture is added into the Scrapbook.

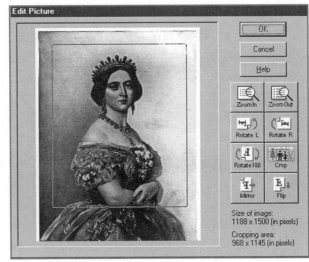

Figure 7.5

You can manipulate pictures at the time you add them to the Scrapbook.

Describing Scrapbook Objects

After you add an object to a Scrapbook, remember to provide as much information about the object as possible. You can add a caption and descriptive information using the More About button in the lower-right corner of each Scrapbook entry. The More About Picture/Object dialog box, shown in Figure 7.6, allows you to enter a caption for each object, as well as a *category* (an organizational field meant to help you keep the objects ordered in a fashion meaningful to you) and the date of origin of the object.

Follow these steps to open the More About screen:

1. Go to the Family Page for the individual whose Scrapbook you want to open (or to the Family Page that contains the marriage whose Scrapbook you want to open).

2. Click the Scrapbook button for the individual or marriage.

3. Click the More About button in the lower-right corner of the Scrapbook object. Alternatively, from the Picture/Object menu, select More About or select the object and press Ctrl+M.

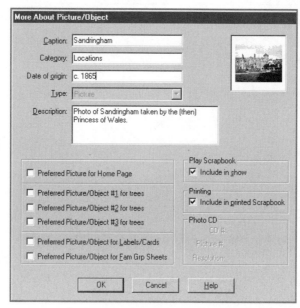

Figure 7.6

This dialog box allows you to specify information about a Scrapbook object, including whether it will appear in various trees, reports, and charts.

4. Enter the information you want in the Caption, Category, Date of Origin, Type, and Description fields.

5. Click the box for whichever feature you want to enable:

- Include in Printed Scrapbook
- Preferred Picture/Object #1 for Trees
- Preferred Picture/Object #2 for Trees
- Preferred Picture/Object #3 for Trees
- Preferred Picture/Object for Labels/Cards
- Preferred Picture/Object for Fam Grp Sheets
- Include in Show

In Figure 7.6, notice that the Type field is grayed out, indicating that when I added the object, Family Tree Maker recognized it as a picture. As a result, I cannot specify the object type. But for items that are not pictures, such as OLE items (see Figure 7.7), you can specify the type of object you are adding, as well as a brief description of the object.

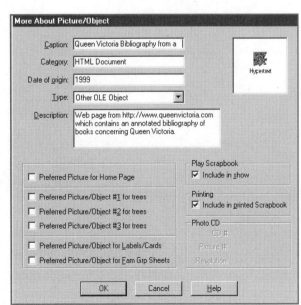

Figure 7.7

When adding an object that is not a picture, you can specify the object type and provide descriptive information.

Specifying Preferred Items

Specifying something as *preferred* is Family Tree Maker's way of letting you choose the default item to be used. In the case of pictures, you can specify which picture to use when you create a Web page via Family Tree Maker, as well as indicating which three pictures you are most likely to want used on trees. For example, you can tell Family Tree Maker to print Preferred Picture/Object #2 on a Descendant Tree. The tree would then be created with the picture or object you specified as being the Preferred Picture/Object #2.

Although you can designate three preferred objects, you can print any of the items in an individual's Scrapbook on a tree; rather than selecting a preferred object, you simply search for the object you want using the category field.

You can also specify which one picture you'd like used when you print up mailing labels and cards, and which picture you want to represent the individual on a Family Group Sheet. See below for more information on adding graphics to trees and reports.

To specify a picture as preferred:

1. In the Scrapbook, click the picture you want to designate as preferred.

2. Click the More About button in the lower-right corner of the Scrapbook entry.

3. In the More About Picture/Object dialog box, click the box pertaining to the choice you want: Preferred Picture/Object for Home Page, Preferred Picture/Object # 1, 2, or 3 for Trees, Preferred Picture/Object for Labels and Cards, or Preferred Picture/Object for Fam Grp Sheets.

The More About Picture/Object dialog box gives you other controls over your Scrapbook objects by allowing you to specify them as preferred items. For more information on telling Family Tree Maker that you want a picture marked as a preferred item, see the sidebar "Specifying Preferred Items."

Scrapbook object descriptions are important when you go to print the Scrapbook. Just as you might label pictures in a photo album, so should you label the objects in a Scrapbook. Names of the individuals contained in the pictures, dates of origin (whenever possible), detailed descriptions of the individuals or objects represented, dates of creation or sources for OLE objects, and similar information help your reader understand who and what is being represented in the Scrapbook object, as well as how valid the item is with regard to your research.

Printing Scrapbooks

Before you go to the trouble of printing your Scrapbook, you'll probably want to see how it will look. Fortunately, Family Tree Maker enables you to preview items before you print them. Figure 7.8 shows an example of how one page of an individual's Scrapbook appears in Print Preview mode.

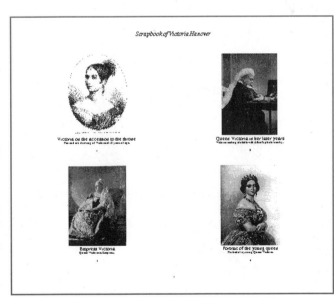

Figure 7.8

A variety of formatting options are available to influence how your Scrapbook is printed. This example shows the 2×2 layout of pictures.

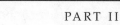
Follow these steps to view a page of the Scrapbook in Print Preview mode:

1. Go to the Family Page for the individual whose Scrapbook you want to open (or to the Family Page that contains the marriage whose Scrapbook you want to open).

2. Click the Scrapbook button for the individual or marriage.

3. From the File menu, click Print Preview.

As with trees and reports, specific options, content and formatting choices, and formatting choices regarding your Scrapbook are all available from the Print Preview screen. The aforementioned are not important unless you plan on printing the Scrapbook itself; if you simply want to use pictures or objects from the Scrapbook on trees and reports, you will not have to bother with Scrapbook-specific options, contents, and formatting choices (however, if you don't enter in captions and descriptions, you will not be able to use the Sort function, mentioned later in this section).

Follow these steps to view the Scrapbook's options:

1. Go to the Family Page for the individual whose Scrapbook you want to open (or to the Family Page that contains the marriage whose Scrapbook you want to open).

2. Click the Scrapbook button for the individual or marriage.

3. From the File menu, click Print Preview.

4. From the Contents menu, click Options.

Two options are available to you when printing a Scrapbook:

➤ Printing all pictures and objects

➤ Printing only those items that fit the specifications of category and type (see Figure 7.9 to view the various types)

Here's how you select the items (as shown in Figure 7.9) to be printed:

1. Open the Scrapbook that you want to print. From the File menu, select Print Preview.

Figure 7.9

You can sort through objects to be printed in your Scrapbook by category and type, or you can print all the items in the Scrapbook.

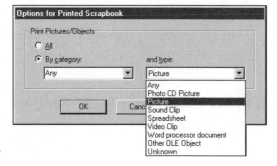

The Scrapbook Print Preview screen opens.

2. From the Contents menu, select Options.

3. In the Options for Printed Scrapbook dialog box, use the pull-down menus to include items by any of the categories you entered when you included pictures or by the object type (picture, word processor document, and so on).

4. Click OK to include the items in the Print Preview screen.

Family Tree Maker gives you two choices for selecting the content to be printed in your Scrapbook:

➤ Items to Include with Each Picture/Object

➤ Title & Footnote

Unlike the items you can include on trees and reports, the items you can include with each Picture/Object are limited to the following:

➤ **Picture/Object.** I'm sure I don't need to remind you to avoid including objects such as sound clips and MIDI sequences, which don't lend themselves to the printed media.

➤ **Picture/Object Caption.** This is the caption (or title) you give to the picture or object. The caption should be brief but descriptive. Save specific details for the description.

- **Picture/Object Category.** You can enter a category for each object when you are entering information in the object's More About section. The category is useful when searching or selecting specific items for printing.

- **Picture/Object Date.** Dates, or estimates of dates, are useful in alerting your reader to what time period the object pertains to. If you don't know a specific date, use *circa* or *est.* (estimated) for dates about which you have an idea, or *unknown* to indicate those for which you have no information.

- **Picture/Object Description.** To my mind, this is the most important field to be filled out for each object. Here is where you can list individuals in a picture, note the source of the document, make comments about what the object contains, and even provide a brief analysis of the validity or value of the object. Be sure to use this field to describe, in as much detail as possible, the Scrapbook object (the description field is four lines long and holds approximately 200 characters).

- **Picture/Object Number on Scrapbook Page.** If you want to have each object numbered, this choice will print the position number for the object.

- **Title & Footnote.** This option is similar to options for trees, reports, and charts; you can use an automatic title or create one for yourself. You can also specify a starting page number and choose whether to have page numbers print on the Scrapbook.

Follow these steps to view the Scrapbook's content choices:

1. Go to the Family Page for the individual whose Scrapbook you want to open (or to the Family Page that contains the marriage whose Scrapbook you want to open).

2. Click the Scrapbook button for the individual or marriage.

3. From the File menu, click Print Preview.

4. From the Contents menu, select the item you want.

Five format options are available that enable you to customize the Scrapbook to your specification. As with reports and trees, I urge you to play with these settings before deciding which format best suits your needs.

⚐ **Scrapbook Format.** This option allows you to tell Family Tree Maker how you want the Scrapbook to appear—that is, the layout. Figure 7.10 shows the Format for Printed Scrapbook dialog box, in which you can see the layout choices. Most of these choices are obvious, but the Custom choice allows you to specify how many objects you want across and down per page. You can go as high as 50 objects in either direction, but that is not recommended unless you are printing a thumbnail contact-type sheet for reference.

⚐ **Sort Scrapbook.** You can sort the pictures and objects within the Scrapbook by caption, category, and date—all of which you can select to sort alphabetically or reverse-alphabetically. This feature allows you to arrange items in the printed version of your Scrapbook without manually reordering them within the Scrapbook. For example, if you want the pictures (arranged at random in your

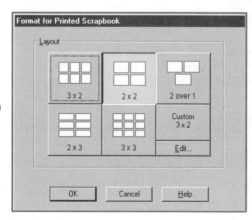

Figure 7.10

You have six layout choices for Scrapbook images, including a Custom layout that you can edit.

Scrapbook) to print chronologically, assuming you have categorized each appropriately, you can tell the Scrapbook to sort by category (*A* first). That will result in a rearrangement of all the objects in the Scrapbook, leaving you with objects ordered alphabetically by category.

* **Box, Line, and Border Styles.** This format option is the same as for trees, reports, and charts. You can specify box, line, and border styles for the pictures and objects to be printed, as well as fill, shadow, line, border, and background colors.

* **Text Font, Style, and Size.** This format option is also the same as for trees, reports, and charts. You can specify the font, size, style, color, and alignment of the text used for the Scrapbook objects (caption, description, date, title, page numbers, and so on).

* **Show Page Lines.** As with other printable items in Family Tree Maker, this option does not affect how the Scrapbook is printed; instead, it shows only page breaks on the screen.

Follow these steps to view the Scrapbook's format choices:

1. Go to the Family Page for the individual whose Scrapbook you want to open (or to the Family Page that contains the marriage Scrapbook you want to open).

2. Click the Scrapbook button for the individual or marriage.

3. From the File menu, click Print Preview.

4. From the Format menu, click the item you want.

Finally, once you have the Scrapbook formatted the way you want it, you'll probably want to print it! To do so, follow these steps:

1. Open the Scrapbook you want to print.

2. From the File menu, click Print Preview. Check through the Print Preview Scrapbook to make sure the Scrapbook meets your satisfaction.

3. From the File menu, click Print Scrapbook.

4. In the Print Scrapbook dialog box, enter the print range you want in the Print Range section, verify that your printer is the one you want to use, and click OK.

Including Graphics in Trees, Charts, and Reports

After you enter your objects into the Scrapbook and include as much information about each object as possible, you can turn your attention to including the pictures and objects in the various trees and charts that Family Tree Maker generates.

Follow these steps to include a picture from the Scrapbook in a tree, chart, or report:

1. Go to the Family Page for the individual who will be featured on the tree, chart, or report.

2. From the View menu, select the item you want. Alternatively, click the appropriate tree, chart, or report button on the toolbar.

3. From the Contents menu, select Items to Include in Each box.

4. From the Available Items list on the left, click Picture/Object and then click the right arrow button to add it to the list of items to be contained in the boxes.

5. Choose the options appropriate for that picture and click OK.

Not all the items you might want to include in your family history book can include pictures or objects; although most of the trees can, the following trees cannot include pictures or objects from the Scrapbook:

- Fan Ancestor Tree
- Fan Descendant Tree
- Fan Hourglass Tree
- Outline Descendant Tree

While the Family Group Sheet can include objects from the Scrapbook, the narrative and miscellaneous reports cannot.

> ❋ **TIP** ❋ *If you really want to include an object from your Scrapbook in a narrative report, a workaround exists. If you export the narrative report to an .rtf (rich text format) or a plain ASCII .txt (text format) file, you can import the narrative report into a word-processing program and insert a graphics file there.*

Picture Options

When including an object from the Scrapbook in one of the trees, you can specify how the object will appear within the tree. Figure 7.11 shows an example of the Options: Picture/Object dialog box. Earlier I talked about assigning a category to your object, and here's where doing so is useful. In Figure 7.11, notice that the dialog box gives you the opportunity to select one of the three preferred objects or to find one by means of a category and type search.

You have several options when inserting a Scrapbook object into a tree:

🐾 **Preferred Picture/Object #1, 2, or 3.** This option allows you to use one of the objects you selected as preferred.

Figure 7.11

If you want to include pictures or Scrapbook objects in your trees, you have control over how the object will appear.

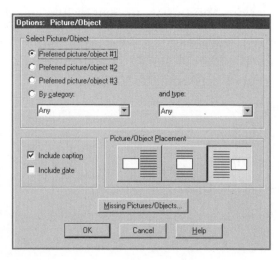

⚹ **By Category and Type.** This feature, as mentioned earlier in this chapter, enables you to select an item that has not been designated as preferred. You can locate non-preferred items by using the Search function via category and type.

⚹ **Include Caption.** If you want to include the caption you entered in the More About facts for each object, select this item.

⚹ **Include Date.** This option allows you to include the date you entered in the More About Facts for each object.

⚹ **Picture/Object Placement.** Select one of the options here to tell Family Tree Maker how you want your object displayed with regard to surrounding text. You can place text to the right of the object, above and below only, or to the left of the object (see Figure 7.12).

⚹ **Missing Pictures/Objects.** If you specify that the tree should include pictures or objects from the Scrapbook, but do not have objects entered into the Scrapbook for each individual, Family Tree Maker will indicate missing objects one of three ways: a blank field (that is,

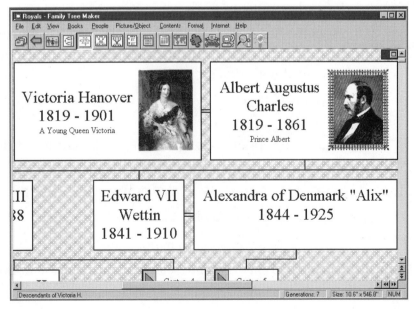

Figure 7.12

You can specify the placement of text and graphic objects in trees using the formatting controls. This example shows two pictures with caption and tree text to the left of the graphics.

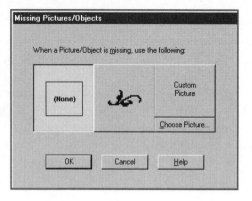

Figure 7.13

Missing objects can be indicated on a tree by a standard symbol, a symbol of your own choosing, or no symbol at all.

no symbol or picture indicating an object is missing), a graphic symbol (see Figure 7.13), or a custom picture that you specify.

SELECTING A PREFERRED OBJECT

Follow these steps to let Family Tree Maker know which object is a preferred object:

1. Open the tree you want to manipulate.

2. From the Contents menu, select Items to Include in Each box.

3. From the Available Items list on the left, click Picture/Object and then click the right arrow button to add it to the list of items to be contained in the boxes.

4. Click the button for Preferred Picture/Object #1, 2, or 3 and then click OK.

5. Choose the options appropriate for that picture and click OK.

INDICATING AN OBJECT'S CATEGORY AND TYPE

Follow these steps to define an object's category and type:

1. Open the tree you want to manipulate.

2. From the Contents menu, select Items to Include in Each box.

3. From the Available Items list on the left, click Picture/Object and then click the right arrow button to add it to the list of items to be contained in the boxes.

4. Click the down arrow for either Category or Type.

5. Click your choice and then click OK.

INCLUDING A CAPTION

These steps enable you to use a caption with an object:

1. Open the tree you want to manipulate.

2. From the Contents menu, select Items to Include in Each box.

3. From the Available Items list on the left, click Picture/Object and then click the right arrow button to add it to the list of items to be contained in the boxes.

4. Click the Include Caption box and then click OK.

INCLUDING A DATE

Follow these steps to include a date with the object:

1. Open the tree you want to manipulate.

2. From the Contents menu, select Items to Include in Each box.

3. From the Available Items list on the left, click Picture/Object and then click the right arrow button to add it to the list of items to be contained in the boxes.

4. Click the Include Date box and then click OK.

PLACING THE TEXT AND OBJECT

Follow these steps to select the placement of the text and object:

1. Open the tree you want to manipulate.

2. From the Contents menu, select Items to Include in Each box.

3. From the Available Items list on the left, click Picture/Object and then click the right arrow button to add it to the list of items to be contained in the boxes.

4. Choose one of the three Picture/Object Placement buttons and then click OK.

INDICATING MISSING OBJECTS

Follow these steps when you want Family Tree Maker to tell you where you have missing objects or pictures:

1. Open the tree you want to manipulate.

2. From the Contents menu, select Items to Include in Each box.

3. From the Available Items list on the left, click Picture/Object and then click the right arrow button to add it to the list of items to be contained in the boxes.

4. Click the Missing Pictures/Objects button.

5. Select one of the three choices and then click OK.

CHAPTER EIGHT

Adding Text to Your Family History Book

History is a pact between the dead,
the living, and the yet unborn.
—Edmund Burke

n the previous chapter, I discussed adding graphics to your family history book to bring life to your ancestors' stories. Although graphics are a great addition to a book, a solid base of research and facts is more important for showcasing those graphics.

One of the ways you can build the base is to include additional text in your family history book. In this case, the phrase "additional text" indicates text that is not created directly in Family Tree Maker—that is, text created in another program or pulled from an unrelated resource such as a public domain document. The text can then be copied and pasted into an individual's More About Notes section or included in a family history book using the New Text item. I discuss the More About Notes and the New Text items later in this chapter.

By the time you finish this chapter, you should be familiar with the following:

- ✻ The benefits of using additional text to enhance your book

- ✻ Different types of text items you can add

- ✻ How to add text into an individual's More About Notes

- ✻ How to add text into a New Text item

Novice users of Family Tree Maker might want to take a look at Figure 8.1, which shows one of the primary buttons you will use to access functions discussed in the following sections.

More button

Figure 8.1

The More button
leads you to the
More About
screen, which has
More About
Notes.

Enhancing Your Book with Additional Text

Many reasons exist for adding additional text items to your family history book—as do graphics, additional text can improve a reader's understanding of the person you are presenting. Informative text can add interest to your book by providing related information or detailed examples about the individuals in the book. In addition, comments and anecdotes and other text can add historical background that puts your ancestors' lives within the perspective of the times in which they lived.

You can include information not found in the database (such as analyses of other research conducted on the same family, arguments for or against evidence, excerpts from other resources, and so on). You can also include extracts or abstracts from supporting evidence such as wills and probate records, census records, and other valuable sources of information.

NOTE *Used in the genealogical sense, an abstract is a summarization of a document—that is, only the important, essential points of a document are noted, and the rest is ignored. An extract is an exact copy of part of a document, with the entire original wording of that part.*

You will find different uses for both abstracts and extracts; for example, land and probate records are good candidates for abstraction because both types of documents are often riddled with legal language that is of no value to researchers. Most other records, however, should be extracted—vital records, census records, immigration records, and so on should be copied in their entirety.

Following are some types of text that you might want to add to your family history book (not all the examples are suited to every type of project, nor is the list comprehensive):

- Legal records
- Government records
- Church records
- Organizational records
- Obituaries
- Book excerpts
- Analyses
- Newspaper and magazine articles

Legal Records

Abstracts of land and probate records offer lots of information without overwhelming your reader with legalese. Following is a sample abstract of a land grant.

Northern Neck Land Grants, VA — Bk X, p. 81

Grant to ISAIAH SCOTT, 27 Feb. 1796, Hampshire Co., VA. 91 acres, Warrant No. 429, issued 26 Apr. 1791. Land granted: ...on the Fort Pleasant road adjourning the Manor line and bounded: beginning at two pines and a black oak standing on the point of a hill, corner to Stewards survey thence with a line of said survey N62W97 crossing the Fort Pleasant road to a hickory and Spanish oak in the Manor line thence with it S51W50 to two pines corner to EBENEZER MCKINLY and JOHN STAG's lots then continuing with the Manor line S25W116 three chestnut oaks on a hill side on said line near PETER UMSTAT's corner thence with his line N85E157 to a white oak and hickory in said line on the east side of a hill thence N19E83 to the beginning.

This abstract gives the reader exact information about the land granted to an individual—the source of the information (book title, volume, and page number), dates and names of parties involved, and a metes and bounds description of the land.

> ❀ **TIP** ❀ *You might be confused about when you should include an image of a document (as discussed in Chapter 7,"Using Graphics in Your Family History Book") or an abstract or extract of the document. The preceding abstract shows a good example of when you should distill information for your readers. Figure 8.2 shows a portion of the original land grant, which, as you can see, might be intimidating to readers unless they have deciphered land grants.*

Government Records

You might already have many records that you want to extract and include in your family history book. Census, vital, church, military, and immigration records are just a few of the items available that go far in presenting a rounded picture of the individuals you detail. Unlike legal documents, which have

Figure 8.2

Records such as this land grant make excellent instruments for abstraction and extraction, giving your readers a glimpse at documents they might otherwise not see.

kernels of information buried in a sea of legal language, government forms such as censuses, immigration records, and military records often are filled with enough clues and information to keep family historians delighted.

Figure 8.3 shows part of a microfilmed copy of the pension record of a Revolutionary War veteran. Although I prefer to use images of actual documents rather than extracts whenever possible, some situations arise in which presenting an image of the original will not benefit your readers—for example, when the handwriting on the original document is difficult to decipher, as is the case in Figure 8.3.

Figure 8.4 shows part of the excerpt in the form of New Text, with a small image of the original document at the top (the image itself is difficult to read, so I include it simply as a point of interest for the reader).

Figure 8.3

Handwritten records might be difficult for readers to decipher. In such cases, consider excerpting the information in the document for your family history book.

Figure 8.4

This sample of New Text illustrates how you can take a graphic that might not be legible and turn it into a useful and informative addition to a family history book.

Extract from Pension File for Christopher Henry Benner

File #12,436
Dennysville, ME

Pension Application for Christopher Benner

I, Christopher Benner of Dennysville in the County of Washington and State of Massachusetts, do testify and declare, that on or about the first of January one thosand seven hundred and seventy six, at Roxbury in the State of Massachusetts, I enlisted as a private soldier in the Continental Army of the United States in Capt. William Reed's Company in Col. John Bailey's Regiment of Infantry in the Massachusetts line and continued to serve in said Company and Regiment till the expiration of my term of Enlistment. I was at the Battle of Trenton in New Jersey the latter part of December in the same year and at the request of the officers continued to do my duty about six

Church Records

You might want to incorporate records related to churches and religious organizations in your book, including records related to baptisms, christenings, communicants, confirmations, deaths, disciplinary records, funerals, marriages, memberships, minutes, church histories, and so on. Because church and religious records are not as commonly found as other records (therefore, readers might not have been aware of the documents), they make especially good choices to include in a family history book.

The following is an excerpt from a list of congregation members. Although all the individuals on the list might not interest your readers, you can extract the names that you think will be of interest and include that information in a More About note for an individual or as a New Text item. If you are creating a family history book about church founders, you might want to include the list in its entirety as a New Text item.

**Extract from William Township
Congregation Membership List**

A list of those, who are minded, to hold to the Congregation here; and, what they are willing to give, annually, as long as each chooses; should however, one or another, quit, he shall inform the deacons that he no longer holds thereto.

	£	s.	d.
Gottfreid Mölich	2	0	0
Peter Mölich	0	15	0
Michel Rosberger	0	6	0
Joust Rosberger	0	6	0

Note: the column headers are amounts in British pounds, shillings, and pence (pence is noted with a d.)

Organizational Records

Records kept by nonreligious organizations can also be extremely helpful, such as those kept by schools and colleges, business organizations, fraternal organizations, funeral homes, financial and employment organizations, health-care facilities, and so on. Don't overlook including texts from nontraditional resources; often the information they provide cannot be found elsewhere.

Obituaries

One of the most common text items you can include is an obituary. You might choose to include a graphic of the actual obituary if you have it, but unless it is an unusual obituary (for example, one that includes a photo of the deceased), you might want to simply provide the text for your readers. Obituaries can take many forms, from front-page news stories about the untimely death of an individual, to a brief mention with little to no useful information (other death-related information that you might seek in newspapers includes funeral notices, death notices, cards of thanks, and death lists).

> **More About Christopher Benner - Notes**
>
> Notice of death from the Edmonds Tribune-Review
> 23 May 1912
>
> Charles Graves, a 16-year-old boy who lived at Meadows point, near Ballard, was killed Thursday afternoon. It has been ascertained that some workmen employed at a manufacturing plant not far from where the body was found on the beach, had been blasting some old iron. A piece of the iron was hurled through the air and imbedded in the boy's skull. The workmen were unaware of the accident. A man walking along the beach discovered the body. The workmen say they never knew a piece of iron to be thrown more than 75 yards and the body was found 360 yards away from the blasting.

Figure 8.5

When you have small quantities of text, try including it in an individual's More About Notes rather than providing it as a New Text item.

Figure 8.5 shows an example of a brief obituary (actually more a notice of death than an obituary) entered into an individual's More About Notes. This obituary will print on all reports that you tell to include More About Notes.

Book Excerpts

Sometimes you might want to include text from a family history book, local history book, or other printed resource. If you are unsure whether you can use the text without permission of the author, review the copyright section in Chapter Two, "Organizing Your Family History Book." Even if the work is in the public domain or is copyright free, be sure to note the source of the text.

In Figure 8.6, you can see how I created a separate New Text item for a family history book. The text contains only excerpts from the now public-domain work by Lytton Strachey.

Analyses

Book excerpts can be interesting on their own, but they might not add a lot of value to your book unless they make a point or provide specific information.

QUEEN VICTORIA

by Lytton Strachey

[New York: Harcourt, Brace and Company, 1921]

Excerpts
Chapter II: Childhood

The child who, in these not very impressive circumstances, appeared in the world, received but scant attention. There was small reason to foresee her destiny. The Duchess of Clarence, two months before, had given birth to a daughter; this infant, indeed, had died almost immediately; but it seemed highly probable that the Duchess would again become a mother; and so it actually fell out. More than this, the Duchess of Kent was young, and the Duke was strong; there was every likelihood that before long a brother would follow, to snatch her faint chance of the succession from the little princess.

Nevertheless, the Duke had other views: there were prophecies... At any rate, he would christen the child Elizabeth, a name of happy augury. In this, however, he reckoned without the Regent, who, seeing a chance of annoying his brother, suddenly announced that he himself would be present at the baptism, and signified at the same time that one of the godfathers was to be the Emperor Alexander of Russia. And so when the ceremony took place, and the Archbishop of Canterbury asked by what name he was to baptise the child, the Regent replied "Alexandrina." At this the Duke ventured to suggest that another name might be added. "Certainly," said the Regent.

Figure 8.6

If you have larger quantities of text than shown in Figure 8.5, you'll probably want to include it by means of the New Text item.

Text such as book excerpts *can* be useful for illustrating points made during an analysis of research done by others, for adding weight to claims or evidences you are trying to prove, or for disputing commonly held facts.

In the Strachey example, however, you might provide another New Text item, going over Strachey's text point by point and arguing those areas that you think are incorrect. You might also want to analyze conflicting evidence, offering pros and cons, evidence, and evaluation of the sources in a section or chapter in your family history book. Analysis is especially useful to readers when they are faced with information that is dated, questionable, or in conflict with other sources.

Personal Writings

Diaries, journals, letters, family stories, autobiographical texts—all are useful and interesting to readers, and all can be included nicely in the form of More About Notes or New Text items. In the example shown in Figure 8.7, I used a journal entry as a New Text item to highlight an important event in this individual's life.

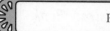

> ### Extracts from Queen Victoria's Journal
>
> **1 May 1851**
> This day is one of the greatest and most glorious days of our lives, with which, to my pride and joy the name of my dearly beloved Albert is forever associated! It is a day which makes my heart swell with thankfulness ... The Park presented a wonderful spectacle, crowds streaming though it - carriages and troops passing, quite like the Coronation Day, and for me, the same anxiety. The day was bright, and all bustle and excitement. At half past 11, the whole procession in 9 state carriages was set in motion. Vicky and Bertie (her two eldest children, the Princess Royal and the Prince of Wales) were in our carriage. Vicky was dressed in lace over white satin, with a small wreath of pink wild roses, in her hair, and looked very nice. Bertie was in full Highland dress. The Green Park and Hyde Park were one mass of densely crowded human beings, in the highest good humour and most enthusiastic. I never saw Hyde Park look as it did, being filled with crowds as far as the eye could reach. A little rain fell, just as we started; but before we neared the Crystal Palace, the sun shone and gleamed upon the gigantic edifice, upon which the flags of every nation were flying.

Figure 8.7

You can use journal, letter, or diary extracts to enhance a section on an individual's life or to illustrate a research point.

Newspaper and Magazine Articles

Although it's true that not everyone has had articles or features written about them, you might find that you have ancestors who have been mentioned in a newspaper, magazine, or other publication. If so, you might want to include the information from that article in the individual's More About Notes, or if the text is lengthy or otherwise proves a point you want to make in an argument or analysis, you could place the text as a New Text item. Figure 8.8 shows an example of how a quotation from a magazine article can be worked into More About Notes.

Adding Text Using More About Notes and New Text Items

As discussed at the beginning of this chapter, adding text to your family history book enables you to flesh out what might otherwise be dull and dry names and dates. Family Tree Maker provides three ways to add text to your family history book:

🏃 More About Notes (for both an individual or a marriage)

Regarding Victoria's journal:

When she first left London for a tour of Wales in 1982, [sic—should be 1832] she began a journal in a book which the Duchess had given her. So fascinating was the coach ride and so tempting the blank pages of the diary that for the first few days she would record the exact time of her arrival and departure at the stages along the route:

"Twenty minutes to nine. We have just changed horses at Barnet, a very pretty little town. Five minutes past half past nine. We have just changed horses at St. Albans. The situation is very pretty and there is a beautiful old abbey there. Five minutes past ten. The country is beautiful here: they have begun to cut the corn; it is so golden and fine that I think they will have a good harvest . . . A quarter to eleven. We have just changed horses at Dunstable . . ."

M. Foster Farley, "Queen Victoria's Childhood" (British Heritage, Oct./Nov. 1998)

Figure 8.8

Quotations or extracts from magazine articles are nice to include. Short clips can add interest to an individual's history via the More About Notes, while longer ones can make up a chapter or part of a chapter in your family history book.

- ⚶ New Text
- ⚶ By manually adding your text to an exported narrative report (for example, if you exported a Register Report, you could open that text in a word processor and add additional text there)

Notice that only the first two text choices can be accomplished within the Family Tree Maker program. The last one requires you to exit the program to add text; therefore, it is not recommended unless you have experience using a word processor and plan to create your family history book outside Family Tree Maker.

Novice users will want to take a close look at the More About screen in Figure 8.9. The Notes button on the right side will lead you to the More About Notes screen.

Including Text in More About Notes

Each individual and marriage has a More About section, which includes a Notes function into which you can enter whatever text you like. Although the text you enter in the Notes dialog box will not appear on the trees, it will appear on narrative reports and family group sheets.

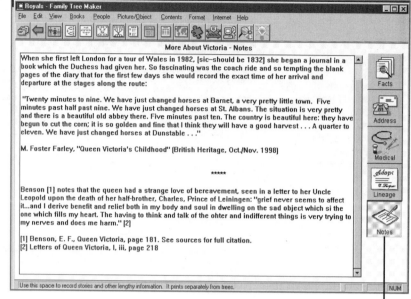

Figure 8.9

Click the Notes button to access the More About Notes screen, where you can enter as many notes as you like for an individual.

Notes button

Follow these steps to add More About Notes for an individual:

1. From the Family Page, click the individual whose notes you want to access.

2. Click the More About icon.

   The More About screen opens, displaying buttons for the five More About features (Facts, Address, Medical, Lineage, Notes).

3. From the vertical toolbar on the right side of the screen, click the Notes button.

   The More About Notes screen opens, with a lengthy Notes field.

4. Click the Notes field, and you're ready to type your text.

In effect, the Notes screen is a miniature word processor. You can enter anything you want to in the Notes screen—miscellaneous bits of information, family stories, biographical notes, comments, and so on.

You can enter text in the Notes page three ways:

* By typing it

* By copying it from another document and pasting it in the Notes page

* By importing an ASCII file

> **NOTE** *An ASCII file is a plain-text file (that is, without any formatting) that most programs can read and create. You can create an ASCII file in any text editor or word processor.*

TYPING TEXT

Entering text in the Notes page by typing the text is easy—just click the Notes field and begin typing. Family Tree Maker takes care of wrapping the lines, so you don't need to press Enter. All the familiar word-processing tools (Backspace and Delete keys, arrow keys to move you around the Notes field, Copy and Paste commands) work in the traditional manner.

PASTING TEXT FROM ANOTHER DOCUMENT

Follow these steps to copy and paste text from another program into the Notes page:

1. Open the program and document containing the text you want to copy.

2. Following the program's instructions, copy the text to your computer's Clipboard.

3. Open your Family Tree Maker file.

4. Open the Notes screen for the person whose notes you want to work with.

5. Position the cursor in the Notes field where you want the text pasted.

6. From the Edit menu, select Paste Text (or right-click to choose the Paste command from the shortcut menu, or simply press Ctrl+V).

IMPORTING AN ASCII TEXT FILE

To import an ASCII text file to the Notes page, follow these steps:

1. From the originating program, save or export the text in ASCII format (the file must have the suffix .TXT or .ASC in order for Family Tree Maker to recognize it as a text or an ASCII file).

2. Open your Family Tree Maker file.

3. Open the Notes screen for the person whose notes you want to work with.

4. Position the cursor where you want to insert the text.

5. From the File menu, select Import Text File.

   The Import Text File dialog box opens.

6. Use the Look In drop-down list to find the drive and directory of your ASCII file. If the file does not show up, be sure the file you are trying to import ends with either .TXT or .ASC. If not, rename the text file so that it ends with either .TXT or .ASC and try to import the file again.

7. Click the filename you want to import and click the Open button.

A WORD ABOUT FORMATTING IN NOTES

Like other text in Family Tree Maker, you can format the text in More About Notes, but the formatting options have certain limitations. One is that you must format all the text in the Notes screen the same way—that is, you cannot highlight one paragraph and have it in one font while other paragraphs are in other fonts. Formatting changes are limited solely to changing the body and endnote text font, style, and size. You cannot underline, italicize, or bold text in the Notes field.

To access the format choices for Notes, follow these steps:

1. Open the Notes screen for the person whose notes you want to work with.

2. From the Format menu, click Text Font, Style, and Size.

3. Read the warning that Family Tree Maker displays regarding formatting changes to notes and click OK.

4. The Text Font, Style, and Size for Notes dialog box will open. In the Items to Format box, click Endnote Body & Text.

5. From the pull-down lists to the right, select the font, style, and font size you want.

6. Click OK to apply the changes. (Don't panic when you don't see the changes on-screen. The Notes format changes only affect the printed version.)

USING FIND, FIND AND REPLACE, AND SPELL CHECK

The Find, Find and Replace, and Spell Check features are enabled for More About Notes. You can use the Find feature, as shown in these steps, to search your notes for certain words or phrases:

1. Open the Notes screen for the person whose notes you want to search.

2. From the Edit menu, choose Find.

3. In the Find dialog box, enter the text you want to find in the Find What field.

4. Click the Find Next button. When a match is found, it will be shown as highlighted text within the Notes field.

5. If you want to find more instances of the text you specified, click the Find Next button again to locate the next match.

NOTE *If the cursor is not at the beginning of the text when you tell Family Tree Maker to search, it will go to the end of the text and then indicate that it has reached the end of the note. At that point, you can have Family Tree Maker either continue searching at the beginning of the text or end the search.*

You can use the Find and Replace dialog box (shown in Figure 8.10) to search for text, replacing it with alternative text that you specify.

To use the Find and Replace command in More About Notes, follow these steps:

1. Open the Notes screen for the person whose notes you want to search.

2. From the Edit menu, choose Find and Replace.

3. In the Find and Replace dialog box, enter the text you want to find in the Find field.

4. In the Replace With field, enter the text that you want to substitute for the existing text.

5. You can replace all instances of the text by clicking the Replace All button, or you can conduct an item-by-item replacement by clicking the Replace button. Once you replace one instance of text, Family Tree Maker will look for more. If you want to continue searching, click Find Next. If you are finished, click the Close button.

Figure 8.10

The Find and Replace command allows you to quickly replace text within your notes and other text in Family Tree Maker. Don't forget to spell-check your text before printing!

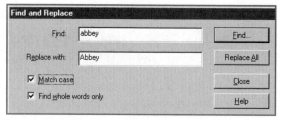

Use the Spell Check feature to catch words with questionable spelling. When Spell Check finds such words, it offers you suggestions for replacements. I highly recommend that you spell-check your text before printing your family history book! To spell-check More About Notes, follow these steps:

1. Open the Notes screen for the person whose notes you want to spell-check.

2. From the Edit menu, choose Spell Check Note.

   The Spell Check dialog box opens, and the spell-check commences.

3. Family Tree Maker looks at your text and alerts you to possible problems. If it finds text that is suspicious, the program highlights the text and waits for you to select Ignore, Change, Add, or Close.

PRINTING MORE ABOUT NOTES

When you finish entering text to More About Notes, you might want to print the notes for proofreading or to save in a work-in-progress file. You can print More About Notes singly or in batches.

Follow these steps to print an individual's More About Notes:

1. Open the Notes screen for the person whose notes you want to search.

2. From the File menu, select Print Notes.

   The Print More About Individual dialog box opens.

3. Click All or specify a page range for your notes. If the other information in the Print dialog box is correct, click OK.

If you want to print the notes for more than one person, use the Batch Print Notes function. You can select multiple individuals whose notes you want printed. To use the Batch Print Notes command, follow these steps:

1. Open the Notes screen for one of the people whose notes you want to print.

2. From the File menu, select Batch Print Notes.

3. From the Available Individuals list on the left side, select the individuals for whom you want notes printed.

4. Click one of the buttons in the center of the dialog box to add the individual, all individuals, all descendants, or all ancestors of that individual to the list of individuals included for batch printing.

5. When each one that you want is included, click OK.

Including Text in New Text Items

Although similar to the Notes feature, New Text is more powerful in that you can include objects from the Scrapbook, format the text with more detail, and even insert page breaks to create separate pages within the text item.

New Text items are created in the Book section of Family Tree Maker. The Book section is where you actually put together the pieces that create a family history book. I discuss the Book section in detail in Chapter 9, "Creating Your Family History Book."

New Text is one of the options you can select from the Add Text Item dialog box, which appears after you click the Text Item entry on the left side of the Book screen, as shown in Figure 8.11. Note that you can create New Text items only from within the Book screen; they are not available elsewhere in Family Tree Maker.

To open or create a book for an individual, follow these steps:

1. In Family Tree Maker, open the Family Page showing the individual who is the focus of the book.

2. From the toolbar, click the Publishing Center button (the fourth button from the left).

3. On the Publishing Center screen, click Create a Family Book if you are beginning a book for the first time; click Edit Your Book if you are opening a book you have already created.

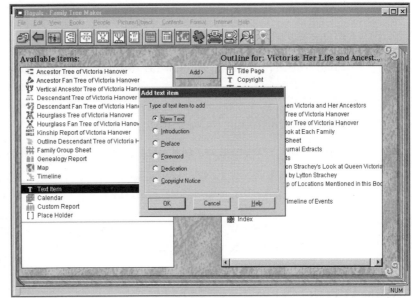

Figure 8.11

One of the text items you can create within the Book feature is New Text. You can use that feature to create whatever you want, from entire chapters of your own text, to just a few pages of notes and comments.

Alternatively, from the Book menu, click New Book, Open Book, or Delete Book, depending on your needs.

4. If you are creating a book for the first time, you will need to enter a book title and an author's name. You can change this information later if necessary. If you are opening an existing book, the Open Book dialog box will display all available books for that Family File. Select the one you want and click OK to open that book.

CREATING NEW TEXT ITEMS

Entering text in the New Text screen is similar to doing so in the More About Notes screen—you can either type the text yourself or copy and paste the text from another program (refer to the earlier section "Pasting Text from Another Document" for more information about copying and pasting text).

To create a New Text item and enter text, follow these steps:

1. Open the book for which you want to create New Text items.

2. From the Available Items list on the left, double-click Text Item.

   The New Text dialog box opens.

3. Click the New Text radio button.

   The empty text item is now added to the Outline list on the right.

4. Double-click the item you just added or click the new item once and click the Edit button in the middle of the screen.

5. Insert the cursor where you want to place text and begin typing (or paste the text you copied from another source).

FORMATTING NEW TEXT ITEMS

Formatting New Text items is similar to formatting More About Notes, but a bit more flexible—you can select the font, size, and style for all the text or for just highlighted portions. From the Format menu, you can choose a font, select the size you want, and select plain, bold, italic, underline, or superscript styles. In addition, you can format paragraphs in the following manner:

* **Left-aligned.** The text is aligned flush to the left side of the page (in the traditional manner). Left-alignment is useful for the body of the text.

* **Centered.** The text is centered in the middle of the page. You will find centered text especially useful for headings and titles.

* **Right-aligned.** The text is aligned flush to the right side of the page. You might right-align captions or special text that you want to emphasize.

* **Fully justified.** The text is arranged with perfect edges (stretching from left to right margins) on either side by adjusting the spacing between words. Justified text can look pleasing, but large quantities

of it are difficult to read. I suggest saving this format for text that you want to stand out rather than using it for the body of your document.

To format text in a New Text item, simply highlight the text you want to edit and from the Format menu, select the font, size, style, or alignment you want to apply.

EDITING NEW TEXT ITEMS

The editing features for New Text items are similar to those for Notes. From the Edit menu, you can undo and redo your last command; cut, copy, and paste text; spell-check the text; use the Find and Replace text command; and insert a page break.

A *page break* indicates where one page ends and another one begins. Family Tree Maker indicates page breaks by using a dotted line; if you find that your text runs over the line or that a picture breaks across pages, you can insert a manual page break before the text or picture begins, forcing it to begin on a new page.

> ❧ **NOTE** ❧ *The page breaks you insert appear as solid black lines, making it clear which breaks you inserted and which were inserted by the program.*

Follow these steps to insert a page break in a New Text item:

1. In the New Text item, insert the cursor where you want the page break to occur.

2. From the Edit menu, click Insert Page Break.

   All text after the cursor is then placed on the next page.

ADDING PICTURES TO NEW TEXT ITEMS

One of the fun things you can do with a New Text item is to add pictures from an individual or marriage Scrapbook (unfortunately, you cannot add nongraphical objects such as tables or OLE objects). After you open the Picture menu, you can view your options, as follows:

- ⚡ Insert from Scrapbook
- ⚡ Size Picture
- ⚡ Delete Picture
- ⚡ Display Caption with Picture
- ⚡ More About
- ⚡ Caption Text Style

Insert from Scrapbook

Select Insert from Scrapbook under the Picture menu to display all the individuals and marriages that have Scrapbooks attached to them. Select the individual for whom you want to include a Scrapbook item in your New Text item and then sort through a list of the pictures that are available from the Insert Scrapbook Picture dialog box, as shown in Figure 8.12. You are not limited to just one picture; you can have as many pictures in your text as you have room for in the New Text item.

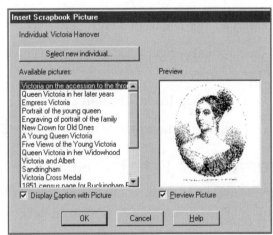

Figure 8.12

Pictures can enhance a text document greatly by adding visual variety and clarity to descriptive passages.

To insert a picture from the Scrapbook into a New Text item, follow these steps:

1. In the New Text item, insert the cursor where you want to place the picture.

2. From the Picture menu, click Insert from Scrapbook (or click the Picture button on the toolbar).

3. In the Individuals with Scrapbook Pictures dialog box, click the person for whom you want to include a picture.

4. In the Insert Scrapbook Picture dialog box, select the picture you want included in the text item.

5. Click OK.

The picture is then placed in the text.

❋**TIP**❋ *Once a picture is added to a text item, you can manipulate it by means of the Picture menu. Commands include sizing the picture, deleting the picture, displaying the caption, displaying the More About information for that picture, and altering the Caption Text Style. For more information about picture options, see the following sections.*

Size Picture

Select Size Picture to change the width (and correspondingly, the height) of a picture. Up and down arrows allow you to change the width by increments of .10 inches at a time.

To size a picture in a New Text item, follow these steps:

1. In the New Text item, click the picture you want to manipulate.

2. Open the Picture menu and click Size Picture (or right-click the picture and select Size Picture from the menu displayed).

3. Using the up and down arrows, scroll the picture width to the size you desire.

Delete Picture

If you want to delete a picture you added to a New Text item, you can easily do so using the Delete Picture command. Here's how:

1. In the New Text item, click the picture you want to delete.

2. From the Picture menu, click Delete Picture.

   Alternatively, you can right-click the picture and select Delete Picture from the menu that appears, or you can click the picture and press the Delete key.

Display Caption with Picture

If you read Chapter 7, you probably remember a discussion about why it is important to enter as much information as possible about pictures in a Scrapbook. Here's one example of this point at work: If you've entered a descriptive caption, you can display it with the picture in the New Text item. To display a caption with a picture in a New Text item, follow these steps:

1. In the New Text item, click the picture whose caption you want to display.

2. From the Picture menu, click Display Caption with Picture.

   Alternatively, you can right-click the picture and select Display Caption with Picture from the menu that appears.

More About

Don't worry if you haven't entered information about a picture in the Scrapbook. By clicking the More About command in the Picture menu, you can enter the information from the New Text screen. Be sure to be as descriptive and detailed as possible!

Follow these steps to add More About information for a picture in a New Text item:

1. In the New Text item, click the picture for which you want to add information.

2. Open the Picture menu and click More About (or right-click the picture and select More About from the menu that appears).

3. Make whatever changes you desire in the More About screen and click OK.

Caption Text Style

You can change the font, size, style, and alignment for the picture caption using this feature. As with other text, you should experiment first to find out what works best within the New Text item.

To change the caption text style for a picture in a New Text item, follow these steps:

1. In the New Text item, click the picture whose caption you want to format.

2. Open the Picture menu and click Caption Text Style (or right-click the picture and select Caption Text Style from the menu that appears).

3. In the Text Font, Style, and Size for Text Items dialog box, make your text style selections and click OK.

PRINTING NEW TEXT ITEMS

As with Notes, you can print your text item if you want to proofread it or save a hard copy. Unlike More About Notes, you cannot batch-print New Text items—each must be printed individually.

To print a New Text item, follow these steps:

1. Open the New Text item you want to print.

2. Open the File menu and click Print.

   The Print Text Item dialog box opens.

3. Select the page range you want to print (All or a specific range). If the printer settings are correct, click OK. If they are not, make the changes you desire and click OK.

CHAPTER NINE

Creating Your
Family History Book

Writing is easy. All you do is stare at a blank sheet of
paper until drops of blood form on your forehead.

—Gene Fowler

 n previous chapters you examined the many tools and skills you
need to build your family history book, but you haven't taken a
close look at the actual mechanics of creating a book in Family Tree
Maker. The Family Book feature is how all the components—
notes, trees, charts, and data—are pulled together to create a book.

This chapter addresses how to gather all these bits and pieces to make a cohesive book. You'll find out how to use the Book Outline feature to order book items, how to edit book item properties, and how to add custom text items. You'll also look at a sample project to understand how to arrange book elements in a coherent and meaningful fashion.

Using the Book Feature

The Publishing Center is where your journey to creating a family history book begins. It acts as a central point for features that present your family history data and allow you to share it with others—whether with a personal home page or a family history book. To access the Publishing Center, click the Publishing Center icon on the toolbar or open the View menu and select Publishing Center.

Once you are in the Publishing Center, you have three options related to a family history book:

❊ You can create a new book.

❊ You can edit an existing book.

❊ You can publish a book to a Web page.

The first two options are discussed in this chapter; the last option is discussed in Chapter Ten, "Printing and Publishing Your Family History Book."

As you know from previous chapters, you can add a number of items to your family history book—trees and reports, charts, calendars, pictures, and text to give a book a well-rounded feeling. The Book feature of Family Tree Maker allows you to access all those items, manipulate them to your satisfaction, and arrange them in a manner that meets your needs.

Creating a New Book

Now that you have entered your data, thought long and hard about what type of family history book you want to create, and familiarized yourself with the various trees, reports, charts, and other items Family Tree Maker allows you to include in a book, you are ready to create a book. To create a new book, do the following:

1. Open the Family Page that includes the individual you want as the primary individual in the book.

2. Click the name of the individual for whom you want to create a book.

3. Click the Publishing Center icon on the toolbar (or open the View menu and select Publishing Center).

4. Click Create a Family Book.

5. In the New Book dialog box (see Figure 9.1), enter a title for the book, the author's name, and click OK

> ❧ **NOTE** ❧ *Although you are required to enter a book title and author now, you can change it later if need be. In any case, be sure to use a title that describes your book accurately, without being too lengthy. If you want to change your book's title later, you can do so anytime from the Book View by going to the Books menu and selecting Book Properties. The Book Properties dialog box opens, allowing you to change the book's title and author, as well as the starting page number.*

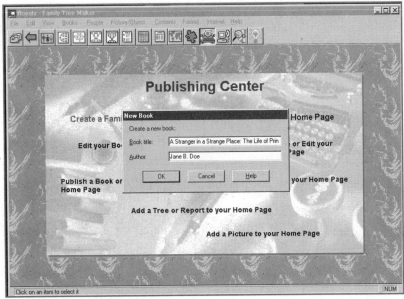

Figure 9.1

Don't worry if you don't like your book's title—you can change it later if the focus of the book changes or if you want a more descriptive title.

Exploring the Book View

After you create a new book, you are taken to the Book View. This is the book headquarters, where you will put together the family history book you've been planning. Figure 9.2 shows the components of the Book View screen.

On the left side, you see a heading titled Available Items. These are the trees, reports, charts, and other items that you can include in your book. Notice that they all focus on the same person—the primary individual.

The Available Items are divided into three categories:

🎄 Standard book items, such as trees and reports, that apply to the primary individual

🎄 Nonstandard book items, such as text, calendars, and Custom Reports.

🎄 Saved View items (if you have created them; if you have no Saved View items, you will only see the first two categories)

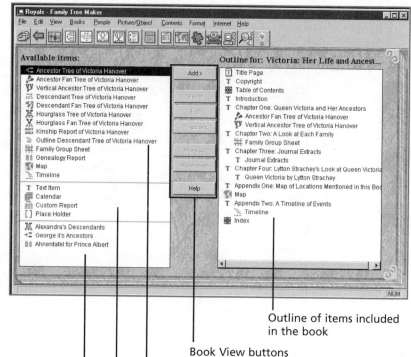

Figure 9.2

The Book View is where you find all the components necessary to create your family history book.

Outline of items included in the book

Book View buttons

List of standard items available to be included

List of nonstandard items available to be included

List of Saved View items available to be included

❧ NOTE ❧   *A Saved View item is one that is not standard—for example, a custom report like a bibliography—that you create and customize. Any one of the custom reports is considered a Saved View item, as are trees or reports that you reformat or customize. Additionally, if you want to include trees and charts for someone other than the primary individual, you can do so by creating a Saved View and including it in the book (you will find more information on Saved Views later in this chapter).*

Saved View Available Items are not available until you create a Saved View item. After you create one, the item displays below the nonstandard Available Items, as shown in Figure 9.2.

You have many standard book items from which to choose:

- Ancestor Tree
- Fan Tree
- Vertical Ancestor Tree
- Descendant Tree
- Descendant Fan Tree
- Hourglass Tree
- Hourglass Fan Tree
- Kinship Report
- Outline Descendant Tree
- Family Group Sheet
- Genealogy Report
- Map
- Timeline

You also have several text and other standard available items to work with:

- Text Item (explained later in this chapter)
- Calendar
- Custom Report (explained later in this chapter)
- Place Holder (explained later in this chapter)

The middle of the Book screen is devoted to these buttons, which enable you to manipulate the items you choose to include in your book:

- **Add.** This button enables you to add the selected item highlighted in the Available Items list to your Outline. The item is added at the end of the list of standard and nonstandard items, but before the index (Family Tree Maker always places the index last).

- **Delete.** You can delete an item from your Outline if you desire. Deleting a standard item from the Outline makes it available once again in the Available Items column.

- **Edit.** This function enables you to edit an item in the Outline. There you can change the formatting, content options, or other options available to the item.

- **Properties.** Here you can give the item a new title, select it to begin a new chapter, specify that it start on an odd-numbered page, or include a header and footer.

❈ **Move Up and Move Down.** These buttons let you move the items in the Outline up or down one step. Using these buttons, you can rearrange the items in the Outline to suit your needs.

❈ **Help.** Click this function to access the Family Tree Maker Help file.

When you are in the Book view, you can also access all the functions in the Books menu, where you can select from the following functions:

❈ **New.** Create a new book. You are asked for the book title and author. The book's primary individual is the primary individual of the book that was open when you accessed the Books menu.

❈ **Open.** Open an existing book. The Available Books box displays all books you created for individuals in your Family File.

❈ **Delete.** Delete a book. The Available Books box displays all the books available.

❈ **Book Properties.** This function enables you to select the title of the book, the author's name, the starting page number, and whether you want the *front matter* (that is, the Table of Contents and preceding items) to use Roman numerals rather than Arabic numerals, as I select to do in Figure 9.3.

❈ **Book Header and Footer.** This function allows you to change the header and footer for the book.

Figure 9.3

You can change certain properties related to your book using the Book Properties command, as well as note the number of pages in the book, the date of the book's creation, and the date of the last edit.

Book Properties

Book title: Victoria: Her Life and Ancestors

Author: Marthe Arends

Number of pages: 42 (approximate)

Date created: May 03, 2000

Date of last edit: August 25, 2000

Page Numbers

Starting number: 1

☑ Use Roman numerals for Table of Contents and preceding items.

[OK]   [Cancel]   [Help]

The following commands can also be issued from the Books menu, but you must select an item from the Available Items list or the Outline first:

- ❋ **Add New Book Item.** This command adds the selected item to the book Outline.

- ❋ **Edit Book Item.** This command allows you to edit the items in the book Outline. It acts the same as the Edit button in the Book View.

- ❋ **Book Item Properties.** This command allows you to change an Outline item's properties; it is the same as the Properties button in the Book View.

- ❋ **Close Book Item.** This command edits the book item mode.

Adding Text Items to Your Family History Book

Family Tree Maker supports eight text items—Introduction, Preface, Foreword, Dedication, Copyright Notice, Text Objects, Table of Contents, and Index—that are intended to be used solely in a family history book. For that reason, with the exception of the last two items, they are completely customizable—that is, because your family history book is different from anyone else's, you can customize the text items to fit your needs and reflect the spirit of your book.

Because these text items are intended only for a family history book, they are not found with other reports; instead, you access them via the Book feature. The custom text items provide you with a way to create introductory material, or front matter, for your family history book. You do not need to include all the items available—you can pick and choose the ones you want for your project.

You have many factors to weigh when considering whether a custom text item is suitable for your family history book project. On one hand, using text items provides a traditional means of introducing or prefacing your book; furthermore, front matter offers you the chance to thank those individuals and groups who have helped you write your book. On the other hand, too much material at the beginning of the book or front matter that rambles from the book's focus or discusses subjects not included in the book does more harm than good. You'll need to consider these issues when deciding the type of text items to include.

⁂ TIP ⁂ *If you are confused about where, when, and how to use front matter in a book, consult the acclaimed* The Chicago Manual of Style *(I use the 14th Edition, published in 1993). This book goes into great detail about the proper way to present, number, and include front matter as well as a host of other useful information.*

Creating an Introduction

An *introduction* can be lengthy or short, but in general, it is a piece that introduces the material in the book. You might want to include your reasons for writing the book, background on your research, information about the family, and so on in an introduction. Figure 9.4 shows an example of an introduction.

⁂ NOTE ⁂ *Notice that in Figure 9.4 a graphic is included in the introduction. Refer to Chapter Seven, "Using Graphics in Your Family History Book," for more on adding graphics to text items.*

To create an introduction, do the following:

1. After you open the book for which you want to create an introduction, double-click Text Item in the Available Items column.

Figure 9.4

An introduction can consist of whatever text you desire, but it should introduce the material you are presenting in the book.

Introduction

Victoria: Her Life and Ancestors is intended to provide readers with a better understanding of the ancestors and descendants of the woman who gave her name to an age--Alexandrina Victoria, Queen of England and Empress of India.

2. In the Text Item dialog box, click Introduction.

   The Introduction is now added to the Outline on the right side.

3. To edit the Introduction—whether to add text or change existing text—click Introduction in the Outline and click the Edit button (or double-click the item or right-click it and select Edit Book Item from the pop-up menu).

4. When you finish editing the Introduction, open the File menu and choose Save (or click the Save button, the first button on the left on the toolbar). Then open the File menu and choose Close to return to the Book View.

Creating a Preface

A *preface* is another type of introductory text. Generally, it is smaller than an introduction and might contain introductory remarks from the author. In a preface for one book I wrote, I thanked individuals who had helped me with the book and acknowledged the societies or agencies that provided information.

To create a preface, follow these steps:

1. After you open the book for which you want to create a preface, double-click Text Item in the Available Items column.

2. In the Text Item dialog box, click Preface.

   The Preface is now added to the Outline on the right side.

3. To edit the Preface—either to create new text or to change existing text—click Preface in the Outline and then click the Edit button (or double-click the item or right-click it and select Edit Book Item from the pop-up menu).

4. When you finish editing the Preface, open the File menu and choose Save. Then open the File menu and choose Close to return to the Book View.

Whether you include a preface is up to you. Some people feel that an introduction alone provides them with the space to make all the acknowledgments and explanations they want. Others like to use the various front-matter elements to present information in an ordered manner—that is, an introduction that explains the history of the author's research, a preface to acknowledge individuals and societies, a foreword written by a family expert, and so on.

If you are unsure whether you need to include any of the front matter material in your book, take the time to consult other family histories. Do they have an introduction? Preface? Foreword? What sorts of things are mentioned in each? How will such items benefit your book?

Creating a Foreword

A *foreword* is yet another type of prefatory text, usually written by someone other than the author. For example, you might have a foreword written by a noted scholar, another author, or an expert in a field related to your family history book. To create a foreword, follow these steps:

1. After you open the book for which you want to create a foreword, double-click Text Item in the Available Items column.

2. In the Text Item dialog box, click Foreword.

   The Foreword is now added to the Outline on the right side.

3. To edit the Foreword, click Foreword in the Outline and then click the Edit button (or double-click the item or right-click it and select Edit Book Item from the pop-up menu).

4. When you finish editing the Foreword, open the File menu and choose Save. Then open the File menu and choose Close to return to the Book View.

   ❧ **NOTE** ❧ *A foreword should not contain text that you have obtained without permission, such as an extract from an out-of-print family history. Forewords should be written about the book you are presenting, the family in general, or you. If you want to include work from another book (and be sure to read the section about copyrights in Chapter Two, "Organizing Your Family History Book"), include it elsewhere, not in the front matter.*

❊ **TIP** ❊ *While Family Tree Maker will not let you arrange "chapters" as such, it will let you set them up by means of the Property button. To create a chapter in your book, follow these steps:*

1. *Add the items you want to make up the chapter to the Outline.*

2. *From the Outline column, select the item you want to start the chapter and click the Properties button.*

3. *In the Properties dialog box, check the box next to This Item Begins a Chapter and click OK.*

4. *If you have more items you want to include in the chapter, select them, click the Properties button, and deselect the box next to This Item Begins a Chapter (the item will not start the chapter, but will be a part of it).*

5. *Repeat until you have all the items you want together in your chapter.*

Creating a Dedication and Copyright Notice

A *dedication* is usually a brief bit of text, usually only a name and a short message in which you offer a tribute to a person (or more than one person) to whom you want to dedicate the book. You can make your dedication as long or as short as you like, but you don't use it to name every individual who helped you with your research or writing. If you're in doubt as to how a dedication is written, consult a favorite book. To create a dedication, follow these steps:

1. After you open the book for which you want to create a dedication, double-click Text Item in the Available Items column.

2. In the Text Item dialog box, click Dedication.

   The Dedication is now added to the Outline on the right side.

3. To edit the Dedication, click Dedication in the Outline and then click the Edit button (or double-click the item or right-click it and select Edit Book Item from the pop-up menu).

   When you finish editing the Dedication, open the File menu and choose Save. Then open the File menu and choose Close to return to the Book View.

To create a copyright notice, follow these steps:

1. After you open the book for which you want to create a copyright notice, double-click Text Item in the Available Items column.

2. In the Text Item dialog box, click Copyright Notice.

    The Copyright Notice is now added to the Outline on the right side.

3. To edit the Copyright Notice, click Copyright Notice in the Outline and then click the Edit button (or double-click the item or right-click it and select Edit Book Item from the pop-up menu).

4. When you finish editing the Copyright Notice, open the File menu and choose Save. Then open the File menu and choose Close to return to the Book View.

The copyright notice, which is automatically generated by Family Tree Maker, says "Copyright 2000 [or whatever year it is] *Your Name* All rights reserved." You can, however, edit this text to say whatever you would like it to say. But because the Family Tree Maker copyright notice is traditional, you don't need to change it unless you have a specific reason to do so. With recent changes in copyright laws, you no longer need to have a copyright notice to claim copyright on a work; however, it is traditional to include one. If you choose not to include one, you still retain the copyright to the book.

Creating New Text Items

The last item that Family Tree Maker classifies under custom text items is *New Text*. This item can be compared to a blank sheet of paper, waiting for you to fill it up with whatever text you desire. You can use New Text to include abstracts, extracts, analyses, lists, or just about any other type of text you can imagine. I have seen people use the New Text item to include census extracts, probate abstracts, descriptions of locations, clips from (public domain) local histories, arguments about conflicting evidences, lengthy biographical passages, comments from contributors, a list of contributing individuals, analysis over prior research, and so on. I like to use New Text items to create brief introductions to each chapter in the book—the introductions explain the reports or charts that are in the chapter, the generations that are included, and any other information I want the readers to have before they dip into the chapter.

To create a New Text item, follow these steps:

1. After you open the book for which you want to create a New Text item, double-click Text Item in the Available Items column.

2. In the Text Item dialog box, click New Text.

   The New Text item is now added to the Outline on the right side.

3. To edit the New Text item, click New Text in the Outline and then click the Edit button (or double-click the item, or right-click it and select Edit Book Item from the pop-up menu).

4. When you finish editing the New Text item, open the File menu and choose Save. Then open the File menu and choose Close to return to the Book View.

You can include any type of text in a New Text item—you are limited only by your creativity. Refer to Chapter Eight, "Adding Text to Your Family History Book," for an extensive discussion on including text items in your family history book.

Format Options for Text Items

Unlike the trees, reports, and charts discussed in the previous chapters, a limited number of formatting choices are available for the custom text items just discussed, and no contents options are available. Along with the traditional editing commands (Copy, Paste, Cut, and so on), you can spell-check your text item, find and replace text, and insert a page break. You can format your text by selecting font, font size, font style, and alignment (left-aligned, centered, right-aligned, or fully justified). If you want to include an object from a Scrapbook, such as an individual's photo, you can size the photo, include a caption, and format the caption text, as well as view the More About information connected with that object. If you need more information about the format options for text items, see Chapter Eight.

Adding Standard Items to Your Family History Book

Adding those items classed by Family Tree Maker as standard items to your family history book is as simple as two clicks of your mouse—literally! Using the buttons in the middle of the Book View (Add, Delete, Edit, Properties, and Move Up and Down), you can easily add as many or as few items from the list in the Available Items column as you think will benefit your book.

To add a standard item to your book, follow these steps:

1. In the Book View, look under Available Items and click the item you want to add to your book.

2. Click the Add button.

   An icon representing that item is now placed in the Outline column.

3. If you want to move the item to another spot in your Outline, use the Move Up or Move Down button to place the item to a different spot in the Outline.

4. If you want to edit the item, click the Edit button.

   This step takes you to the item's edit screen (which should be familiar if you've examined all the trees, reports, and charts in Family Tree Maker).

5. If you want to give the item a new title, click the Properties button and change the item's title in the Properties dialog box.

Creating an Index

Family Tree Maker automatically indexes all individuals found in the reports, trees, and other items you include in your family history book using the Book feature. Family Tree Maker also updates your index each time you add a new item to the list of items contained in your book and keeps track of page numbers as they change.

To create an index, follow these steps:

1. After you open the book for which you want to create an index, double-click Index in the Available Items column.

   The Index icon is moved from the Available Items column to the Outline column, indicating that you added the Index to the book.

2. To edit the Index—change the Index options, title and footnote, or the font used in the Index—click Index in the Outline and then click the Edit button (or double-click the item or right-click it and select Edit Book Item from the pop-up menu).

3. You can select the default title for your Index ("Index of Individuals") or you can create a title of your own. To change the title, from the Outline column, click Index and the Properties button. In the Properties dialog box, you can enter a new title if you choose.

4. When you finish editing the Index, click the Go Back button, the second button from the left on the toolbar, to return to Book View.

5. Family Tree Maker asks you if you want to save the changes you've made. If you want to, click Yes, and you are returned to Book View. If you decide against your changes, click Cancel and no changes will be saved.

   ❧ **NOTE** ❧ *The index is generated only after you start putting your book together using the Book feature.*

Unfortunately, Family Tree Maker enables you to index only individuals, not locations or topics. If you want to include a location index or some other type of index, you must do so manually and insert it using the New Text function.

Formatting the Index

Unlike most other text items, an index is treated as a report, so you have several options and formatting styles you can use to customize an index to your preference. For example, you can specify the number of columns in an index (Figure 9.5 shows an example of a two-column index), the grouping of first names under the same surnames, and so on. You set these preferences in the Options for Book Index dialog box, shown in Figure 9.6.

To change the options for an index, follow these steps:

1. In the Book View, click Index and then the Edit button.

2. In the Edit Index screen, go to the Contents menu and click Options.

3. In the Options for Book Index dialog box, you can select the following options:

   • One Column, Two Columns, or Three Columns

   • Group First Names Under Each Surname

   • Display Index Letters

4. Once you make your choices, click OK to return to the Edit Index screen.

Figure 9.5

With just the click of the mouse, you can automatically create a comprehensive index of individuals for your family history book. Page numbers are updated as you add or delete individuals and items from your book.

Index of Individuals

Prince (Frederick) Christian Charles: 11, 19

(Sophia) Charlotte: 5, 6

Adela: 31

Adeliza of Louvain: 29

King of Belgians Albert I: 30

Duke Albert Victor Christian: 35
Albertin -
Elizabeth of Saxe-Hildburghausen: 5, 6

Earl of Ulster Alexander Patrick Gregers: 32

Tsarina Alexandra Fedorovna "Alix": 30

Princess Alexandra of Denmark "Alix": 11, 16, 30

King of Spain Alfonso XII: 32

Prince Alfred Ernest Albert: 11, 18

Augusta of Saxe-Gotha: 5, 6

Countess Augusta Reuss-Ebersdorf: 5, 6
Baels -
Mary Liliane: 32

Princess Beatrice Mary Victoria: 12, 23, 32

Queen Beatrix of Netherlands: 33

Blanche: 31
Boleyn -
Anne: 33
Bowes-Lyon -
Lady Elizabeth Angela Marguerite: 32
Campbell -
Duke of Argyll John: 12, 20

Caroline: 30

Countess Caroline Erbach-Schonberg: 5, 6

Caroline of Ansbach: 5, 6

Catherine: 30

Figure 9.6

Index options allow you
to specify how you
want the index to
appear. Try out the
options before you
decide which layout
suits you best.

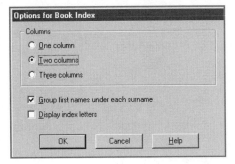

*※TIP※ If numerous individuals will be referenced in your family
history book, you might want to select the two- or three-column layout.
Doing so will cut down on the number of pages in your index. Of
course, avoid making the index unreadable by cramming too many
columns on each page!*

In addition, you can specify the font, size, and style for the following text elements within an index:

- ※ Title
- ※ Index Letters
- ※ First Names
- ※ Surnames

When formatting the text in an index, keep in mind that the text must be readable. Avoid squishing the font size down to accommodate more text per page
(thus shortening the index).

Creating a Table of Contents

Family Tree Maker automatically generates a table of contents for all the items
you include in your family history book using the Book feature. As you add new
items or delete existing ones, the table of contents is automatically updated to
reflect the changes. Figure 9.7 shows an example of a table of contents.

Figure 9.7

A Table of Contents is generated automatically by Family Tree Maker and is updated as you add or delete items.

To create a table of contents, follow these steps:

1. After you open the book for which you want to create a table of contents, double-click the Table of Contents icon in the Available Items column.

    The Table of Contents icon is now moved from the Available Items column to the Outline column, indicating that you added the Table of Contents to the book.

2. To edit the Table of Contents—that is, to change the title and footnote or the font—click Table of Contents in the Outline and then click the Edit button (or double-click the item or right-click it and select Edit Book Item from the pop-up menu).

3. You can select the default title for your Table of Contents ("Table of Contents"). Or you can create a title of your own by clicking the Table of Contents icon, clicking Properties, and entering a new title in the Table of Contents Properties dialog box.

4. When you finish editing the Table of Contents, click the Go Back button to return to the Book View.

5. Family Tree Maker asks if you want to save the changes you've made. If you want to, click Yes, and you return to the Book View. If you decide against your changes, click Cancel, and no changes are saved.

❦ **NOTE** ❦   *A table of contents, also often called a TOC, is generated only after you start putting your book together using the Book feature.*

Formatting the Table of Contents

A table of contents offers few options for formatting. You can, however, select the font, size, and style for the following TOC elements:

- 🏃 Chapters
- 🏃 Normal Items (that is, items included under the heading of a chapter)
- 🏃 Title

To change the format of a table of contents, follow these steps:

1. From the Book View, click the table of contents icon and then click Edit.

2. In the Table of Contents Edit screen, go to the Format menu and select Text Font, Style, and Size.

3. In the Text Font, Style, and Size for Table of Contents dialog box, select the item you want to format (Chapter, Normal Items, Title) and pick the font, style, and size you want from the boxes on the right.

4. When you are happy with your changes, click OK to return to the Table of Contents Edit screen.

Adding Saved View Items to Your Family History Book

As I mentioned earlier in this chapter, a Saved View item is a customized item that you saved using the Save As command—items such as a tree or report that you have formatted and customized. Figure 9.8 shows three Saved View items

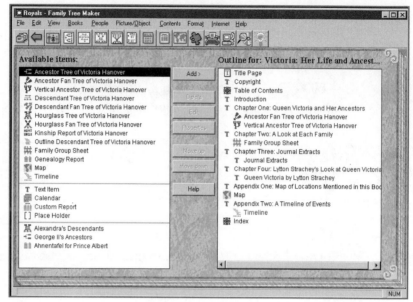

Figure 9.8

New Saved View items are added at the bottom of the Available Items list. In this figure, you see three Saved View items.

at the bottom of the Available Items column. These three items were modified until they no longer fit the original title. I saved each as a New Item, gave them an appropriately descriptive title, and Family Tree Maker automatically included them in the list of Available Items as a Saved View.

To create a Saved View item, follow these steps:

1. Open the item upon which you want to base your Saved View item.

2. Reformat and customize the item as desired.

3. Open the File menu and choose Save *[item name]* As.

4. Enter a new name for the item and click OK.

To open or edit an existing Saved View item, follow these steps:

1. Open the File menu and choose Open Saved View.

2. In the Open Saved View dialog box, select the Saved View you want to open and click Open.

✤ **NOTE** ✤ *If you create more than one book, you might want to include some of the Saved Views you made for other books. Family Tree Maker automatically makes available existing Saved Views to any book you created within that Family File, no matter who the primary individual is. To add a Saved View to your book, simply click the Saved View and the Add button; the item is now added to your book outline.*

Using Place Holders

A time might come when you need to make room in your book for items you have created in other programs. For example, if you have a spreadsheet table of census extracts and you want to maintain the formatting of that table, you might want to print it using the spreadsheet program and manually insert it into the book later. Using the Place Holder function, you can tell Family Tree Maker to allow a specified number of pages to be allotted to that document.

To insert a place holder, follow these steps:

1. From the Book View, select Place Holder from the list of Available Items.

2. Click the Add button.

3. In the Place Holder Properties dialog box (see Figure 9.9), make your selections and click OK.

Figure 9.9

The Place Holder function allows you to accommodate items created outside Family Tree Maker by leaving a place for the documents in your book.

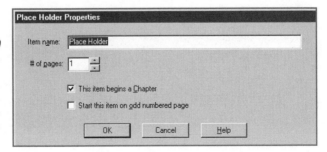

Changing Item Properties

After you include the items you want in your book Outline, you can customize them to meet your needs. For example, you can edit trees, charts, and reports just as you would directly in the tree, chart, or report view (in fact, clicking the Edit button takes you to each item's view, where you can use the Contents and Format menus to make changes). In addition, you can change the properties for each item in the Outline using the Item Properties dialog box (shown in Figure 9.10).

Properties you can change in this dialog box are as follows:

- **Item Name.** This is the title that you give the item. If you have the Title option turned on for the item, this is the title that prints at the top of the page (for more information about titles and footnotes, consult the item's description in Chapter 3, "Using Trees in Your Family History Book"). Be descriptive in your title—*Three Generations of Mary Jones's Ancestors* will give your reader more information than just *Jones's Ancestors*.
- **This Item Begins a Chapter.** If you want the item in question to start a chapter, select this box. Notice in Figure 9.11 that certain items are indented in the Outline column; the indented items are the ones that are *not* marked to begin a chapter.
- **Start This Item on Odd Numbered Page.** If you want to start an item *recto* (that is, on the right page), select this item. According to

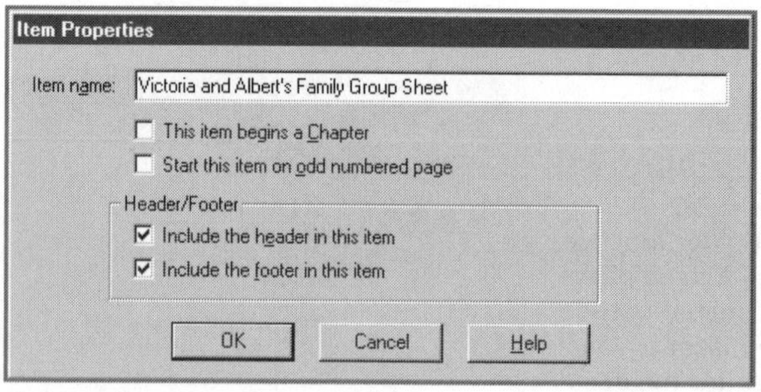

Figure 9.10

You can change a book item's properties using the Properties button in the Book View. The Item Properties dialog box then opens, allowing you to make your changes.

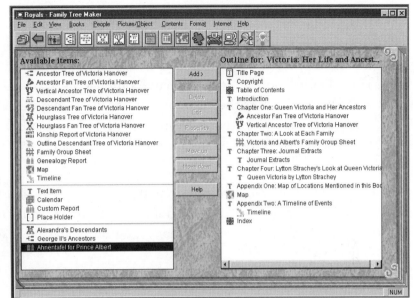

Figure 9.11

Items you select
to begin as
chapters are
aligned to the
left in the
Outline column;
items that make
up chapter
contents are
indented.

The Chicago Manual of Style, chapters can begin either verso (left side) or recto. For a consistent look throughout your book, you can enable this feature so that all the chapters start on the right (odd-numbered) side.

Include Header and/or Footer in This Item. If you want to include the header and/or footer that you specified for an item, here is where you tell Family Tree Maker to do so.

To change an item's properties, follow these steps:

1. Click the item in the Outline whose properties you want to change.

2. Click the Properties button.

   The Properties dialog box opens.

3. Make your selections and click OK.

Arranging Your Book's Outline

The Outline column is where you arrange the items you added in the order you want them to appear in your book. For example, notice in Figure 9.12 that the items in the Outline appear in no particular order. Material that should be at the front of the book—such as the introduction—is in the middle, related trees and charts are not grouped together, a Descendant Tree is in conflict with the stated title of the book, and all the chapter introductions are not placed in front of their chapter material.

To organize this material into an outline that makes sense, you need to gather together all the front matter at the beginning of the book, group the reports and charts together, group the trees together, and group the New Text and nonstandard items together.

To move an item in the Outline, follow these steps:

1. Click to select the item and then click either the Move Up or Move Down button until the item is exactly where you want it (or click the item and without releasing the mouse button, drag it to the place in the Outline where you want it to be).

Figure 9.12

Here is the Outline for a sample book, showing a confusing mishmash of items before they are arranged into a meaningful order.

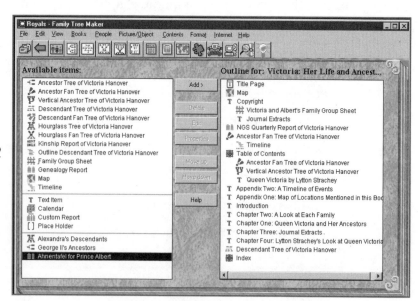

2. Repeat these steps for each item you want to move until the items in your outline are in the correct order.

Figure 9.13 shows the newly ordered Outline.

> ❧ **NOTE** ❧ *You cannot move an item below the index—that is, Family Tree Maker assumes that the Index is the last item you want in your book, so you cannot place anything after it. Should you want to do so, you must print the item separately and add it manually after you print your book.*

Take a close look at the order of the items in my sample book. The book is arranged so that it unfolds information in small, easily digested chunks.

The journey starts with a detailed overview of the primary individual and her ancestors in the form of an NGS Quarterly Report. Following that, I take the readers through each family one at a time via the Family Group Sheets. To facilitate understanding of the material I've just presented, I show the readers graphical versions of Queen Victoria's ancestry using two ancestor-only views (the Fan Ancestor Tree is included only to add interest; it doesn't present information

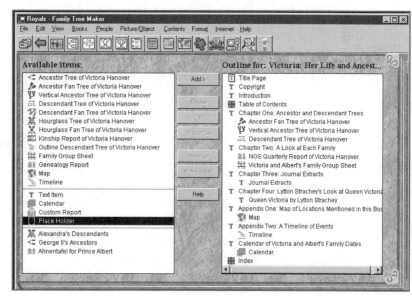

Figure 9.13

Et voilà! The final Outline for my sample book should move readers through the material in a manner that is cohesive and easy to understand.

that is not on the Standard Ancestor Tree). I provide an all-encompassing look at her ancestors and descendants in the Hourglass Tree.

Once I'm sure that my readers have a good grip on the primary individual's ancestry, I move them into a detailed look at Queen Victoria's life using journal extracts and excerpts from a public domain text. To finish, I present maps showing all the locations mentioned in the reports and trees and provide a timeline to ground the readers, giving them an understanding of when events occurred.

Striving for Clarity

When ordering items in your outline, you should not be thinking so much "I must group like items together regardless of their content" as "I want to make this book coherent so that material flows from one chapter to the next." When organizing the material in the Book View Outline, consider your readers and think about what you want them to know first. If you present a Descendant Tree first, will they get enough information from the tree to understand the next bit of information that you present?

One of the basic precepts of fiction writing is to make sure that every scene pushes the plot along in some manner. Writing nonfiction, such as a family history, is really no different. As you present each item, make sure that it furthers your readers' understanding of the material you are presenting. If you have created a family history book about an immigrant ancestor and his descendants, you will probably want to begin the book at the beginning—that is, with the immigrant's parents (if known) or with his birth.

Give the readers the information they need to move to the next chapter, where you can offer information of a different type, go into more detail about something you presented in the prior chapter, or display material covered in a different manner that will benefit reader understanding.

> ❋ **TIP** ❋ *If you have lengthy reports or trees, you might want to use each one as a separate chapter. When planning your book, try to keep the items within each chapter related. For example, you might create a chapter per generation, one family per chapter, one topic per chapter, and so on.*

Another way to make a book coherent, consistent, and professional is to ensure that all the elements in it are formatted in the same way. If you use the same text styles for titles, text body, footnotes, captions, and so on throughout the book, you will end up with a product that is well designed and that won't distract readers with sudden font or style changes.

Of course, you can find exceptions to every rule, and this one is not immune. For example, if you are creating a fun, informal family book, in which you are more interested in amusing the reader than disseminating information, you can go a little wild with the fonts, colors, and styles. For those projects that present a family history in more a conventional manner, however, be sure to check the items you plan to include in the book to make sure that you use consistent formatting.

You have an opportunity to see a variety of specific book projects in Chapter Eleven, "Family History Book Projects." For now, take a quick look at the Outline for a family history book project and notice the book's organization, as shown in Figure 9.14.

The front matter of the book deals specifically with the book's creation: a dedication, a preface from a noted member of a Whitney family association, and an

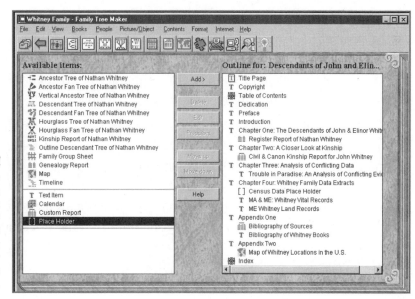

Figure 9.14

This sample book represents a formal family history that focuses on a specific ancestor and his descendants.

introduction detailing the research project and acknowledging people who helped with the research. The other front matter—title page, copyright, and table of contents—are all standard items and should be included in most books. Readers may or may not read the front matter, but it is nice to include at least an introduction giving readers background on your research project.

The first section of the book covers the genealogical information standard in a family history book—the bulk of the information is presented by means of a Register Report, but an additional Kinship Report is included to stress family connections in a database of more than one thousand individuals. Readers should come to this information primed by the introduction, knowing what the book will be about and what sorts of information will be included. The Register Report gives them information in a readable, narrative fashion, and the Kinship Report solidifies the relationships in the readers' minds by offering the information in an easy-to-understand format. Finally, a discussion is provided to guide the reader through the intricacies of conflicting evidences, giving insight into how the author analyzed and used source material. By providing this material, the readers are able to judge the evidence presented.

The second part of the book offers a collection of data from primary resources collected for the individuals in the book. Census abstracts are presented in an easy-to-read table format (printed in a different program and added manually to the book at the time of printing), followed by vital records and land records extracts. By now, your readers have a good understanding of the individuals in the book—in this section, you provide some of the solid facts that add weight to your conclusions and offer proof of your evidence.

The third part of the book provides tools for the readers' benefit—the bibliography shows the resources used in the book and a list of related books, while the map displays all the locations mentioned on the trees and reports found in the book (if you include a legend on the map, it serves as an index of locations). The index ends the book with an alphabetized list of all individuals mentioned in the book (with the exception of anyone found on the document created outside Family Tree Maker).

The History of George Howard Lafferty

George Howard Lafferty was born September 2, 1894 in Lenox township, Ashtabula County, Ohio, to Amber Amelia Wescott Lafferty and George Edwin Lafferty. A sister, Maud Irene, was born May 21, 1892.

A family of farmers, the Laffertys harvested the land where they lived. On May 9, 1919, they moved to Warren, Ohio, to a house on Forest Street NE. They lived next door to their daughter Maud, her husband Jay Rood Webster, and their three beautiful daughters, Reta, Shirley, and Marion.

As a youth, Lafferty went by "Howard" rather than "George" and signed his name as G. Howard Lafferty. After graduating from Lenox Township schools in 1911, he received a Teachers Certificate and became an educator and later a high school Principal. He then switched careers and ventured into banking just before World War I.

As a student at Ohio State University during the war, Howard Lafferty hoped to join the army but was classified 5G due to his glasses and other restrictions. In 1923 he received an L.L. B. degree and passed

Ancestors of George Howard Lafferty

Samuel Lafferty
1801 - 1871

Edwin E. Lafferty
1834 - 1907

Margaret McDowell
1803 - 1861

George E. Lafferty
1867 - 1936

Erastus Fowler
1793 - 1875

Celia Fowler
1914

Temperence Merrill
1796 - 1871

Nathan Wescott
1818 - 1900

Hiram Wescott

Sarah Ann McMichael
1820 - 1901

Samuel C. Amsden
1822 - 1899

Theresa Jerusa Amsden
1845 - 1934

Clarissa Hubbard
1820 - 1870

CHAPTER TEN

Printing and Publishing
Your Family History Book

History is a pattern of timeless moments.
—T. S. Eliot, *Four Quartets*

fter your book is organized the way you want it, the items are formatted and customized to meet your needs, the text is checked for spelling, your sources are cited, and graphics are included in the Scrapbook, you're ready to print a copy of your book. In this chapter, you'll look at the mechanics of printing your book, what to do with it once it's printed, and electronic forms of printing.

❧ **NOTE** ❧ *Many people find that it's easier to edit text on hard copy (a printed copy) than on-screen, so you might want to print a copy with the intention of checking it closely for errors, typos, and other mistakes before printing your final copy.*

Preparing to Print

Before you print your book, you should create and look over a checklist of items to make sure that everything you meant to accomplish with your family history book is indeed accomplished. You might ask yourself the following questions:

- 🏃 Are all events sourced and citations noted?
- 🏃 Did you generate an error-checking report to note problem areas?
- 🏃 Did you run a spell check?
- 🏃 Did you add pictures to the Scrapbook and include full descriptions?
- 🏃 Did you print sample reports to determine the best format and layout?

※ Did you use consistent font and style throughout the book items?

※ Did you add all the components desired in the book to the Outline (in the Book View)?

※ Does the order of items in the Outline lead the reader through a cohesive reading experience?

After you can check off all the items on your checklist, it's time to turn your attention to Family Tree Maker and take a look at the Print Setup dialog box (see Figure 10.1), which you access by going to the main menu and clicking File, Print Setup.

The Print Setup dialog box enables you to configure the following settings.

※ **Default or Specific Printer.** The default printer is designated in your Windows Control Panel and is the printer you normally use when printing. If you want to use a printer other than your default printer, click the Specific Printer button and use the drop-down list to select the printer you want.

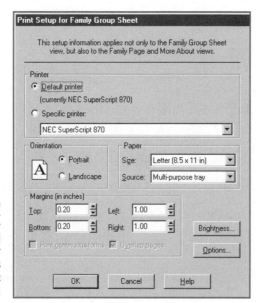

Figure 10.1

You can control how your printer turns out items using the Print Setup dialog box.

❋ **Portrait/Landscape.** This option allows you to choose the orientation of the paper. *Portrait* means the paper prints in the traditional manner (vertically), while *Landscape* indicates the page will print sideways (horizontally).

❋ **Size/Source.** Here you specify whether you want to use a different paper size or get your paper from a source other than the one your printer generally uses.

❋ **Margins.** If you want to change the margins on your paper, you can do so for all four sides (top, bottom, left, and right). If you are binding your book yourself, you might want to leave a larger margin on the left side to allow a certain amount of space for the binding.

❋ **Print Continuous Forms.** If your printer uses continuous forms (like an older dot-matrix printer), this box enables you to set Family Tree Maker to print over the page perforations. Note: If your printer does not support this option, it will not be available.

❋ **Overlap Pages.** If you want the information at the edge of a page to be repeated on the next page, select this function. This option is useful for large wall charts, because overlapping makes it easier for you to line up the pages when assembling them. Note: If your printer does not support this option, it will not be available.

❋ **Brightness.** Click this button to view a dialog box that allows you to control the color level for pictures and objects. If you have particularly dark images to print, you might want to increase the brightness level so that the picture or object does not print so dark.

❋ **Options.** The options you'll see when you click this button depend on your printer. Because of this, the options you find here are not standardized; for example, the options for my laser printer are many—Paper Source, Resolution, Image Controls, Accessories, Toner Usage, Special Effects—and are probably different from the options that are available for your printer.

Printing Your Book

After you have your printer settings the way you like, you're finally ready to print your book! To do so, follow these steps:

1. Go to the Book View for the book you want to print.

2. Go to the main menu and click File, Print Book.

   The Print Book dialog box opens (see Figure 10.2).

3. Select one from among the Page Range options:

   - **All.** Print the entire document.

   - **Selected Item.** Print the selected portion of the document (that is, the portion you clicked and highlighted in the Outline).

   - **Pages (from *x* to *y*).** Print the specified page range.

4. If you have a color printer and want to print your family history book in color, check the Print Color check box. Or if your printer is capable of printing in grayscale, leave this option selected to print colors in corresponding shades of gray.

5. If you want both left and right margins to switch on alternate pages, select the Mirror Margins option. Mirroring margins allows you to have the larger margin on the side of the page that will be bound if you have the book published in back-to-back page format.

6. In the Copies check box, enter the number of copies you want to print.

7. Click OK, and the book begins printing.

Figure 10.2

The Print Book dialog box gives you options for how to print your family history book.

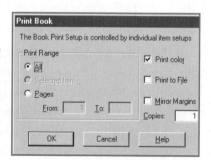

> ❊ **TIP** ❊ *Suppose that your printer is lousy—it won't print in color, and it takes forever. Your neighbor's printer, however, works great. To print your family history book on your neighbor's printer, select the Print to File option in the Print Book dialog box. Doing so saves the book to a file on your hard drive or on a disk, depending on your specifications. Save the file to a disk, and wander next door!*

Family Tree Maker prints according to the printer settings you choose for each individual item. That is, if you select certain margins for a Descendant Tree and different margins for an Ancestor Tree, the two items will print with different margins.

To change printer settings for individual items in your book, follow these steps:

1. Select the item you want to change from the Available Items column in Book View.

2. Click the Edit button.

3. When the item appears, go to the main menu and click File, Print Setup.

4. Make the changes you desire and click OK.

   The setup you changed for that item is then saved.

Publishing Your Book

After you print the book and check it for errors or mistakes, you are probably ready to take your project to the next step—printing it professionally or printing it yourself. You also need to decide whether you want to print the book electronically (that is, on a disk, CD-ROM, or on the Web).

Each type of publishing has its own benefits and drawbacks—the biggest drawback being cost—and choosing a means of publishing suitable for your project and needs is not a decision to take lightly. Before you jump in with both feet, take a moment to consider all your publishing options and to weigh the pros and cons.

Electronic Publishing

Deciding between publishing your book electronically or on paper has come up only recently because of technological advances. Rocket Readers, Web-based family history books, and books on disk or CD-ROM are all viable options for the new author. No matter which avenue of electronic publishing you choose, however, all require one thing—that you publish your book in HTML format on the Family Tree Maker Online Web site.

> ✤ **NOTE** ✤ *HTML (HyperText Markup Language) is the language (also called code) that is used to create World Wide Web (WWW) documents, commonly called Web pages. HTML uses tags and attributes to affect how a Web page appears and can be created by means of a text editor (assuming that you understand how to use code in HTML) or by a specialized HTML editor such as HotDog by Sausage Software (http://www.sausage.com). Many word processors can also now save a document in HTML format. Two helpful books on the subjects of HTML and Web pages are Learn HTML In a Weekend, Revised Edition, and Create Your First Web Page In a Weekend, 3rd Edition, both by Steve Callihan and published by Prima Tech.*

Unfortunately, Family Tree Maker will not allow you to convert your family history book directly into a series of HTML files. In order to obtain HTML files of your book, you must first upload it to the Family Tree Maker Web site. Once your book is in HTML format, however, you can use the HTML code to create a book on disk or CD-ROM that can be read by a Web browser, or you can transfer the HTML code to an electronic reader such as NuvoMedia's Rocket Reader, and voilà! Instant electronic book, complete with graphics.

PUBLISHING YOUR BOOK TO THE INTERNET

To publish your book to the Family Tree Maker's Web site (http://www.familytreemaker.com), you must first create a Web page on the site (for instructions on creating a Web page, see the sidebar titled "Registering a Web Page with Family Tree Maker Online"). This is a free service of Broderbund, but one available only to users of Family Tree Maker. At the time of this writing, Family Tree Maker was allowing users 22MB of space for images and unlimited space for other items.

Registering a Web Page with Family Tree Maker Online

In order to upload your book to the Family Tree Maker Web site, you must first register and create a Web page at the site. If that sounds intimidating, it isn't—Family Tree Maker does most of the work for you, leaving you with just a few basic decisions.

To register a Web page with Family Tree Maker, follow these steps:

1. Open the Family File you want to use to create the Web page.

2. From the toolbar, click the Publishing Center button.

3. In the Publishing Center screen, click Create a Family Home Page.

4. A wizard appears (see Figure 10.3), guiding you through the creation of your Web page.

   The wizard shows you the elements that can make up your Web page (surnames from your family tree, an index of everyone in your tree, biographical information on individuals, and a tree showing all connected individuals). The wizard enables you to choose which family members to include on your Web page and whether to include pictures from the Scrapbook. It also prompts you to hide information on living individuals by using the Privatize function.

   After you make your Web page choices using the wizard, you are reminded that you need to be connected to the Internet before the process can continue.

5. The wizard alerts you that your Web page is being created. Your Web browser is then opened (if it isn't already), and you are taken to your new Web page so that you can select the page style and customize the appearance of your Web page.

For an example of what a Web page at the Family Tree Maker Web site looks like, see Figure 10.4.

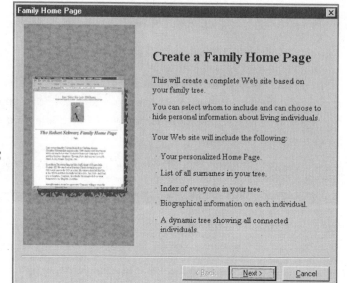

Figure 10.3

The Create a
Family Home
Page wizard
helps you create
your own Web
page at Family
Tree Maker's
Web site.

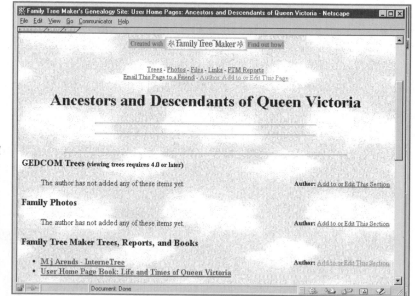

Figure 10.4

Your genealogy
page at Family
Tree Maker
Online gives you
the opportunity
to share your
information with
other interested
researchers.

❋ **TIP** ❋ *If your family history book consists solely of a narrative report (for example, a Register Report or NGS Quarterly Report), you can also create an electronic book by exporting the report in RTF (rich text format) and using a word processor to save the RTF file in HTML or using a program such as RTF-2-HTML by EasyByte Software (http://www.easybyte.com) or Arachnophilia (http://www.arachnoid.com).*

Once your Web page is created at the Family Tree Maker Web site, you can publish your family history book to your Web page (you might have to be a little patient. As Figure 10.5 shows, Family Tree Maker cautions you that adding the book into your Family Tree Maker Web site takes a few minutes).

Some users may want to obtain the HTML code for their family history book, but don't necessarily want to make it available online. In that case, the book must still initially be published to the Family Tree Maker Web site, but after the resulting HTML code has been saved, the online version of the book can be removed from the Web site.

To publish your book to the Internet, follow these steps:

1. Open the Family File that contains the book you want to publish to a Web page.

2. Click the Publishing Center button and in the Publishing Center screen, select Publish Your Book on Your Home Page (or from the Book View, go to the Internet menu and select Publish Book to the Internet).

3. From the Select Book to Upload dialog box, choose the book you want to publish online, as shown in Figure 10.6. Click OK.

Figure 10.5

There is a slight delay between the time you upload your family history book and the time it appears on your Family Tree Maker Web site.

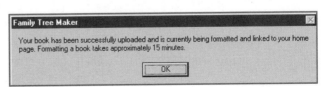

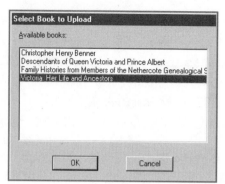

Figure 10.6

You can upload any of your family history books to the Family Tree Maker Web site.

❧ **NOTE** ❧ *Your book must meet certain requirements before it can be published on the Family Tree Maker Web site; namely, your book must include a table of contents and an index. If your book does not include these two items, you are prompted to create them. Family Tree Maker will not upload your book until you do so.*

4. Family Tree Maker displays a box telling you it will prepare your book for publication on your home page. If you want it to do so, click OK.

5. A status bar is displayed while the book is copied to your Web page. While it is working, you are asked if you want to contribute your Family File to the World Family Tree Project. If you want to do so, click Yes. If not, click No.

❧ **NOTE** ❧ *The World Family Tree (WFT) Project, which began in 1995, consists of voluntarily donated Family Files that are placed on CD-ROM and sold to interested users. All individuals who submit WFT files are indexed in the FamilyFinder Index (available online at the Family Tree Maker Web site or on CD-ROM), making it easy for other researchers to locate the individuals being researched. You can submit your family data to the WFT Project for free; however, there is a charge for purchasing the WFT CDs.*

6. After your book is transferred, the title appears on your Family Tree Maker Web site. Click the book's title to view your online book. Figure 10.7 shows an example of the title page for a family history book online, and Figure 10.8 shows an ancestor tree.

❧ **NOTE** ❧ *Your book probably will not appear immediately; in fact, it might be several hours before it appears on your Web page. If you have uploaded your Web page and are waiting with your browser open to see it, you may need to refresh or reload the page to see the changes.*

You might find that some of the text styles in your book items are not duplicated in the online version. Family Tree Maker will try its best to create an identical version of your book, but some stylistic changes might occur. You need to be aware of other limitations too. For one, each tree in your online book is limited to only 2,000 individuals (but you can have a combined total of up to 60,000 individuals in all the trees included in your book). Additionally, your book must contain fewer than 10,000 pages.

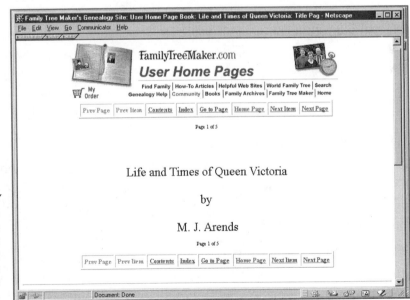

Figure 10.7

Your online family history book can contain the same elements as the version you print.

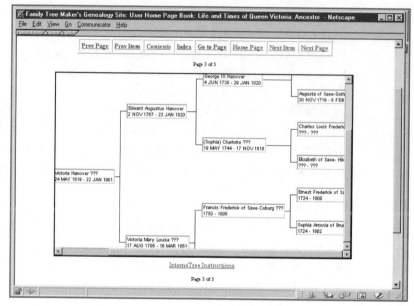

Figure 10.8

When you
upload a book
containing a tree,
it is automatically
translated into
InterneTrees—a
Java applet that
allows visitors to
view box-style
trees on your
Web page.

❧ **NOTE** ❧ *As always, be aware of privacy issues. Remember that the material you are uploading will be freely available to anyone. For this reason, make sure that information in your family history book concerning living individuals is excluded. (When you create a Web page based on your Family File, you are asked if you want to exclude information about living individuals. It's a good idea to accept this option.)*

CONSIDERING E-BOOKS

If you want to publish your book in electronic format (commonly known as an *e-book*), but don't want to make it freely available to everyone as an Internet published book is, consider going with either an electronic publisher or self-publishing your book in electronic format.

With the advent of e-book readers such as Softbook Press, Inc.'s Softbook (http://www.softbook.com) and NuvoMedia's Rocket eBook (http://www. rocket-ebook.com), more and more people are interested in downloading books. By manipulating the files created when you upload your family history book to the Family Tree Maker Web site as previously discussed, you can make your book available in HTML format. For an example of just what HTML looks like, check out Figure 10.9 (but don't be worried if you don't understand it).

HTML-formatted books can be saved on a floppy disk, burned to a CD-ROM, or downloaded directly to a computer or e-book reader. You'll find little to no cost in creating an electronic version of your book, although to view it, you must use a Web browser.

If you want someone else to handle marketing and selling the electronic version of your family history book, you might consider contacting an electronic publisher. For a list of electronic publishers, visit the Association of Electronic Publishers Web site at http://www.welcome.to/AEP.

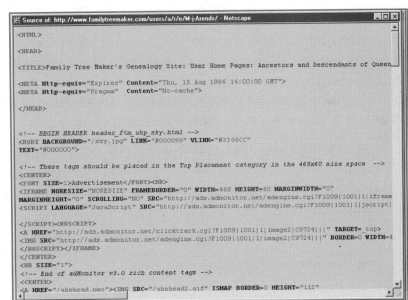

Figure 10.9

You might not be able to understand HTML, but your Web browser loves it!

Print Publishing

If you want to publish your book on paper rather than electronically, you will need to do one of the following:

- ❋ Print and bind it yourself.

- ❋ Contract a printer at a print shop or service bureau to print your book.

- ❋ Utilize the services of a vanity press or print-on-demand publisher.

- ❋ Sell your book idea to a traditional publisher.

> ❋**CAUTION**❋ *Of these options, the last is likely the most difficult—publishers, even those who specialize in genealogical books—are inundated with family histories, and many will not consider them at all.*

A QUICK LOOK AT SELF-PUBLISHING

If you decide to self-publish your book—that is, arrange the printing of the book and market it yourself—you'll want to educate yourself in a number of areas. With regard to family history books, self-publishing is probably the most common choice because it gives you control over how the book will appear, its price, how many copies to create at a time, and so on.

To begin, you need to contact a print shop, copy shop, or printer with the basic information about your book. You will probably want to get an estimate from the shop and compare it to estimates from other print shops in order to find the best deal.

The printer will expect you to provide the following information:

- ❋ The number of pages in your book

- ❋ Whether you will provide *camera-ready* copy (copy that can be printed just as you provide it)

- ❋ Whether you want color in your book

- ❋ The type of paper on which you want the book printed

* How many copies you want printed (initially—you can usually order more as you need them)

* What sort of binding you want (plastic comb, stapled, soft-cover book binding, and so on)

* What you want on the book cover

* Any other special information

> ❋**TIP**❋ *You might be able to save money when having your book printed if you provide the printer with camera-ready copy. With the affordable price of high-quality laser printers, it's now possible to create your own camera-ready pages and save time and money in the production of your book.*

After your book is printed, promoting and marketing your book is up to you (for more on those topics, see Chapter Twelve, "Marketing and Promotion"), so keep price in mind when you negotiate a printing deal. If you decide on several expensive options, you will end up with a lovely book, but one that might be priced beyond the range of most people.

> ❋**TIP**❋ *If you are interested in self-publishing your book, you might want to check out at an excellent guide to the subject, titled The Self-Publishing Manual: How to Write, Print and Sell Your Own Book, by Dan Poynter (Para Publishing). This book gives you great advice on the ins and outs of self-publishing.*

Vanity Presses and Print-on-Demand

A vanity press, also known as a *subsidy press*, has long been one of the standard ways family history books are published. Such publishers accept any book, and for a fee (sometimes quite hefty), they will produce copies of your book. Prices vary depending on the number of pages, pictures, and on the binding, but usually you can expect an outlay of anywhere from a few hundred to a few thousand dollars to create the books. One popular vanity press, Gateway Press, specializes in genealogical books (you can read about Gateway at http://www.GatewayPress.com). As with self-published books, you are left with the responsibility of selling the books.

A recent newcomer to the world of publishing is *print-on-demand;* as book orders are placed, copies of books are printed and sent out. One of the largest print-on-demand publishers, iUniverse (http://www.iuniverse.com), has several publishing programs available, including one intended solely for family history books. Although print-on-demand is less expensive than vanity presses (at the time of this writing, the setup fee was $299), it is much the same as a vanity press—you are still responsible for creating, editing, and marketing your book.

Print-on-demand does offer one bonus over traditional vanity publishers, however. Rather than being left with several cartons of expensive hard-bound books, you can request as few or as many books as you have orders for, thus you have little out-of-pocket cost.

GENEALOGICAL PUBLISHERS

Rarely will a genealogical publisher agree to publish a family history, and I recommend that you not approach one unless you have a unique, highly researched family history that has the potential for a wide audience. Most genealogical publishers, such as the Genealogical Publishing Company (and its affiliate, Clearfield Company), rarely accept family histories.

Generally speaking, interesting a genealogical publisher in your book is not going to be a viable option, and you should consider self-publishing, vanity presses, or print-on-demand technology first.

PART III

Pulling It All Together

CHAPTER ELEVEN

Family History Book Projects

If you would not be forgotten
as soon as you are dead and rotten,
either write things worth reading or
do things worth the writing.

—Benjamin Franklin

y now you should have all the skills needed to plan, organize, and print a family history book. But the phrase "family history book" can be a misleading one. In fact, you can use Family Tree Maker to create more than just a book concerning a specific family. Using the program, you can create fun, informal books such as printed Scrapbooks, books for grandparents or parents, or a biography of a loved one. You can also use Family Tree Maker to create a book based on a project initiated by more than one person; for example, societies can enter member pedigrees and print the results. Local histories revolving around founding fathers or members of an organization or group (such as descendants of the pioneer families who traveled together on a wagon train or of immigrants to a small Canadian town) can also form the basis for a book.

Using blank tree and chart features in conjunction with New Text items, you can even print a book of blank forms to take with you when researching. Portable research books showing missing family information can also be of help to the researcher who doesn't have the energy to tote large files to every library or courthouse.

This chapter reviews a number of family history projects and other book projects. This information is only a starting point. When thinking of the many types of books you can create, you are limited only by your imagination!

> ❧ **NOTE** ❧ *To create most of the fun projects in this chapter, you can use the information that you have already entered into your Family File. If you have not created a Family File yet, refer to Chapter One, "Setting the Stage," to get started. The lists within each project will give you recommendations about additional information to incorporate into your Family File.*

Fun Family Projects

You can create innumerable book projects that are not intended to inform or expound on a family's history. Instead, these books are meant to entertain and amuse. All are quick and easy to create, and all would benefit from the availability of a color printer. These types of books are best duplicated at a photocopy shop and bound by stapler or plastic comb. You can create attractive covers with some heavy card stock and a color printer.

> ❧ **NOTE** ❧ *Photocopy versus print shops—which is best? The answer depends on your needs (see Chapter Ten, "Printing and Publishing Your Family History Book," for a discussion on the various ways you can publish your book). Most photocopy shops will take your camera-ready copy and photocopy and bind it for you. Print shops use a more advanced method to create a book, creating a master image of each page and printing copies from that. Generally speaking, a book that is printed rather than copied has a higher quality, but you will pay a higher price for the end product.*

Project #1: Grandparent Book

This project is meant for a grandparent, featuring his or her grandchildren. Little family data is included; instead, the focus is on pictures, stories, poems, and drawings—all created by the grandchildren.

For this type of book, consider these questions:

> ❧ **Whom should you include in the book?** Consider whether you are in contact with all the grandchildren or only some.

❀ **What sorts of things should you include?** Stories written by the grandchildren, images of paintings and drawings, handmade cards, reminiscences about the grandparent, scanned handprints, poems, and pictures of the grandchildren are all popular suggestions.

❀ **Who will gather the items to be included?** Will each parent be responsible for gathering the material to be scanned or otherwise included, or will you gather it yourself?

Okay, it's time to start. Enter the following information into your Family File.

1. Enter basic information for each child (name, birth date, and birth place).

   ❀ **TIP** ❀ *You will also want to enter each child's parents' and grandparents' information so that you can show how all the grandchildren are related.*

2. Enter as much information in the More About section as you can. This includes basic facts (christening, baptism, Bar or Bat Mitzvah, confirmation, and so on), height and weight at the time of the writing (if you are working with adult grandchildren, they might appreciate your skipping that information), a nickname, and any general notes of important events in the grandchild's life.

3. Open each grandchild's Scrapbook and insert scanned or digitized photos, artwork, and other items. Be sure to describe and date the items to the best of your ability and to include captions and descriptions. For more information on using the Scrapbook, be sure to read Chapter Seven, "Using Graphics in Your Family History Book."

4. Gather any stories, poems, or reminiscences the grandchild has about his grandparent. You might want to conduct a mini–oral history with the grandchild, prompting him to recall his favorite holiday memory about the grandparent, what he likes best about the grandparent, and so on. For hints on adding text, check out Chapter Eight, "Adding Text to Your Family History Book."

5. Pick an easy-to-understand descendant tree to display the family. The Standard Descendant Tree and Fan Descendant Tree are good choices. Be sure you include pictures in the trees, and if you have a color printer, use bright, vibrant colors when formatting the trees. Not sure which tree to use? Read over Chapters Three ("Using Trees in Your Family History Book") and Four ("Using Miscellaneous Trees and Charts in Your Family History Book").

6. Create a book for the grandparent, giving the book a creative title and using your name or the family's name for the author. You can find more information about the process of creating the book in Chapter Nine, "Creating Your Family History Book."

7. Organize the book as shown in the book Outline in Figure 11.1.

In the book represented in Figure 11.1, notice that most of the items are New Text items. The book has a standard title page and introduction and a Fan Ancestor Tree to show the grandmother and her progeny, as well as a calendar to display birth dates and anniversaries, but the rest of the items are New Text.

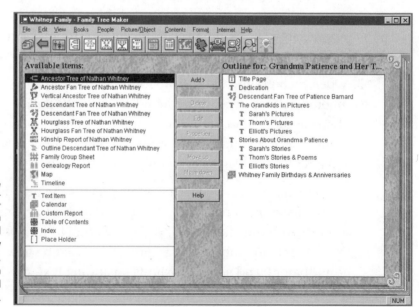

Figure 11.1

A book for a grandparent will likely include very little genealogy, but should use a lot of images and pictures.

In order to include pictures in your book, you must either include them in the tree or chart selected to be part of the book, or you must paste them into a text item like New Text. In this project, I created two chapters ("Pictures" and "Stories"), and gave each child his own New Text page. On one page, I placed graphics from each child's Scrapbook, while on the other, I placed stories and poems that the child wrote about his grandmother.

The various sets of steps in the next section explain how to create a Grandparent book.

SETTING UP THE GRANDPARENT BOOK PROJECT

To set up this project, just follow these steps:

1. Add all the individuals you want in the book to your Family File (see Chapter One for more information about beginning a Family File).

2. Enter information for all the individuals, More About information, and pictures in their Scrapbooks.

3. From the Family File page, choose your primary individual; then from the main menu, click Books, New Book.

4. Give your book a title and fill in the author's name.

ADDING THE FRONT MATTER

To add front matter, just pick up where you left off in the preceding section and follow these steps:

1. From Book View, in the Available Items, double-click Text Item and then click Dedication, OK.

2. Select Dedication from the Outline and click Edit and enter your dedication text.

3. When you finish, from the main menu, click File, Save, Close to return to Book View.

ADDING THE FIRST CHAPTER

To add the first chapter, again just pick up where you left off in the preceding section and follow these steps:

1. From the Available Items, double-click Text Item and then click New Text, OK.

2. From the Outline, click Text Item, Edit and enter your chapter introduction text, if any.

3. From the main menu, click File, Save, Close to return to Book View.

4. Click Text Item, Properties. Title the chapter introduction (in this project, the title is "The Grandkids in Pictures") and click OK.

5. From the Available Items, double-click Text Item and then click New Text, OK.

6. If you have text to enter for this chapter, from the Outline, click Text Item, Edit and enter your chapter text.

7. Place your cursor where you want the first picture inserted. From the main menu, click Picture, Insert from Scrapbook. Select the individual whose Scrapbook you want to access by clicking her name and then click OK. From the Insert Scrapbook Picture dialog box, select the Scrapbook item and click OK.

8. Repeat the process of inserting pictures as many times as needed. When you finish with that item, open the File menu and click Save, Close to return to Book View.

9. Click Text Item, Properties and title the chapter element (in the first element project, the title is "Sarah's Pictures"). Deselect the This Item Begins a Chapter option and click OK.

10. Repeat the process as many times as needed to add Scrapbook items in this chapter.

❧ **NOTE** ❧ *In creating a chapter in this book, notice that one of the first things I did was to use a Text Item as what I call a chapter marker; that is, I used the Text Item to mark the beginning of the chapter. Although you do not have to do this in your family history book, I find it's an easy way to set up chapters.*

The Text Item serves a dual purpose. First, the chapter marker can have a chapter header on it, marking the beginning of a chapter; second, it can contain introduction of or explanation about the contents of that particular chapter. For example, if you have a chapter made up of ancestor trees, you can use the chapter marker to indicate the chapter number and follow it with a brief explanation of how to read an ancestor tree and what sort of information will be found on the trees.

In this chapter's instructions, I often use chapter markers. Rather than waste space repeating the instructions for creating one, just refer to the steps in this section (Steps 1–3) whenever you need to create a chapter marker.

ADDING THE SECOND CHAPTER

Again, continuing from the steps in the preceding section, follow these steps to add the second chapter:

1. Create a chapter marker as you did in the preceding section.

2. Be sure to title the chapter introduction appropriately (in this project, the title is "Stories About Grandma's Patience") and click OK.

3. From the Available Items, double-click Text Item and then click New Text, OK.

4. If you need to enter text in this chapter, from the Outline, click Text Item, Edit. Enter your chapter text, if any, including stories, poems, and reminiscences.

5. When you finish, open the File menu and click Save, Close to return to Book View.

6. Click New Text, Properties. Title the chapter element (in the first element project, the title is "Sarah's Stories"). Deselect the This Item Begins a Chapter Option and click OK.

7. Repeat the process as many times as needed to add additional text to the chapter.

ADDING THE CALENDAR

To add a calendar to your Grandparent book, continue with these steps:

1. From the Available Items, click Calendar, Add.

2. If you want to change the Calendar formatting or content, click Edit.

3. If you want to change the Calendar's title, from the Outline, click Calendar, Properties. Change the title if you desire and click OK.

PRINTING THE BOOK

Finally, you get to print your book! To do so, continue with these steps:

1. From the main menu, click File, Print Book.

2. Select your printing options and click OK.

Project #2: Biography of Ancestor

A *biography* is a book that focuses on the life of one individual. If your target individual is living, you might make her biography a type of memoir, filled with personal reminiscences, oral-history interviews, and so on. If the individual is no longer living, you might create a book to reflect her life and how she touched the lives of others. This example will show the latter—a biography of a deceased grandparent—and is intended for an audience of immediate family members.

For this book, you'll want to consider the following questions:

- 🏃 **Whom should you include in the book?** Because it will be a biography, you might want to keep the focus on the immediate family and include only information about the individual's parents, children, and grandchildren.

- 🏃 **What sort of external (non–Family Tree Maker) items should you include?** Excerpts from journals, letters, diaries, and other writings are particularly effective. Interviews conducted with siblings, children, and grandchildren also make for interesting reading. Pictures are a plus.

- 🏃 **What sort of Family Tree Maker items should you include?** Family Group Sheets detail the families, a descendant tree shows the relationships, a timeline offers an understanding of where the individual's life fell in regard to historic events, and New Text items add interest and a personal look at the individual's life.

With these questions answered, you need to enter everything into your Family File. You'll need to complete these preliminary steps:

1. Enter basic information for each individual to be included in the book. Be sure to include More About information where available.

2. Gather, scan, and add pictures to each individual's Scrapbook. Be sure to enter descriptions and captions.

3. Collect the text you will use in the book: oral histories, transcribed journals, letters, and so on.

4. Plan any introductory text you intend to use in the book. Mention all those who helped you with the project.

5. Pick a descendant tree that you want to use in the book. Print copies of the tree, map, and timeline to make sure the format is satisfactory. If you make changes, save the item as a Saved View for use in the book.

6. Print a copy of the Scrapbook to insert into the book manually after it is printed. Note the number of pages in the Scrapbook (you'll need this for the book's place holder).

7. Create the book for the primary individual (see upcoming steps), giving it a descriptive title and entering the author's name.

8. Organize the book as shown in the book Outline in Figure 11.2.

Once you complete the preliminary work, you are ready to get down to the nitty-gritty of creating the book.

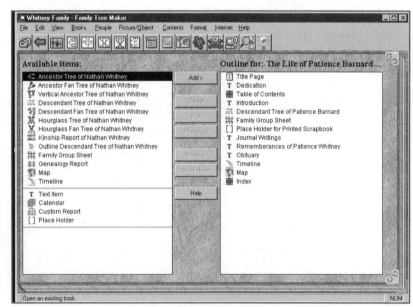

Figure 11.2

When creating a biography, the focus should be on the individual's life rather than on her ancestors or descendants.

Setting Up the Biography of an Ancestor Project

You begin the book as you did in Example #1 (Grandparent's book) by creating a Family File and entering the necessary data, picking the primary individual, selecting a book title, and filling in the author's name.

Adding the Front Matter

After you finish setting up the book, continue with the creation of the front matter as follows:

1. From the Outline, click Title Page, Edit and enter your Title Page information.

2. When you finish, open the File menu and click Save, Close to return to Book View.

3. In the Available Items, double-click Text Item and click Dedication. Continue creating the Dedication as described in "Adding the Front Matter" in the section "Grandparent Book," earlier in this chapter.

4. From the Available Items, click Table of Contents, Add.

5. From the Available Items, double-click Text Item and then click Introduction, OK.

6. From the Outline, click Introduction, Edit. Enter your book Introduction.

7. When you finish, open the File menu and click Save, Close to return to Book View.

Adding the First Chapter

When you finish with the front matter, you'll want to turn your attention to the trees and charts in the first chapter. Note that this particular project does not contain chapter markers, but you can add chapter markers if you think they are

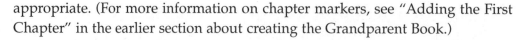

appropriate. (For more information on chapter markers, see "Adding the First Chapter" in the earlier section about creating the Grandparent Book.)

1. From the Available Items, click Descendant Tree, Add. If you want to change the tree formatting or content, click Edit.

2. When you finish editing the tree, click the Go Back button to return to the Book View. You are asked if you want to save your changes before returning; click Yes to do so or No if you do not want to save the changes.

3. From the Available Items, click Family Group Sheet, Add. If you want to change the chart formatting or content, click Edit.

4. When you finish editing the Family Group Sheet, click the Go Back button on the toolbar to return to the Book View. Click Yes if you want to save your changes or No if you do not.

5. From the Available Items, double-click Place Holder. In the Place Holder dialog box, enter the number of pages you want skipped (for the copy of the Scrapbook you printed earlier) and click OK.

6. From the Available Items, double-click Text Item and then click New Text, OK.

7. From the Outline, click Text Item, Edit and enter the text you want to make up this chapter; in this project, this chapter contains journal extracts.

8. When you finish, from the main menu, click File, Save, Close to return to Book View.

9. From the Available Items, double-click Text Item and click New Text, OK.

10. From the Outline, click Text Item, Edit and enter whatever text you want to include in the chapter. In this project, this chapter contains family members' memories of the primary individual.

11. When you finish, from the main menu, click File, Save, Close to return to Book View.

12. From the Available Items, double-click Text Item and then click New Text, OK.

13. From the Outline, click Text Item, Edit and enter the last section of text you want to include in the chapter. In this project, this chapter contains a transcript of the primary individual's lengthy obituary.

14. When you finish, from the main menu, click File, Save, Close to return to Book View.

ADDING THE TIMELINE, MAP, AND INDEX

Now that you're finished with the text portion of the book, you can add those items that make up the last portion of the book—the timeline, the map, and finally, the index. To do so, follow these steps:

1. From the Available Items, click Timeline, Add. If you want to edit or format the Timeline, click Edit.

2. When you finish editing the Timeline, click the Go Back button on the toolbar. Family Tree Maker asks you if you want to save your changes; if you want to do so, click Yes; otherwise, click No to return to the Book View without saving your changes.

3. From the Available Items, click Map, Add. If you want to edit or format the Map, click Edit.

4. After you finish editing the Map, click the Go Back button on the toolbar. As with the Timeline, Family Tree Maker asks if you want to save your changes—click Yes to do so and return to the Book View, No if you do not want to save the changes, or Cancel to go back to the Map view.

5. From the Available Items, click Index. If you want to format the Index, click Edit.

6. When you finish formatting the Index, click the Go Back button to return to the Book View. You are asked if you want to save your changes before returning; click Yes to do so or No to not save the changes.

PRINTING THE BOOK

When you finish adding all the book elements, you are ready to print a copy and give it the once-over. You can print the book directly from the Book View. To do so, follow these steps:

1. From the File menu, click Print Book.

2. Select your print options and click OK.

As I mentioned at the beginning of this project section, this project uses no Text Items as chapter markers. You don't need text to introduce each chapter, but it does add a professional look to your book. Also, each item in this book is considered a separate chapter, as shown earlier in Figure 11.2. (Remember, items that are part of a chapter are indented. Items that begin a chapter are shown flush left.) Finally, this book makes use of a place holder to skip pages in order to allow for a printed copy of the primary individual's Scrapbook. I could have added Scrapbook images into a Text Item as mentioned in the first project, but there might be a time when you want to print the Scrapbook rather than manually add pictures to your book.

Society and Organization Projects

If you are a member of a group or organization that wants to produce a book of its findings or member information, consider using Family Tree Maker to produce the book. Although most people traditionally think of a family history book as being about one particular family, it doesn't have to be. Family Tree Maker enables you to include individuals who are unrelated, thus allowing you to have a database of separate families who are not related by birth or marriage. This capability gives you great freedom to write books that are genealogically related, yet not a traditional family history.

Many projects are well suited to being used in Family Tree Maker—projects such as cemetery mapping (each individual included in the database with a note of his or her headstone inscription, maps to show lot locations, and even pictures of individual headstones), a local history with founders of a town (information on all the founders' families can be included in the database, as well as pictures and facts about businesses, schools, churches, and so on), a group of immigrants who traveled together and settled an area, or even a collection of genealogies from a genealogy society's members. This section shows you two examples: a cemetery mapping book and genealogies from a society's members.

Cemetery Mapping Project Book

The goal of this book is to create a resource detailing all the graves in a small cemetery. Because many of the individuals buried in this small cemetery are related, family units are so noted. Not all the individuals are related, however, which means an index is vital to this project.

For this book, you'll want to consider these questions:

> ✻ **Who will conduct the actual work of gathering information?** The amount of work involved in mapping even a small cemetery is overwhelming for an individual, so this is a project best suited to a group. You'll need to designate tasks.

> ✻ **What will you want to include in this book?** If this resource is to be of real help to you, consider all the information you will want. Probably, you'll want to add more than just the names and dates found on the headstones.

To get the project underway, you'll need to complete these preliminary steps:

1. Have someone walk the cemetery and take pictures of all the headstones.

2. Have someone walk the cemetery and write down all the headstone transcriptions (yes, it's best to record transcriptions off the

headstone rather than rely on pictures of the headstones).

3. Have someone who has a copy of the cemetery map walk along and verify that all the graves are located where they are indicated on the cemetery map.

4. Have someone *digitize* (scan) a copy of the cemetery map to include in the book.

5. Likewise, have someone *digitize* or scan the pictures of the headstones if they were not taken with a digital camera.

6. Assign someone to input the family data into the database. Add photos and notes for each individual. Specify headstone photos as Preferred Photo #1 so that they appear on the Family Group Sheet.

7. Create Saved Views for all the families' Family Group Sheets (be sure to set the content so that Preferred Photo #1 will be included on each person's Family Group Sheet). If you are unfamiliar with Saved Views, read Chapter Nine.

> **NOTE** *When you create this book, you will have to pick someone to be the primary individual (it can be the first burial if you like). It doesn't really matter who it is because you will not be including genealogy forms other than the Family Group Sheets, which you saved as Saved Views.*

8. Research the history of the cemetery and include any notes of interest as separate text in the book.

9. Organize the book as shown in the book Outline in Figure 11.3.

The following sections explain how to set up this particular project, beginning with the planning stage and moving through the actual book creation. It's important to remember that the steps in each section follow where the preceding ones leave off.

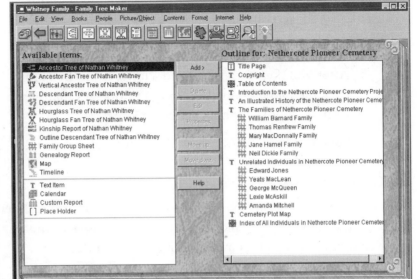

Figure 11.3

You are not limited to books about a specific family; you can also create books about a number of families related by place or circumstances.

SETTING UP THE CEMETERY MAPPING BOOK PROJECT

You begin this project as you do any other—gather your data first, then turn to entering it in the computer and finally preparing your Family File for conversion to book form.

1. After you enter the information for all the individuals in the cemetery, headstone inscriptions in More About Notes, and pictures of the headstones in each person's Scrapbook, be sure to designate one picture per individual as preferred so it will print on the Family Group Sheet.

2. From the Family File page, load an individual's Family Group Sheet and from the main menu, click File, Save Family Group Sheet As.

3. Enter a title for the Saved View (in this project, I formed groups of those families who had more than one family member buried in the cemetery separate from those individuals who were unrelated to anyone else buried there) and then click OK.

4. Repeat the Saved View process for all individuals in the database (you can exclude creating a separate Saved View for children if they are included on their parents' headstone).

5. After you create all the Saved Views, from the Family File page, click the name of any individual (it doesn't matter whom) and then from the Books menu, click New Book.

6. Give your book a title and fill in the author's name.

ADDING THE FRONT MATTER

Next take a look at what you need to do to add the front matter for this book (many of the steps below are covered in other sections in this chapter—be sure to check them out if you are not familiar with them).

1. From the Outline, click Title Page, Edit and enter your Title Page information.

2. When you finish, open the File menu and click Save, Close to return to Book View.

3. In the Available Items, double-click Text Item and click Copyright Notice, OK.

4. If you want to edit the Copyright Notice, select it from the Outline and click Edit and then enter your copyright text.

5. When you finish, open the File menu and click Save, Close to return to Book View.

6. Next you need to add a Dedication; follow the instructions given in "Adding the Front Matter" in the section "Biography of an Ancestor," earlier in this chapter.

7. Following the instructions in the same section, add a Table of Contents and an Introduction. Edit and format as you desire and then return to the Book View to continue.

8. From the Outline, click Introduction, Edit and enter your book Introduction. Be sure to acknowledge everyone who helped with the project.

9. When you finish, from the main menu, click File, Save, Close to return to Book View.

ADDING THE FIRST CHAPTER

After you add your front matter, you can begin filling the book with chapters. Begin with Chapter One, which you can create by doing the following:

1. As described in "Adding the Front Matter" in the "Grandparent Book" section, add a chapter marker to mark off the first chapter.

2. From the Outline, select the New Text item, click Edit, and enter your text (in this project, it's a history of the cemetery, complete with historical pictures saved in one individual's Scrapbook).

3. When you finish, from the main menu, click File, Save, Close to return to Book View.

4. Following the instructions in "Adding the First Chapter" in the "Grandparent Book" section, title your Text Item appropriately and make sure it does not begin a chapter.

ADDING THE SECOND CHAPTER

Continuing from where you left off in the preceding section:

1. Repeat the process of adding a new chapter marker. Enter the introductory text you want, title the chapter marker, and return to the Book View.

2. From the Available Items, click the first Family Group Sheet Saved View (I separated the families from the single individuals; only families are included in this chapter) and click Add.

3. From the Outline, click the Family Group Sheet you just added and click Properties. Deselect the This Item Begins a Chapter option and click OK.

4. Repeat the process until you add all the Saved View Family Group Sheets for families.

ADDING THE THIRD CHAPTER

Now it's time to add the second batch of Family Group Sheets. Do so by following these steps:

1. Create another chapter marker for this chapter. Be sure to enter the text you want to introduce the chapter and give it an appropriate title.

2. Repeat the process of adding the remainder of the Saved View Family Group Sheets—this time for the individuals who are buried in the cemetery without any family members.

ADDING THE FOURTH CHAPTER

Here is where you can add extra text items that you created for the project:

1. Create a chapter marker for this chapter, complete with introduction and title.

2. From the Outline, select the New Text item, click Edit, and enter your chapter text (in this project, I included a brief description of the plot arrangements and any corrections to the map; then I included an image of the cemetery map in the document).

3. When you finish, from the main menu, click File, Save, Close to return to Book View.

4. Following the instructions found in "Adding the First Chapter" in the earlier section "Grandparent Book," title the Text Item and make sure it is not marked to begin a chapter.

ADDING THE INDEX AND PRINTING THE BOOK

Finally, include an index so that readers can easily locate their ancestors in your book, as follows:

1. From the Available Items, double-click Index.

2. If you want to rename the Index, from the Outline, click Index, Properties, type the new title, and then click OK.

3. If you want to format the Index, follow the instructions in "Adding the Index" in the "Biography of an Ancestor" section earlier in this chapter.

   Once you are happy with the Index, you can print the book.

4. To print the book, open the File menu and click Print Book.

5. Select your print options and click OK.

You'll notice that the bulk of this book is taken up in Family Group Sheets—that's because the intrepid authors used Family Tree Maker to enter all the cemetery data—individuals' names, death dates, headstone inscriptions, and any other data they could find.

Nethercote Genealogical Society Member Genealogies Book

This book is created to share with people interested in the families of a specific area. Society members submitted the fruits of their research, along with notes, photos (if available), and contact information. The book is intended for an audience of genealogists.

For this book, you'll want to consider these questions:

> ❋ **Will your group establish a standard for acceptance, or will all member genealogies be accepted?** Decisions will have to be made regarding the quality of material accepted for the book. At the very least, sources for facts should be required.

※ **What will you want included in this book?** Will the book contain just bare-bones genealogies, or genealogies with photos, notes, and additional texts as needed?

※ **In what format will the information be presented?** Narrative Reports? Family Group Sheets? Trees? Decisions will have to be made about the best way to present the information. In order to keep the format of the book consistent, I don't recommend letting each individual choose the type of reports and trees he or she would use.

To get the project underway, you'll need to complete these preliminary steps:

1. You or a committee must make the decisions just mentioned regarding what will be included and how the information will be presented.

2. Coordinate the importing of member information. The best way to do this is via GEDCOMs.

3. Write introductory text explaining the project and providing contact information for all the members.

4. Gather additional text files from all members that introduce their families and offer any notes about their research project.

5. Scan and add the pictures into the appropriate person's Scrapbook if pictures are to be added. For my sample project, I decided not to include pictures because coordinating the scanning and adding hundreds of pictures into the database was too time consuming.

6. Create Saved Views. As with the last project, this book concerns several unrelated families, and as such, the designation of primary individual is meaningless. For that reason, each family's report (or tree or chart, if that is the chosen item for presenting information) must be saved as a Saved View to be added to the book later.

7. Organize the book as shown in the book Outline in Figure 11.4.

Now that the project is planned, you can turn your attention to getting things organized on the computer.

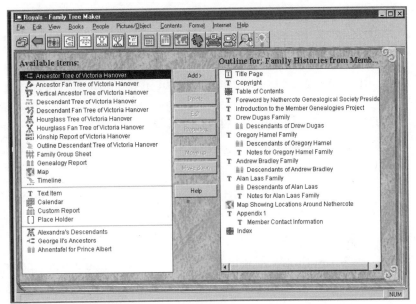

Figure 11.4

A collection of genealogies by members of a group or society can be a popular book with area researchers.

SETTING UP THE NETHERCOTE GENEALOGICAL SOCIETY MEMBER GENEALOGIES PROJECT

You begin setting up this project as you do the others—make sure you have gathered the data you want to use and entered it in the computer.

1. Begin a new Family File and import via GEDCOM all the members' data. Make note of any import errors and correct problems and be sure to check for duplicate individuals!

2. From the Family File page, load an individual's Register Report (this project is using Register Reports to present information). From the main menu, click File, Save Genealogy Report As.

3. Enter a title for the Saved View (in this project, I used the name of each member's primary individual); then click OK.

4. Repeat the Saved View process for each member's primary individual.

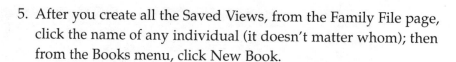

5. After you create all the Saved Views, from the Family File page, click the name of any individual (it doesn't matter whom); then from the Books menu, click New Book.

6. Give your book a title and fill in the author's name.

ADDING THE FRONT MATTER

Once you complete the beginning work, you can move on to the book's front matter.

1. Following the instructions found in "Adding the Front Matter" in the earlier section "Biography of an Ancestor," edit your title page and add and edit the Copyright Notice and a Table of Contents.

2. From the Available Items, double-click Text Item, select Foreword, and click OK.

3. From the Outline, click Foreword, Edit and enter the text for the book's Foreword. When you finish, from the main menu, click File, Save, Close to return to Book View.

4. Finish your front matter by adding an Introduction (for instructions on how to do that, see "Adding the Front Matter" in the "Biography of an Ancestor" section, earlier in this chapter).

ADDING THE FIRST, SECOND, THIRD, AND FOURTH CHAPTERS

Taking up where you left off with the front matter, you can start adding the elements for the first chapter.

1. Create a chapter marker as demonstrated in "Adding the First Chapter" in the earlier section "Biography of an Ancestor." Enter the chapter introduction and give it a title.

2. From the Available Items, click the appropriate Saved View and click Add. If you want to rename the item, click Properties and give it a new name (in this project, I used "Descendants of" and the name of the member's primary individual). Click OK.

3. From the Outline, click Saved View, Properties. Make sure the Saved View does not begin a chapter and then click OK.

4. If you have Text Items associated with this chapter (that is, this particular family), add them at this point, following the instructions for adding Text Items in the "Grandparent Book" section.

5. Repeat the preceding steps for the Second, Third, and Fourth chapters, selecting a different family as the focus for each chapter.

ADDING THE MAP, APPENDIX, AND INDEX

Once you have the bulk of the book added, you can add the remainder of the material—in this case, the map, appendix, and the always important index.

1. From the Available items, select the Map and click Add.

2. From the Outline, select the Map and click Properties. If you want to change the Map's title, do so and click OK.

3. Add a chapter marker to indicate the beginning of the Appendix. Enter any introductory text you want and give the Text Item a title.

4. From the Available Items, double-click Text Item and select New Text. Click OK.

5. From the Outline, click New Text, Edit. Enter the Appendix text; in this project, I used the Appendix to list member names and addresses (after verifying it was allowable to do so) so that interested researchers could contact them. When you finish, from the main menu, click File, Save, Close to return to Book View.

6. Don't forget to give your Text Item a title and to make sure it does not begin a chapter.

7. From the Available Items, double-click Index.

8. If you want to give the Index a new title, from the Outline, click Index, Properties. Rename the Index if you desire and click OK.

PRINTING THE BOOK

When you finish adding everything you want to the book, it's time to print a copy of the book!

1. Open the File menu and click Print Book.

2. Select your print options and click OK.

Because not all members have gathered copious research on their families, this book is organized to allow those members who have significant research to share their information by way of additional notes. Members can include data analysis, information about their research, conflicting sources, and so on.

Research Tools

In addition to creating books intended to share your information with others, you can use Family Tree Maker to create useful research tools to help you when you are researching the family. The examples mentioned here—a portable research reminder and a research notes organizer—are just two of the types of book projects you can create to aid you in research. Research Calendars, Research Journals, Correspondence Logs . . . all can be created within Family Tree Maker and included in a book meant solely for your use. As with other book project ideas, here you are limited only by your imagination!

Portable Research Reminder Book

This book is intended to nudge your memory when you are out researching. The book will contain only information on the family line you are researching and will show information you have (so you know where and when to research) and missing information (so you know what it is you need to find). Books like these serve as quick references to remind you of the names, dates, and locations while you're juggling microfilms or hunting through courthouse archives for information.

For this book, you'll want to consider these questions:

> ☀ **What information do you want to include in the book?** Because the book's purpose is not to inform other readers, you can stick to the bare facts.

> ☀ **In what format will the information be presented?** Because you don't need a detailed look at the family, you can dispense with narrative reports and go with an ancestor or descendant tree because they use less space and show more information per page.

To get the project underway, you'll need to complete these preliminary steps:

1. Make sure the information in your database is correct and updated.

2. Make sure you have sources cited wherever possible.

3. Decide whether to go with an ancestor-ordered report or descendant-ordered report.

4. Set up place holders. If you want to include a copy of your Research Journal in the book, you need to print it separately and insert a place holder in the book to skip the required number of pages.

5. Organize the book as shown in the book Outline in Figure 11.5.

Enough organization! It's time to move on to the actual work of creating this book.

SETTING UP THE PORTABLE RESEARCH REMINDER BOOK PROJECT AND ADDING THE FRONT MATTER

When creating this book, remember that you are making the book for yourself—it's a reminder of all of the families you are researching.

1. Open the Family File that you want to work with.

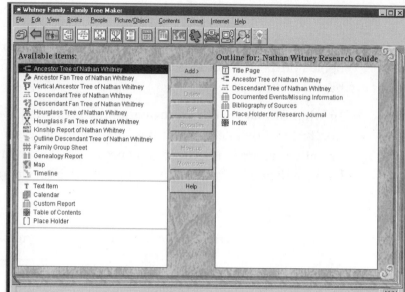

Figure 11.5

When you go
researching, take
along something
to remind you of
all the names and
dates—try
printing your
own Portable
Research
Reminder.

2. Identify the person you want to designate as the primary individual;
   click that person's name. From the main menu, click Books, New
   Book.

3. Give your book a title and fill in the author's name.

4. Edit the Title Page as described in the instructions in the earlier
   section "Biography of an Ancestor."

ADDING CHAPTERS ONE AND TWO

The first two chapters are made up of ancestor and descendant trees. Pick up
the steps where you left off in the prior section.

1. From the Available Items, click the ancestor tree of your choice for
   your primary individual. Click Add. If you want to format or
   customize the tree, click Edit.

2. From the Available Items, click the descendant tree of your choice for your primary individual. Click Add. If you want to format or customize the tree, click Edit.

ADDING CHAPTERS THREE AND FOUR

After you've added in the trees, turn your attention to including two Custom Reports.

1. From the Available Items, click Custom Report and click Add.

2. From the Outline, click Custom Report, Edit. Select the report format you want (in this project, I used the Documented Events Report to note which events were documented, and which weren't— indicating missing information).

3. From the Outline, click Custom Report, Properties. Give the report a title and click OK.

4. Repeat the process shown in Steps 1–3, but select a Bibliography Report rather than the Documented Events Report. Using the Properties button, give the report a new title if desired. (The Properties button brings up the Properties dialog box, in which you can decide whether an item should begin a chapter or not.)

ADDING THE PLACE HOLDER

Because I want to include my Research Journal in this book, I need to include a place holder. Here's how you add it to the book:

1. From the Available Items, click Place Holder, Add. In the Place Holder dialog box, indicate how many pages you want skipped (this should correspond to the number of pages you printed earlier for your Research Journal). Click OK.

2. If you want to change the title for the Place Holder, click Properties and enter a new title and click OK.

ADDING THE INDEX AND PRINTING THE BOOK.

Finally, you can add an index (so you can locate individuals quickly and easily) and print a copy of the book.

1. As described in "Adding the Index" in the "Biography of an Ancestor" section, add your Index here, and format it if necessary.

2. To print the book, open the File menu and click Print Book.

3. Select your print options and click OK.

You'll notice that in this book, the only genealogical data that is presented is found on the two trees—that's because I don't need to know every bit of data when I'm out researching, I just need a reminder of the basic details of each person's life. Also, including a Research Journal reminds me what tasks I have assigned, what is completed, and what remains to be done. The bibliography shows me the sources I've used so that I don't waste valuable time duplicating research.

Research Note Organizer

If you are like me, you love blank charts and forms. I used to haul around a big attaché case full of my family files, blank charts and forms, scribbled notes, photocopies, and a thousand other bits of research ephemera. Now when I trot out to a library or archive, I am armed with my Portable Research Reminder (see preceding section) handsomely bound in a paper file folder and a Research Note Organizer containing blank charts and forms just waiting to be filled out. Usually I spend the money to have the Research Note Organizer bound with a comb binding so that the charts and forms don't slide out and get lost. With a spiral binding, I can just yank out the forms after I fill them in.

For this book, you'll want to consider the following questions:

> ✻ **What charts and forms do you use?** If you do not use a pedigree chart to record information when you are researching, you probably will not want to include blank pedigree charts (what Family Tree

Maker calls ancestor trees) in your book. If you make copious notes, be sure to include several blank sheets with appropriate headers ("Notes for the Whitney Family," "Notes for Jellybone Tinney," "Notes About Old Town, Maine," and so on).

☀ **What size font is best for the charts and forms?** If you have vision problems or anticipate making notes while hunched over a microfilm reader in a darkened Family History Center, it's best to reformat the items to a larger or bolder font.

To get the project underway, you'll need to complete these preliminary steps:

1. Know how many and which blank versions of charts and forms you want. Print them from any Family Page. (To print blank charts and forms, open the File menu from the chart's view or the tree's view and choose Print Family Group Sheet. In the Print dialog box, click the Print Empty box to print a blank Family Group Sheet.) You need to print the blank forms ahead of time because you cannot print blank forms within the Book View. Instead, you need to use place holders to skip the blank forms and charts pages.

2. Make a list of all the note subjects you will need (*note subjects* is my terminology for making blank sheets headed up by subjects; examples might be Benner Family Notes, Miscellaneous Sauber Notes, Interested Researcher Names and Addresses, and so on).

3. Create a Research Log as a Text Item so that you can keep track of every resource you use.

4. Create Census Extract Logs as Text Items so that you can extract information from a census directly to the appropriate forms.

5. Organize the book as shown in the book Outline in Figure 11.6.

Once you organize your Research Note Organizer, it's time to get down to work and get those blank charts and trees created! You can do that by following the steps in the next few sections.

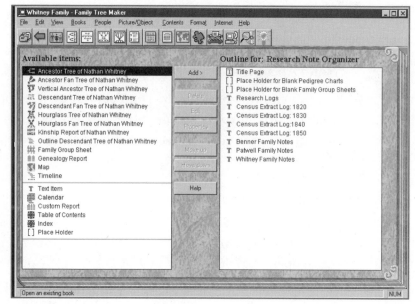

Figure 11.6

Blank forms are
excellent to take
with you when
researching—as
are research logs.
You can include
both in your
Research Note
Organizer.

SETTING UP THE RESEARCH NOTE ORGANIZER PROJECT

This is a quick and easy project to create because all the forms are blank—
there's no pesky picking of individuals in this project!

Just begin as you always do—open the Family File you want to work with (if
your trees and charts are all blank, it doesn't really matter what Family File you
use) and create a new book, giving it a title and filling in the author's name.

ADDING THE FRONT MATTER,
CHAPTER ONE, AND CHAPTER TWO

1. Edit the Title Page per the instructions in "Adding the Front Matter"
   in the "Biography of an Ancestor" section, earlier in this chapter. For
   books like this one, I just enter my name and contact information, in
   case my handy book of charts and forms should get lost.

2. Add a Place Holder (for instructions, see "Adding the Place Holder" in the "Biography of an Ancestor" section, earlier in this chapter), making sure that you indicate the number of pages you want skipped (which should correspond to the number of blank pedigree charts you are including).

3. Repeat the process, this time making sure that the Place Holder represents the number of blank Family Group Sheets you are including.

ADDING CHAPTERS THREE, FOUR, FIVE, SIX, AND SEVEN

These next five chapters use the Text Items to create customized logs for your research.

1. Add the Text Item you want to for the next item (in this chapter, my text item is a research log that allows me to keep track of all the books, magazines, and other resources I use, as well as whether I found any information in each resource). If you need instructions on adding a Text Item, refer to "Adding Chapter One" in the earlier section "Grandparent Book." Don't forget to give the text item a title (in this project, it's "Research Log"). Click OK.

2. Repeat the process in Step 1 for Chapters Four, Five, Six, and Seven. Note in this project that these text items are census logs that allow me to enter data found in a microfilmed census record.

ADDING CHAPTERS EIGHT, NINE, AND TEN

To add these three chapters, just continue with these steps:

1. Add another Text Item to be used as your Notes sheet. To keep these sheets organized, I put a header on each sheet. In this project, the Notes sheet is for the Benner family.

2. Repeat Step 1 for Chapters Nine and Ten, creating Notes sheets for two additional families.

PRINTING THE BOOK

Now is the time to print your forms, trees, and charts! You may want to initially print one copy of each, just to make sure that the items all look the way you want them to before you print several copies of each.

1. Open the File menu and click Print Book.

2. Select your print options. Be sure to note how many copies you want to make—if you tell Family Tree Maker to print one copy, you will have only one copy of each blank form. I generally print 1–20 copies of blank charts and forms at a time. After you select your Print options, click OK.

Formal Family History Books

The last type of book I discuss is the one most commonly thought of when the term "family history book" is used—that is, a book containing a thoroughly researched, documented family history. Such books are geared to other genealogists, and as such, they are as complete and accurate as possible. Unlike the first book project, wild colors and bold fonts are not appropriate in a formal family history. Consistency and format are almost as important as the actual content.

Descendant-Ordered Family History Book

The goal of this book is to illustrate the descendants of a primary individual with supporting evidences, analyses, and additional text items where appropriate. Pictures from the Scrapbook are included in New Text items, but are not limited to just photographs—scanned census returns, postcards, newspaper articles, and more are also included. Because the book adopts a scholarly tone, the bulk of the genealogical information is presented in NGS Quarterly Report format (see Chapter Five, "Using Narrative Reports in your Family History Book," for more information about the NGS Quarterly Report).

For this book, you'll want to consider the following questions:

* **Which trees, reports, or forms will best present the information?**
  Because I expect other interested researchers to read this book, I used
  a narrative report to present the information in a formal manner. In
  order to let my reader see the primary individual's ancestors (and to
  insert a little variety), I also chose to include an Hourglass Tree in an
  appendix (Hourglass Trees are not items found in traditional family
  histories, which is why I've relegated it to an appendix).

* **How much additional information do you want to include?**
  Transcripts, abstracts, and extracts of material all benefit the book by
  rounding out the reader's understanding of the individual and the
  society in which the individual lived. In this project, I added a
  couple of texts that should interest my reader.

To get the project underway, you'll need to complete these preliminary steps:

1. Make sure all the data for the family is entered accurately and
   completely. Run Error Checking reports to catch problems before
   you create the book.

2. Make sure all the events are sourced thoroughly.

3. Scan or digitize pictures and enter them into the appropriate person's
   Scrapbook. Be sure to accurately describe each one. Print the
   Scrapbooks you want to include, being sure to make a note to add a
   place holder to the Outline to compensate for those additional pages.

4. Create any additional text you want to include in the book.

5. Experiment with the format and option settings for the report you
   choose to use in the book. Test-print sample pages to make sure they
   are legible. Be consistent in your use of font and style for all the
   elements in your book.

6. Organize the book as shown in the book Outline in Figure 11.7.

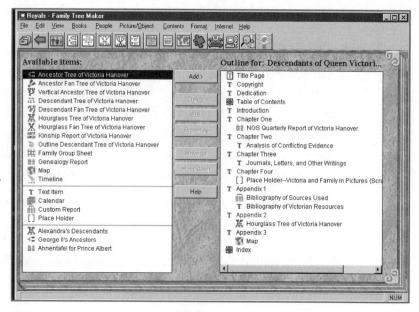

Figure 11.7

Even a formal family history can have a few fun elements in it, such as a map and an Hourglass Tree.

By now you should have a good idea about what you want to include in this book—both individuals' and Family Tree Maker's items. If you're ready to move forward, you now tackle getting the project underway.

SETTING UP THE DESCENDANT-ORDERED FAMILY HISTORY BOOK PROJECT

This book will feature the descendants of a primary individual (or individuals, if you are using a couple); be sure you have gathered all the information you can on the descendants before you begin this project.

1. Begin as you would any other book project—by entering all the information you have gathered pertaining to your primary individual and their descendants into Family Tree Maker (see Chapter One if you are new to entering data in Family Tree Maker). Be sure to include sources for as many events and facts as possible.

2. Check for errors and duplicate individuals (see Chapter Two, "Organizing Your Family History Book," for more information on

both subjects); then following the steps earlier in this chapter in the section, "Grandparent Book," create a family history book for the primary individual.

ADDING THE FRONT MATTER

The material you're going to add as front matter—title page, copyright notice, dedication, table of contents, and introduction—are all standard items that you should be familiar with now. To add them, just follow these steps:

1. Using the steps detailed in "Adding the Front Matter" in the earlier section "Biography of an Ancestor," add the Copyright Notice, the Dedication, the Table of Contents, and the Introduction.

2. Edit the front matter items as appropriate and do not forget to give each a new title if you so desire.

ADDING THE FIRST CHAPTER

When you finish adding and editing the front matter, you can focus on including the meat of the book—the narrative report detailing the primary individual's descendants.

1. Following the steps shown earlier in "Adding the First Chapter" in the section, "Grandparent Book," add a chapter marker, write the introductory text you need, and give the chapter a title.

2. From the Available Items, click Genealogy Report. In the Genealogy Report dialog box, select the type of narrative report you want (for this project, I chose the NGS Quarterly Report). Using the Properties button, be sure this item is not marked to begin a new chapter. Give it a new title if you desire.

ADDING THE SECOND AND THIRD CHAPTERS

The second and third chapters focus on additional text. You might want to have your text already written and ready to be copied and pasted into the Text Item (for more information on including additional text in a book, consult Chapter Eight).

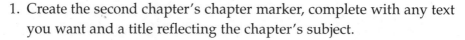
1. Create the second chapter's chapter marker, complete with any text you want and a title reflecting the chapter's subject.

2. From the Available Items, double-click Text Item and select New Text. Click OK.

3. From the Outline, click New Text, Edit and enter the chapter text (for this project, I used an analysis of evidence as a way to support or contradict existing research).

4. When you finish, from the main menu, click File, Save, Close to return to Book View.

5. Using the Properties button, give your Text Item a title and make sure it's not marked to begin the chapter.

6. Repeat the process for the third chapter. Note that in this project, I used text written by the primary individual as a point of interest for the readers and to give them a better understanding of the individual). Give the new Text Item a title, and be sure it doesn't begin a chapter.

ADDING THE FOURTH CHAPTER

Because this chapter is meant to show a printed copy of the Scrapbooks for various individuals, a place holder is used to mark the spot that the Scrapbook pages will fill.

1. Following the steps found in "Adding a Place Holder" in the earlier section "Biography of an Ancestor," add a Place Holder to represent the number of pages you printed in the Scrapbooks.

2. Because this item will not print, you don't have to worry about assigning it a new title unless you want to for organization's sake.

ADDING THE FIRST APPENDIX

This first appendix will contain a bibliography—which means you need to make a Custom Report.

1. Following the instructions in the section "Grandparent Book," add a chapter marker to designate this appendix. Give it a title and enter any introductory text you want to include.

2. Using the steps provided in "Adding Chapters Three and Four" in the earlier section "Portable Research Reminder Book," add a Bibliography. Be sure to give it a title (in this project, I used "Bibliography of Victorian Resources") and mark it as *not* beginning a chapter.

ADDING THE SECOND APPENDIX

This second appendix will contain a tree not traditionally found in a formalized family history book. If you want to format the tree ahead of time, you can do so and save it as a Saved View, adding the Saved View to the book rather than the tree mentioned in this section.

1. Begin as you did for the first appendix—by setting up a chapter marker for the appendix, giving it a title, and entering any text you desire.

2. From the Available Items, select the Hourglass Tree and click Add. If you want to format or manipulate the tree, click Edit; otherwise, click the Properties button, give the tree a customized title (if you want), and make sure it is not selected to begin a chapter.

ADDING THE THIRD APPENDIX

In this last appendix, you will include a map to give your readers an idea of location.

1. Create a chapter marker to begin this appendix, complete with chapter title and any text you want to introduce or explain the appendix.

2. From the Available Items, select the Map and click Add. If you want to format or manipulate the Map, click Edit. If not, click the Properties button, give your Map a new title if desired, and make sure it's not marked to begin a new chapter.

ADDING THE INDEX AND PRINTING THE BOOK

The last steps should be familiar to you now—adding an index and printing your book.

1. From the Available Items, double-click Index.

2. If you want to give the Index a new title, from the Outline, click Index, Properties. Rename the Index if you desire. Click OK.

3. Open the File menu and click Print Book.

4. Select your print options and click OK.

Ancestor-Ordered Family History Book

The purpose of this book is similar to the purpose of the preceding one, with the exception that it features the ancestors rather than the descendants of a primary individual. This book is also created to be a bit less formal and is suitable for distribution at a family reunion—it has trees rather than a narrative report, as well as Family Group Sheets to detail each family.

For this book, you'll want to consider the following questions:

> ❧ **What will your audience's level of experience be with genealogy?**
> Because I expect this book to be shared at a family reunion—which has people both experienced and inexperienced with genealogy—I will include trees so that those people new to genealogy can understand the relationship of family members, and Family Group Sheets for those people more experienced with genealogy and who crave a bit more information.

> ❧ **How much additional information do you want to include?**
> Calendars, additional text (letters and diary extracts), a timeline, maps, and so on enhance the book, especially if you have an audience of varying expertise in genealogy.

To get the project underway, you'll need to complete the following preliminary steps:

1. Make sure all the data for the family is entered accurately and completely. Run Error Checking reports to catch any problems before you create the book.

2. Make sure all the events are sourced thoroughly.

3. Create any additional text you want to include in the book.

4. Decide which of the ancestor trees you want to use and then experiment with the format and option settings. Print sample pages to make sure the tree is legible. Be consistent in your use of font and style for all the elements in your book.

5. Organize the book as shown in the book Outline in Figure 11.8.

Are you ready to jump into the creative process? If you've completed all the tasks in the preceding list, dive into the project and get it underway!

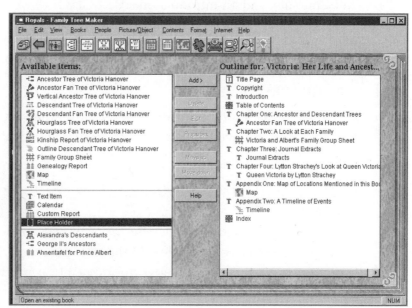

Figure 11.8

Trees, maps, and timelines add life to a family history—if your audience is not experienced in genealogy, give them something fun to look at.

SETTING UP THE ANCESTOR-ORDERED FAMILY HISTORY BOOK PROJECT

This project is similar to the previous one, although the focus is on the ancestors of a primary individual, rather than the descendants. For that reason, some different items are included in the book, although the desire to provide a valuable resource to researchers means that some necessary elements, such as the front matter, may be similar.

To get your Family File up and running and error free, you can just follow the steps in the section "Setting Up the Descendant-Ordered Family History Book Project."

ADDING THE FRONT MATTER

This book does not contain as much front matter as the previous one, but it does have an important introduction, which can serve to ease your readers into your subject and prepare them for the information you present in the book.

1. Following the steps in "Adding the Front Matter" in the earlier section "Biography of an Ancestor," add a Copyright Notice, a Table of Contents, and an Introduction.

2. Edit those three items, as well as the Title Page, returning to the Book View when you finish.

ADDING THE FIRST CHAPTER

Because this book focuses on the ancestors of an individual, it's not surprising that the first chapter starts with a look at the ancestors via an ancestor tree.

1. By now you should have a good idea about what comes first in a chapter—the chapter marker—and how to add it. So, I will not belabor that step here.

2. From the Available Items, click the ancestor tree you want to include and click Add. If you want to edit the tree, click the Edit button. When you finish, be sure to give your tree a title and verify that it is not marked to begin a new chapter.

3. Repeat Step 2 if you want to add a second ancestor tree.

ADDING THE SECOND CHAPTER

This chapter is meant to give the reader a closer look at individual families in the primary individual's ancestry. For that reason, Family Group Sheets are included.

1. Set up the chapter marker, complete with title and chapter introduction, if needed.

2. From the Available Items, click the Family Group Sheet and click Add.

3. From the Outline, click Family Group Sheet, Properties. Give the chart a different title if you want and make sure it is not marked to begin a chapter. Click OK.

4. If you want to format or manipulate the chart, click Edit. When you finish, return to the Book View.

ADDING THE THIRD AND FOURTH CHAPTERS

To add the third and fourth chapters, just continue as follows:

1. Set up the chapter marker as described in earlier sections. Be sure to title it and include any text needed to explain the chapter contents.

2. From the Outline, click New Text, Edit. Enter the chapter text (in this case, I chose to include extracts from the individual's journal).

3. When you finish, return to the Book View, and using the Properties button, give your Text Item a title (in this project, I used "Journal Extracts"), making sure that it's not marked to begin a chapter.

4. Repeat this process to create the fourth chapter (in this project, I extracted text from a public domain book).

5. When you finish, give your chapter marker and Text Item a title, making sure that the Text Item does not begin a chapter.

ADDING THE FIRST AND SECOND APPENDIXES

As with the descendant-ordered book outlined in the previous section, I have included two nontraditional items in my book (nontraditional in the sense that they do not often appear in formal family history books): a map and a timeline.

1. Following the instructions set out in previous sections of this chapter, add a chapter marker for the first appendix, giving it a title and adding any text you think is needed to explain the appendix contents.

2. Using the steps in "Adding a Map" in the earlier section "Biography of an Ancestor," add (and edit, if necessary) a Map. Make sure that it is not marked as beginning the chapter.

3. Repeat Steps 1 and 2 to add the second appendix, replacing the Map with a Timeline, as mentioned in "Adding a Timeline" in the earlier section "Biography of an Ancestor." Don't forget to give it a new title if you like and to mark it as not beginning a new chapter.

ADDING THE INDEX

The last few steps are almost always the same in a family history book—adding an index (no self-respecting family history book should be without one!) and then printing the book. You're almost finished!

1. From the Available Items, double-click Index.

2. If you want to give the Index a new title, from the Outline, click Index, Properties. Rename the Index if you desire. Click OK.

3. Open the File menu and click Print Book.

4. Select your print options and click OK.

If you've made it this far, give yourself a big pat on the back. You've accomplished quite a bit on the journey to creating a family history book—from planning and organizing your book, to experimenting with trees and reports, to exploring the number of family history book projects available. There's only one last hurdle to overcome before you can sit back and rest on your laurels—marketing and promoting your book—but you'll find out about those topics in the next chapter!

Ancestors of George Howard Lafferty

Samuel Lafferty
1801 - 1871

Edwin E. Lafferty
1834 - 1907

Margaret McDowell
1803 - 1861

George E. Lafferty
1867 - 1936

Erastus Fowler
1793 - 1875

...elia Fowler
...1914

Temperence Merrill
1796 - 1871

Nathan Wescott
1818 - 1900

...ram Wescott

Sarah Ann McMichael
1820 - 1901

...na Wescott

Samuel C. Amsden
1822 - 1899

Theresa Jerusa Amsden
1845 - 1914

Clarissa Hubbard
1820 - 1870

The History of George Howard Lafferty

George Howard Lafferty was born September 2, 1894 in Lenox township, Ashtabula County, Ohio, to Amber Amelia Wescott Lafferty and George Edwin Lafferty. A sister, Maud Irene, was born May 23, 1892.

A family of farmers, the Laffertys harvested the land where they lived. On May 9, 1919, they moved to Warren, Ohio, to a house on Forest Street NE. They lived next door to their daughter Maud, her husband Jay Rood Webster, and their three beautiful daughters, Reta, Shirley, and Marion.

As a youth, Lafferty went by "Howard" rather than "George" and signed his name as G. Howard Lafferty. After graduating from Lenox Township schools in 1911, he received a Teachers Certificate and became an educator and later a high school Principal. He then switched careers and ventured into banking just before World War I.

As a student at Ohio State University during the war, Howard Lafferty hoped to join the army but was classified 5G due to his glasses and other restrictions. In 1923 he received a L.L.B. degree and passed

CHAPTER TWELVE

Marketing and Promotion

To be clear is the first duty of a writer;
to charm and to please are graces to be acquired later.
—Brander Matthews

or many people, creating a family history book is its own reward—just holding their book in their hands makes them happy. Those people usually create books for their families or for special groups, and their books are either not for sale or only for what it cost them publish their books.

If you have created such a book, you'll probably want to skip parts of this chapter; perhaps only the sections on filing for a copyright and ISBN or on donating copies to repositories are of interest to you. If you have created a book to sell to other interested researchers, you'll probably want to read the sections on marketing and promotion.

Registering Your Book for Copyright

Cast your mind back to Chapter Two, "Organizing Your Family History Book." Remember when I said that the moment a work is created in tangible form (for example, when it is written down), by U.S. law, it is copyrighted? Well, that's still true, but there are advantages to officially registering your copyright with the U.S. Copyright Office—advantages like having a public record of your claim of copyright. This advantage becomes important if anyone infringes on your copyright!

Copyright registration is completely voluntary and can be done for both published and unpublished works. Reasons for registering your work for copyright revolve around proving ownership of the work. For example, copyright registration is required to bring a copyright infringement lawsuit (that is, if someone uses your work without permission). If you register your work and someone infringes on your copyright, you are eligible to receive not only statutory damages, but legal costs as well. Although it might seem unlikely that someone would want to steal your work or use it without permission, it's better to protect yourself and be aware of your rights.

To register a work for copyright, first fill out Form TX from the Library of Congress (you can download a copy online at http://www.loc.gov/copyright, as shown in Figure 12.1). The form is intuitive and should take only a few minutes to fill out. Then enclose the completed form in an envelope along with $30 (application fee) and one copy of the work if it is unpublished or two if it is published and mail it to this address:

> Library of Congress
> Copyright Office
> Register of Copyrights
> 101 Independence Avenue, S.E.
> Washington, D.C. 20559-6000

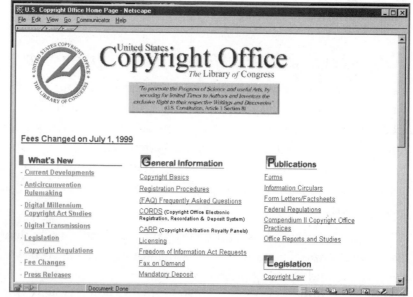

Figure 12.1

The U.S. Copyright Web site has all the information you will need regarding copyright dos and don'ts.

Understanding ISBN

If you want your book to be sold through a bookstore, you need to obtain an ISBN (International Standard Book Number). The ISBN system was introduced in 1968 to standardize book identification. All book databases, distributors, and bookstores use the ISBN to identify and track books.

If you want your book included in the Books in Print directory (a catalog of every book in print with an ISBN number), you need an ISBN. Even if your book is never sold through a bookstore, you should consider getting an ISBN for identification purposes (libraries love ISBNs!). The process of obtaining one is not difficult; simply fill out the ISBN application (you can download forms from http://www.bowker.com, as shown in Figure 12.2, or request one from R.R. Bowker—see following address). You can request one ISBN, or if you are

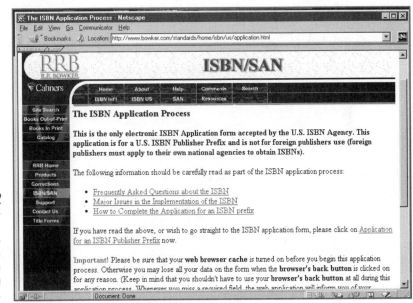

Figure 12.2

Contact the R.R. Bowker Web site for information and forms on obtaining an ISBN.

paying online with a credit card, blocks of numbers. Processing generally takes about ten business days. To get an ISBN in the U.S., contact the following:

> R.R. Bowker
> 121 Chanlon Road
> New Providence, NJ 07974
> 908-665-6770
> Fax: 908-665-2895

After you have an ISBN, include it on the copyright page and at the lower-right corner of the back cover of your book (in small font). If you make significant changes to your book—for example, adding new data or a new family line— you should apply for a new ISBN.

Selling Your Book

Assuming that you want to sell your book (either for profit or to pay for publishing costs), you have three basic ways in which to do so:

- ❋ You can sell it yourself.
- ❋ You can sell it to a bookstore, which will then sell it to customers.
- ❋ You can sell it to a distributor, which will then sell it to bookstores.

For a family history book, the first two are the only reasonable options; few family histories are of sufficient interest that a book distributor will be interested in carrying it. Selling a book yourself has lots of benefits. You know exactly how many copies are being sold and to whom, and you get the full profit from the book sale, rather than a discounted price. Besides, you have the satisfaction of being in contact with other researchers interested in the same family. The sidebar "Internet Resources for Book Promotion" also has ideas on how to promote your family history book.

Internet Resources for Book Promotion

The Internet is a boon to genealogists because it makes it so easy to get in contact with other researchers, share information, and utilize online resources. Also of interest are the number of online articles and guides to book promotion. Although none of the following are intended specifically for family history books, you will find lots of good advice:

- "Promoting Your Book on the Internet" (http://www.themestream. com/gspd_browse/browse/view_article.gsp?c_id=118723&id_list=&c ookied=T)

- "Promoting Your Book" (for e-book authors, but has good advice for everyone—http://www.suite101.com/article.cfm/e-books/29358)

- "Writing is an Art . . . Publishing is a Business" (http://www. writershelpdesk.com/Report_13_art.htm)

- "26 Ideas for Promoting Your Book!" (http://www.hodi.com/ promo.html—a commercial site, but offers useful free information)

- "Promote Your Piece" (the first in a series of articles regarding book promotion—http://www1.mightywords.com/writerscorner/ getnoticed/david_yale.asp)

- "Book Writing, Publishing, and Promoting Resources" (http://www. parapublishing.com/getpage.cfm?file=/homepage.html&user=%%u ser%%—a commercial site, but has a good number of free, helpful articles that carry no obligation for purchasing the company's books or services)

Before you sell your book, however, you need to let people know that it's available. Promotion will create a buzz about your book and alert those readers who are interested in its availability. So before you look at places to sell your book, explore briefly how to let people know about your book.

Family History Book Promotion Basics

Many ways exist to drum up interest in your book—too many to be fully discussed here. However, in this section you can take a look at the most common forms of promotion. The concept of family history book promotion is pretty basic when you think about it—you want to let interested researchers know about your book. To do so, you can use the following tools:

 ❊ **Obtain a mailing list (the U.S. Mail kind, not the Internet kind) from a related family association and conduct a bulk mailing.** This approach involves creating some sort of advertising copy about your book (generally a flyer with details about the book, a table of contents, perhaps a brief excerpt, and an order form). This can be expensive if the mailing list runs to the thousands, but you can target those individuals who live in the locations relevant to your book.

 ❊ **Mention your book on Internet mailing lists.** Many Internet mailing lists are devoted to one surname or family, and they make an excellent spot to mention your book, although you need to be careful you do not post a spam (in this case, a *spam* is an unsolicited commercial message). Some mailing lists have policies against commercial posts. If you want to post a mention of your book, check with the list owner first to make sure it's allowed.

 ❊ **Mention your book on Internet surname newsgroups or bulletin boards.** Like mailing lists, many surname-specific newsgroups and message areas (bulletin boards) exist that can be useful for publicizing your book. However, you need to make sure that your information is not considered a spam (see the preceding bullet).

❧ **Place an advertisement in a genealogical publication.** Many genealogy societies have newsletters or quarterly publications that accept advertisements. This is another good way to reach potential readers at a minimum cost. Don't neglect general genealogy magazines, such as *Everton's Genealogical Helper*—they accept ads for all sorts of books, including family histories.

❧ **Send review copies to publications.** One of the best ways to generate word-of-mouth publicity about your book is to have someone review it and publish the review. Many genealogy-society publications (such as the *National Genealogy Society's Quarterly*, or NGSQ) carry book reviews, as do general genealogical publications.

❧ **NOTE** ❧ *The National Genealogy Society Quarterly publishes a number of articles in each issue as well as book reviews. The space devoted to family histories is limited, but the NGSQ does review some. For more information about book reviews in the NGSQ, contact the Book Review Editor:*

> *Thomas W. Jones, Ph.D., CG*
> *Department of Education*
> *Fowler Hall*
> *Gallaudet University*
> *800 Florida Avenue NE*
> *Washington, D.C. 20002*

❧ **Create a Web site with your book information.** The Internet is a powerful tool that can greatly assist you in contacting other researchers interested in the same family. By creating a Web site with information about your book, you have the potential of reaching millions of people. You can include such items as a table of contents, a brief excerpt, and an index so that people will know whether their family is in your book.

❧ **Make sure that your book is easy to purchase.** If you sell the book yourself, consider using some of the free or low-cost credit card services so that you can accept credit card sales online or via the phone.

❧ **Give a talk about the book.** I've found that I sell more books when I conduct an in-person appearance. Contact local societies or related family organizations and offer to give a talk about the family in your book, your research process, or your experience writing the book. Make sure copies are available for purchase at your talk!

*❧ **NOTE** ❧ The National Genealogy Society (NGS) conducts a yearly contest to recognize excellence in the field of family history—the Award for Excellence: Genealogy and Family History. According to the NGS, this award is for "a specific, significant, single contribution in the form of a family genealogy or family history book published during the past five years which serves to foster scholarship and/or advances or promotes excellence in genealogy." At the time of this writing, these are the requirements for contents:*

- *Length: Three to four generations, 4,000–10,000 words*
- *Originality: Not previously published and not submitted elsewhere for publication*
- *Documentation: Individual, specific citations (footnote form) for every statement of fact that is not public knowledge*
- *Appearance: 11- or 12-point type, 1-inch margins, laser-quality print*
- *Numbering system: NGSQ*

For more information about this award, visit the NGS Web site at http://www.ngsgenealogy.org or write to them at

> *The National Genealogical Society*
> *4527 17th Street, North*
> *Arlington, VA, 22207-2399*

Getting Your Book into Bookstores

Although *hand-selling* (one-on-one selling) is often the best type of selling because you get to meet the buyer, don't overlook the convenience of having your family history book sold in a bookstore. You can use both online and offline bookstores to sell your book, although the chances are much higher that an online bookstore will carry your book. Offline bookstores are limited by space restraints, and they must restrict books they carry to ones they believe will sell. For the purpose of this discussion, I refer only to online bookstores because they are the best option for family history authors.

Before you consider having your book sold in a bookstore, you need to do the following:

- ❋ Set a price for your book. See the sidebar " Setting the Price for Your Book" for ideas on how to determine a price.

- ❋ Register your book for copyright.

- ❋ Get an ISBN. This is a must-have for any bookstore.

- ❋ Make sure you have books on hand (unless your book is published print-on-demand).

After you have your ISBN, your book will be listed in the Books in Print database, and any bookstore should be able to order it. Three major online bookstores can sell your book: Amazon.com, BarnesandNoble.com, and Borders.com. All three allow you to enter information about your book, making it available to customers.

The following is basic information about what you will need to do to get your book listed. For more details or for help getting your book listed, contact the company of your choice.

SELLING YOUR BOOK AT AMAZON.COM

An online form that takes about five minutes to fill out makes adding your book to Amazon.com's catalog a snap. To be included in the catalog, you must have an ISBN, and the book must be available from a North American source

Setting the Price for Your Book

The price you charge for your book depends on a number of factors:

- The cost, per book, to publish
- The cost to deliver the book to the purchaser
- The costs for registering the copyright and ISBN
- The costs for promotion and advertisement
- Your profit level (do you want to make a profit from the book, or is it a not-for-profit venture)

Add all these figures together and then add a little on top to account for increases in postage and other unforeseen expenses. Be wary of setting the price too high—people balk at paying a huge price for a book they consider nonessential. Check to see what other family histories are selling for, and if possible, price yours in that range.

(publisher, distributor, and so on). For specialty books like family histories, Amazon notifies you when it receives an order, and you send the number of books it needs. Amazon takes a discount on the sale price (usually around 40–50 percent), and pays you the remainder. Its Web site, shown in Figure 12.3, is at http://www.amazon.com.

You can join the "Amazon.com Advantage" program to sell your books via Amazon.com by filling out your book's information at http://www.amazon.com/exec/obidos/subst/partners/direct/advantage-for-books.html (see Figure 12.4). The program is free and is recommended for people who are publishing and selling their own books.

Figure 12.3

Amazon.com is one of the largest online bookstores—and a good place to list your book for sale!

Figure 12.4

Amazon.com Advantage gives you worldwide distribution for your book.

SELLING YOUR BOOK AT BARNESANDNOBLE.COM

You can send your book information to BarnesandNoble.com via e-mail. To be included in its catalog, you need an ISBN. BarnesandNoble.com takes a percentage of your book, paying you the balance. Its Web site is at http://www.barnesandnoble.com or http://www.bn.com (see Figure 12.5).

BarnesandNoble.com does not have an online book submission form as does Amazon.com, but it does have information for publishers on submitting their books for inclusion in the BarnesandNoble.com catalog. You can find the information at http://www.barnesandnoble.com/help/b_faq.asp?. Figure 12.6 shows an excerpt from the Publishers' Frequently Asked Questions.

SELLING YOUR BOOK AT BORDERS.COM

This is the hardest online bookstore on which to be listed—your book must be in Books in Print to be included in their catalog. Once your book is listed in Books in Print, your book should be added to the Borders.com catalog, although like the other two stores, you'll take a whopping discount on every book sold.

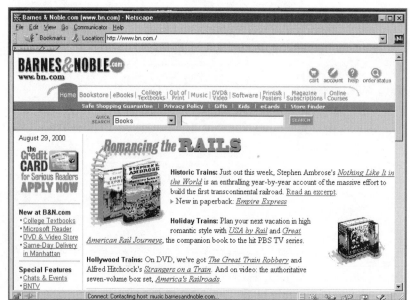

Figure 12.5

BarnesandNoble.com is the Internet version of this popular chain bookstore.

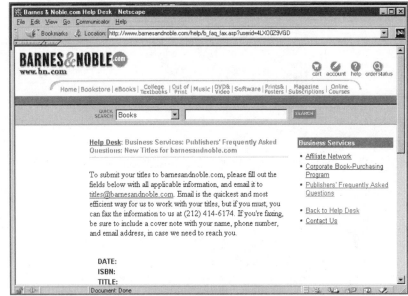

Figure 12.6

BarnesandNoble. com requires you to send book information to them via e-mail.

You can see the main screen of the Borders.com Web site (http://www. borders.com), in Figure 12.7.

Selling Your Book Yourself

Considering the amount of discount that bookstores take to carry a book, it's not surprising that many people opt to sell their books themselves and retain all the profits. In this age of Internet commerce, personal toll-free numbers, and mass-market publications reaching thousands of readers, it's completely reasonable to sell your book yourself.

The best way to make people aware of your book is to conduct a mass-mailing to interested people (members of a related family history society, members of a family reunion, and so on) and to advertise the book in a large genealogical publication. Include order information in the mailing. If you are online, you can also sell your book from your Web site, utilizing one of the free credit card companies such as PayPal.com (see Figure 12.8), which allows people to pay you online in a secure environment. The PayPal Web site is at http://www.paypal.com or http://www.x.com.

Figure 12.7

Borders.com is part of another large bookstore chain with an Internet presence.

Figure 12.8

PayPal.com enables you to receive and send payments via credit cards online.

Keeping a contact list of interested researchers is an important tool for finding buyers for your book. I once bought a family history book from a man whom I had contacted several years earlier about a family line that I was tracing. After he completed his book, he contacted everyone who had ever written to him, as well as members of the local genealogy society who were interested in the family, and offered them copies of the book at cost. He sold later copies at a slightly higher price. Eventually, with information donated by book purchasers, he released a second, updated version of the book.

※ **TIP** ※ *You can use Family Tree Maker's capability of printing labels from the addresses you entered in the More About section to create a mailing list of people who might be interested in your book. To create labels, as illustrated in Figure 12.9, follow these steps:*

1. *Load the Family File you want to use.*
2. *From the View menu, select Labels/Cards.*
3. *From the File menu, select Print Labels/Cards and click OK.*

Mr. George Abbott	Ms. Abigail Adams	Mr. Amos Adams
Ms. Elizabeth Adams	Ms. Elizabeth Adams	Ms. Elizabeth Adams
Mr. George F. Adams	Ms. Hannah Adams	Ms. Hephzibah Adams
Mr. Isaac Adams	Mr. J. R. Adams	Mr. James Adams
Mr. James Adams	Mr. James W. Adams	Mr. Joel Adams
Mr. Joel Adams	Mr. Joseph Adams	Mr. Joshua Adams

Figure 12.9

Use Family Tree Maker to create labels from the mailing addresses you enter.

Being the Good Samaritan: Donating Copies of Your Book

You should not donate copies of your book to libraries and other repositories just to get the warm fuzzy glow of having done something nice. Instead, donate copies of your book in order to share the fruits of your long, hard research with others and to preserve your work for later generations. I strongly urge all who write a family history book that features the ancestors or descendants of an individual to send copies of their books to the following repositories:

The Library of Congress
Thomas Jefferson Building, Room 5010
Washington, D.C. 20540

Family History Library (The Church of Jesus Christ of Latter-day Saints)
35 N. West Temple Street
Salt Lake City, UT 84150

> ❧ **NOTE** ❧ *Be sure to include a note giving permission for the Family History Library (FHL) to microfilm your book. Because the FHL does not circulate original copies of books, they microfilm them instead, sending out the microfilmed copies to requesting Family History Centers.*

The Allen County Public Library
900 Webster Street
Fort Wayne, IN 46802

> ❧ **NOTE** ❧ *The Allen County Public Library has the second largest collection of genealogical books in the country—only the National Genealogy Society's library has more. For that reason, you should send a copy of your book to both libraries.*

National Genealogical Society Library
4527 17th Street North
Arlington, VA 22207

Finally, if your book concerns a family with roots in the New England area, contact this organization:

> New England Historic Genealogical Society
> 101 Newbury Street
> Boston, MA 02116-3007

In addition, consider sending copies to all libraries in the region that you discuss in your book and to all family associations and regional genealogical societies that might have ties with the individuals in your book. By donating copies, you make sure that libraries (which often have very tight budgets) and other organizations have access to a work that might otherwise be unavailable to them.

Looking Ahead to the Future

After your book is written and published, you might think that's the end of the journey. But just as you never really finish researching a family, you always have the opportunity to continue your family history book projects. You can either begin working on a different family, join a society or group's project, or you can update the information in your previous book.

The desire to update information in a book can bring up many questions—how much new information should you have before you add it? Should you publish an addendum or add the new information to the book and republish it? Should you publish the new information separately? These are questions that really only you can answer. No written guidelines tell you that when you have x amount of information, you should publish an addendum or that when you have y amount of information, you should update the entire book.

Because Family Tree Maker makes it so easy to create a family history book, updating the entire book should not be too much trouble—the table of contents and index are automatically regenerated if you add new trees, reports, or other items to the book. If you have new data to include in existing trees and reports, printing a new version of the items includes the updated information. The only concern you might have regarding updating is the price of publishing. If you have a box of 40 books on hand, you'll probably want to print an addendum to slip inside the books rather than throw away the books and start again.

> ❋**TIP**❋ *As you gather new information or make corrections to existing information, keep a file of all the new information. Doing so enables you to keep track of when you have enough new material to warrant republishing, and it keeps the new information separate in case you want to publish only an addendum.*

My rule of thumb is this: If the new information is minor and doesn't influence a large number of individuals, print an addendum and include it with the book. If the information adds an entire new branch of the family or requires you to chop off one of the branches, republish the book. You will have to weigh these matters and go with a choice that works with your time and budget.

Writing a family history book is a creative endeavor like any other form of writing. You must choose what to say, how to say it, and what will appeal to your readers. Like other authors, you strive for a balance between clarity and interest, and you try to take your readers on a journey that gives them something to remember when they are finished. Creating a family history book with Family Tree Maker can be a fun, exciting experience. So fire up that Family File, kick your creativity into high gear, and dazzle everyone with your genealogical creations!

Index